LEARNING
&TEACHING
for BUSINESS

CASE STUDIES OF
SUCCESSFUL INNOVATION

EDITED BY ROLAND KAYE & DAVID HAWKRIDGE

ltsn
Learning and Teaching
Support Network

Business Education Support Team

**KOGAN
PAGE**

London and Sterling, VA

First published in Great Britain and the United States in 2003 by Kogan Page Limited

120 Pentonville Road
London N1 9JN
UK
www.kogan-page.co.uk

22883 Quicksilver Drive
Sterling VA 20166–2012
USA

ISBN 0 7494 4025 2

British Library Cataloguing-in-Publication Data

A CIP record for this book is available from the British Library.

Library of Congress Cataloging-in-Publication Data

Learning and teaching for business : case studies of successful
innovation / edited by Roland Kaye and David Hawkridge for the Business
Education Support Team of the UK Learning and Teaching Support Network
    p. cm.
Includes bibliographical references and index.
  ISBN 0-7494-4025-2
  1. Business education--Great Britain--Case studies. 2.
Management--Study and teaching (Higher)--Great Britain--Case studies.
3. Educational innovations--Great Britain--Case studies. I. Kaye,
Roland, 1948- II. Hawkridge, David G.
  HF1141.L43 2003
  658'.0071'1--dc21
                                    2003005108

Typeset by Saxon Graphics Ltd, Derby
Printed and bound in Great Britain by Biddles Ltd, Guildford and King's Lynn
www.biddles.co.uk

Contents

Figures

Tables

Contributors

Colin Allison is a Senior Lecturer in the School of Computer Science at the University of St Andrews; his current interests include systems support for distributed learning environments.

Tom Bourner is Professor of Personal and Professional Development and leader of the Management Development Research Unit at the Brighton Business School at the University of Brighton; his current interests are in self-managed action learning, supporting student learning and developments in higher education.

Colin Clarke-Hill is Reader in Strategic Management in the Business School at the University of Gloucestershire; his current interests include internationalization of retailing, service as a strategy in industrial markets, and international alliances and joint ventures.

Graham Clayton is a Teaching Fellow at the University of Plymouth; his current interests include problem-based learning, games and simulations, work-based learning, and methods for teaching large classes.

Anne Cook is a Senior Lecturer in the Liverpool Business School, Liverpool John Moores University; her current interests include the use of computer-based learning in financial accounting and management accounting.

David Edelshain is a Senior Lecturer in International Business in the Faculty of Management at the Sir John Cass Business School, City University, and New York University in London; his current interests include currency risk management.

Stephen Flowers is a Principal Research Fellow in the Centre for Research in Innovation Management, University of Brighton; his current interests include complex software systems and management development.

Wendy Fowle is a Project Officer at the Open University and was involved in the development of B823 Managing Knowledge; her current interests include management of intellectual capital for innovation.

Anne Gregory is Professor of Public Relations and Director of the Centre for Public Relations Studies at Leeds Metropolitan University; her current interests include public relations as a management function and the ethics of communication.

David Hawkridge, Emeritus Professor of Applied Educational Sciences, is a member of the Business Education Support Team (BEST), and was formerly Director of the Institute of Educational Technology at the Open University; his current interests include innovations in education and training, distance learning and the impact of globalization on education.

Christine Helliar is a Senior Lecturer in the Department of Accountancy and Business Finance, University of Dundee; her current academic interests include derivative products, treasury management, management control, corporate governance, auditing and accounting education.

Roland Kaye, Dean of the Open University's Business School and Professor of Information Management, is Co-Director of BEST; his current interests include strategic information management and decision supports.

Ismo Kuhanen, a consultant, was formerly a Senior Lecturer in Strategic Management at the University of Plymouth; his current interests include corporate leadership development, e-commerce, innovation and entrepreneurship, competence-based learning and distance learning.

John Lawson is course leader for the MA in Change Management and head of the management development subject group in the Brighton Business School, University of Brighton; his current interests include action learning, learning and teaching, group development, personal development and management development.

Stephen Little, a Senior Lecturer in Knowledge Management in the Open University's Business School, was Course Team Chair for the initial presentations of B823 Managing Knowledge (an MBA elective); his current interests include the internationalization of the School's learning materials.

Rosa Michaelson is a Fellow in Business Computing in the Department of Accountancy and Business Finance, University of Dundee; her current interests include critical and social issues in information systems, and the impact of cycles of technological change and policy uptake on higher education.

Sue Moon came into BEST at the Open University in 2001–02 after working for the University of Central England and is now a researcher at the University of Derby; her current interests include guidance, work placement and graduate employability.

Becci Newton is a Research Officer (Learning Technologies), Brighton Business School, University of Brighton; her current interests include student-centred learning and a systems review of the School's postgraduate programme.

Suzanne O'Hara is a leading member of the Business School's Management Development Research Unit at the University of Brighton; her current interests include self-managed action learning and innovative approaches to manager learning and development.

Roger Ottewill, formerly a Lecturer in Public Sector and Related Studies in Sheffield Hallam University, is now a part-time researcher (while semi-retired) in the Centre for Learning and Teaching at Southampton University; his current interests include student self-managed learning, academic skill development, video streaming and educational development.

Cameron Paine is a Research Officer (Learning Technologies) and a systems engineer in the Faculty of Information Technology, University of Brighton; his current interests include development of a managed learning environment, particularly integration of student records and legacy data systems.

Ashok Patel is Director of Computer-Assisted Learning Research and Principal Lecturer at the School of Business, De Montfort University, Leicester; his current interests include human cognition, human–computer interaction, intelligent learning environments and knowledge management.

Joanne Powell, a Senior Lecturer at Leeds Metropolitan University, is deputy course leader for the BA Hons in Public Relations and module leader for Public Relations Planning and Management; her current interests include corporate communications strategy and internal communication.

David Power is Professor of Business Finance in the Department of Accountancy and Business Finance, University of Dundee; his current interests include corporate finance, particularly emerging markets, share issues and corporate communication to shareholders.

Paul Quintas is Professor of Knowledge Management in the Open University's Business School and led the initial development and launch of B823 Managing Knowledge (an MBA elective); his current interests include management of intellectual capital for innovation, and knowledge management in design and innovation networks.

Steve Reeve is MBA programme leader in the Business School at the University of Brighton; his current interests include adult learning, particularly the communication of tacit experience among managers.

Donald Sinclair is an Honorary Senior Lecturer in the Department of Accountancy and Business Finance, University of Dundee; as a statistician, he includes all aspects of quantitative research methods in his current interests.

Tudor Spencer is the course leader for the Accounting and Finance Degree Programme at the University of Hertfordshire. He specializes in financial management and his current interests include constructivist learning in accounting and finance.

Greg Stoner is a Lecturer in Accounting and Information Systems in the Department of Accounting and Finance, University of Glasgow; his current interests include information systems, managerial accounting, financial modelling, the integration of learning technologies into student learning, and the use and flows of information in organizations.

Carol Vielba is a Senior Lecturer in Management in the Sir John Cass Business School, City University; her current interests include student learning.

Ann Wall is a Lecturer in the School of Business and Finance, Sheffield Hallam University; her current interests include public and social administration, particularly health care policy.

Liz Yeomans is a Principal Lecturer in Public Relations at Leeds Metropolitan University; her current interests include internal communication and its link to organizational learning.

Foreword

Educating people for the effective management of enterprises is a more and more important activity. This is evidenced in many ways – but two examples are the great rise in demand for this kind of education over the last 30 years or so, and current government concern that management inadequacy lies at the heart of the UK's productivity problems. What is done in business education has also changed substantially during this period and continues to change. Thirty years ago management training centres focussed on developing management capabilities, while universities, if they taught business and management at all, taught the principles of economics and psychology using the traditional methodologies of lectures, books and written, unseen examinations. But now, skills and knowledge are both seen to be important to management education in management education establishments of all kinds: the traditional education methods have been superseded by student-centred learning – a move from sage-on-the-stage to guide-at-the-side; new kinds of assessment methods have been increasingly employed – to be formative as well as summative; and information technology is making many new learning methods possible.

In this environment, experiments in business education have been developed in many different parts of the higher and further education system. Some of these have been motivated by a need to achieve improved cost efficiency – a very strong pressure in British universities and colleges in the last decade. Others have been designed to improve learning outcomes – perhaps driven by teaching quality audits. While these may have helped the institution in which they were developed, other institutions may well gain from using them as well. This is the issue addressed by this very welcome volume. BEST is the organization set up by the UK Learning and Teaching Support Network (which is funded by the Funding Councils for Higher Education) to support the development and dissemination of good practice in teaching management and business studies and accounting. BEST carried out a detailed search process and identified the 12 innovations described in this book as worthy of description for a wider audience.

What we have here are some fascinating innovations – and I certainly encourage any business-school teacher to dip into this book for ideas on how to improve the practice of business education. Although business schools are increasingly competitive, and so less willing to share the details of their successes, they are also (for the most part) in receipt of public funds to support their teaching. So it is not only useful, but also highly desirable, that good innovations get passed on. This volume makes an important contribution to this important aim and I commend it warmly.

Professor Stephen Watson
Principal
Henley Management College

Acknowledgements

The editors are grateful to the Higher Education Funding Council's Learning and Teaching Support Network, which provided the funding to establish the Business Education Support Team (BEST), the discipline support centre for business, management and accounting; to the directors and staff of BEST for their encouragement and assistance; to all those who responded to the BEST surveys and who answered our subsequent enquiries regarding their work and methods; and to all the authors of the BEST stories.

Chapter 1

Success in the new world of learning and teaching

Roland Kaye and David Hawkridge

This book contains what we have called the 'BEST stories', case studies of successful innovation in the new world of learning and teaching in business schools. BEST is the Business Education Support Team, of which we are members. BEST is the UK Learning and Teaching Support Network's node for the disciplines of business, management and accounting in higher and further education. BEST's Web-based survey of opinions of deans and heads of department in UK business schools in late 2000 provided leads to 126 innovations in learning and teaching. Our searches located 'success stories' among these innovations, and BEST invited the authors to write these up for publication as examples of good practice. The stories range across business, management and accounting. Some draw on information technology but others do not. Most are from newer universities and colleges. Some are tried and tested over 5–10 years; others are more recent. All employ methods of learning and teaching that are transferable to other business school settings.

In this chapter we describe briefly the methods and criteria we used in the searches. We summarize each story to give an overview, and then explain how the innovations chosen for the stories differ from those excluded. Lastly, we discuss the evidence of success (and failure).

The Web-based survey

BEST's first national landscape survey of views about learning and teaching the academic disciplines of business, management and accounting was in November 2000. With help from the Association of Business Schools, we sent a letter to several hundred deans and heads of department asking them, or their nominated representatives, to answer a short questionnaire on a Web site at the Open University. After e-mail follow-up of non-respondents, we received responses from 71 individuals at 49 universities and five institutions of higher or further education.

Our respondents gave us their opinions on many current major issues and concerns. They also furnished us with a large set of 'elevator pitches' they would make to important stakeholders – see BEST's annual report (http://www.business.ltsn.ac.uk/) or the executive summary, *Managing Better* (BEST, 2002). This book, however, is based on some of the 126 innovations in learning and teaching that they considered newsworthy and 'wrote in' for us. We grouped these as in Table 1.1.

Changing the curriculum, teaching and assessment

Many of the 59 listed innovations in curriculum were new programmes of study, mostly at the post-graduate level, some for doctorates. Entrepreneurship, strategic management and leadership were the most frequently mentioned topics, but there were also programmes aimed at niche markets in creative management, leisure management, insurance management and management accounting. Others sought to increase relevance by building strong links with companies and incorporating work experience of various kinds. A few claimed to be grounded in research.

Among the innovations in teaching (other than those involving ICT – see below), problem-based learning, action learning, portfolios, case studies and simulations were prominent, together with provision of learning materials. Innovations in assessment were seldom listed but focused on peer assessment.

Table 1.1 *Groups of innovations in learning and teaching*

Groups of innovations	No.
1. Changing the curriculum, teaching and assessment	59
2. Using information and communication technology for learning	41
3. Changing student attitudes and improving their skills	24
4. Staffing	4
5. Dealing with competition and rivalry	3
6. Assuring quality of provision	2
Total (a few responses fell into two categories)	133

Using information and communication technology for learning

Our respondents listed 41 innovations that used ICT for learning. Among them were instances of teaching materials being delivered to students on CD ROM or the Web. Interactive Web sites featured in many, although there was no indication of whether these sites achieve economies of scale; some required students to use commercial software such as Lotus Learning Space and Blackboard, or UK-developed software (eg Byzantium). A few instances of national or international videoconferencing were mentioned.

Changing student attitudes and improving their skills

We noticed that serious concern about student attitudes was reflected less in the 24 innovations listed than was the desire to improve students' skills. Many examples involved teaching relevant study and ICT skills or providing support services for students. Others were aimed at enabling students to work in teams or groups. A few tested students' abilities on admission.

Staffing

Among the four innovations in this group, one involved recruiting appropriately qualified staff. The other three were aimed at staff development: the topics included improving lecture delivery, training tutors well and teaching e-learning competencies.

Dealing with competition and rivalry

Only three innovations fell clearly into this group. One involved international taught doctorates, another was based on partnership with overseas companies and the third gave students opportunities for consultancies in a multinational company.

Assuring quality of provision

Although many of the innovations may well contribute to improved quality, only two were aimed specifically at quality assurance. One involved the use of focus groups to explore quality considerations within units. The other involved accreditation of an innovative accounting course.

The search for 'newsworthy' stories

In early 2001 we started a search for further information on the innovations, with a view to creating and publishing 'success stories' in partnership with the authors concerned. The search was not easy. For the 126 innovations, there were 134 contacts. Some contacts were unreachable owing to wrong e-mail addresses. Some were the wrong contacts. Some had no e-mail addresses. So much for the accuracy of a few of our informants!

We told each e-mail contact that BEST was trying to find out more about the newsworthy innovations listed by the respondents. We asked the contacts to post to us any published or unpublished papers – or CDs/videos! – they had that described and/or evaluated that particular innovation. We said we would like internal committee papers, student handbook entries, student guides or course award documentation if these were available. We accepted them electronically as well as by snail mail. We also told the contacts that BEST might invite them to prepare a case study for national dissemination.

The next stage was to read and/or view what was sent and get back to the contacts to find out more details if necessary. When we had enough information, we compiled summaries of about 40 of the better ones and asked senior BEST members to choose the most newsworthy among these. In the end, we selected 12 innovations. We invited the authors of these to write them up for publication as examples of good practice, in return for the publicity, sharing the copyright and a modest honorarium.

For the authors chosen by BEST, writing up included adopting (in most cases) a straightforward rubric with a set of headings. Authors also agreed to work with the editors in 'telling the story', clarifying meaning and meeting a word limit of 6,000 words. In fact, this arrangement worked very well.

Our original plans for publishing the BEST stories were that, first, they would go on the BEST Web site (http://www.business.ltsn.ac.uk/); second, they would be printed by BEST as a series of individual booklets, complete with ISBNs, and, third, they would appear in a book. The first two stages have been completed, and this book is the third.

Since innovation is occurring continuously, further innovations in learning and teaching come to light each year. We started the search for more success stories when we decided to follow up on innovations reported as still in the early stages of development in 2001. But we also mounted a second Web-based survey. In BEST's first survey respondents prioritized 11 potential tasks for BEST (see Table 1.2).

The top priorities by far were 1) the use of electronic resources for learning and teaching, and 2) adding or switching to e-learning and e-teaching, followed by 3) improving student assessment strategies and methods. As we had already collected quite a few stories relating to the first two priorities, BEST decided that the second survey, in late 2001, would focus on innovations in assessment of student performance. We used BEST's own extensive database of postal addresses. As before, a letter invited respondents or their representatives to go to a Web site at the Open University. On the site was a short questionnaire asking about the range of assessment methods in use and any newsworthy innovations. We received 42 leads, and sought further information about each innovation. In particular we

Table 1.2 *Ranking of potential tasks for BEST*

Potential tasks for BEST	No.	Rank
Use electronic resources for learning and teaching	56	1.5
Add, or switch to, e-learning and e-teaching	56	1.5
Improve student assessment strategies and methods	44	3
Forecast changes in learning and teaching in your environment	40	4
Set up local or regional benchmarking groups	35	5
Help students in learning to learn	33	6.5
Prepare for teaching quality audits	33	6.5
Collaborate across disciplines	30	8
Raise student completion rates	26	9
Review curriculum changes and introduce new courses	22	10
Introduce staff to quality assurance procedures	13	11

wanted any papers, published or unpublished, written about these and any other innovations in this field. This search did not yield any additional BEST stories, however. Instead, Chapter 14 summarizes the findings, including some interesting minor innovations in assessing students' achievement.

The stories so far

We say 'so far' because we are sure there are more stories worth telling and the search will continue as long as funds are available through the Learning and Teaching Support Network. The 12 newsworthy stories in this book, BEST's first set, range across business (4), management (5) and accounting (3). Some draw on information and communication technology but others do not. Most are from newer universities and colleges. Some are tried and tested over 5–10 years; others are more recent. The stories are accessible on the BEST Web site (http://www.business.ltsn.ac.uk/). All employ methods of learning and teaching that are transferable to other business school settings. Our summaries follow, in the order in which they were published and in which they appear in this volume.

Chapter 2, Resource-based learning in the business environment, by Roger Ottewill and Ann Wall, School of Business and Finance, Sheffield Hallam University

This is the story of how tutors responsible for a business environment unit of study, driven by the desire to enhance the quality of their students' learning experience and under pressure to secure efficiency gains, provided an innovative form of resource-based learning. Their students gained access to four types of resource to support them in achieving learning outcomes: a unit learning scheme; learning support materials; a Web site; and timetabled weekly 'learning encounters' with tutors. Assessment was through a seamless web of coursework and examination tasks, the former being both formative and summative. The unit was well received and greatly valued by students, and the delivery mode enabled tutors to play to their strengths while ensuring equivalent experience for all students.

Chapter 3, From leading edge to mainstream: the evolving Brighton Business School intranet, by Becci Newton, Cameron Paine and Stephen Flowers, Brighton Business School, University of Brighton

An intranet is an 'in-house' computer network that facilitates information and file sharing within a closed group of users. An intranet in an educational context is an innovation that enhances student access to information relating to their studies. A pilot intranet was introduced in Brighton Business School in late 1997. A second version using industry-standard software went operational in September 2000. This story is about the school when the system first arrived and compares it with the context in 2001, tracing changes in the system's conceptual design and underlying technology. It analyses student and staff reaction at the two release dates. Finally, it discusses how such a project, in an established school with established learning and teaching methods, can be evaluated.

Chapter 4, The International Consultancy Assignment, by David Edelshain, Sir John Cass Business School, City University, and New York University in London, and Carol Vielba, Sir John Cass Business School, City University

This story is about the development and introduction of an innovative course taught jointly by City University Business School (CUBS, now Sir John Cass Business School) in London and Fordham Business School in New York, originally in conjunction with Chase Manhattan Corporation. The course ran in 1998, 1999 and 2000, and is continuing in expanded form. Fordham Business School wanted to develop international links with other schools and approached CUBS. At that time the authors were directing the MBA programme at CUBS and had been developing international business as a prime feature of it. The two schools set up a joint course that would stress learning of knowledge and skills needed for international business. Read the story to find out how students from both schools were briefed and worked together before presenting their work to each other. The practical assignment topic for 1998 was the euro; in later years, e-commerce. The project's style shifted from research on behalf of a client to an international consultant's assignment. Like many innovations, this one raised pedagogical and academic issues.

Chapter 5, Introducing action learning into a business school, by Tom Bourner and John Lawson, Brighton Business School, University of Brighton

This story is about action learning in the business school at the University of Brighton. The authors tell how action learning began, and, following its successful introduction, how the innovation spread throughout the school and beyond. They analyse its development and application as self-managed action learning. They reflect on the worst and best aspects of its introduction, and what they might have done differently to ensure its wider adoption in the business school. Finally, they consider what helped and hindered the overall establishment of action learning.

Chapter 6, Byzantium for learning accounting in English business schools, by Ashok Patel, De Montfort University, Anne Cook, Liverpool John Moores University, and Tudor Spencer, University of Hertfordshire

Byzantium is interactive computer-aided learning software for introductory financial and management accounting. Innovatively, it emulates a human tutor and enables business school students to learn, practise and test their skills. Byzantium was developed by a consortium of six universities within the Teaching and Learning Technology Programme of the Higher Education Funding Councils of the United Kingdom (1993–97). This story is about Byzantium's design, development and evaluation, and how students and staff can use the software. It includes details of Byzantium's successful use at business schools in two English universities, Liverpool John Moores University and the University of Hertfordshire.

Chapter 7, Using Monopoly© as an introduction to financial accounting, by Graham Clayton, Department of Accounting and Law, University of Plymouth Business School

Playing the board game Monopoly© enables students to run their own property businesses and, thereby, create their own financial transactions. At Plymouth, students are actively involved in this innovation. Theory and practice meet. As a result basic financial accounting techniques are assimilated very effectively and students develop as autonomous learners. The authors have used Monopoly© since 1998 for the initial stages of a first-level financial accounting module. The module leader's main role is to plan and administer the exercise. The students, to a large extent, run each session themselves. The students prepare balance sheets and profit and loss accounts for four trading periods. In addition, the exercise demands that they can interpret, at a basic level, their own and their peers' financial statements. In playing the game, they develop a range of personal skills. They have greeted Monopoly© with much enthusiasm and feedback has been very posi-tive. They enjoy being actively involved. Creating and recording their own finan-cial transactions is an effective way of developing an understanding of how to draft simple financial statements. Adding a 'betting' element helps to develop the students' skills in interpreting financial statements. Because of the success of this approach, Monopoly© is now also used on other modules at both undergraduate and postgraduate level. Again the impact on, and feedback from, students has been positive.

Chapter 8, Peer assessment and enhancing students' learning, by Anne Gregory, Liz Yeomans and Joanne Powell, Leeds Business School, Leeds Metropolitan University

This is the story of how the authors innovatively used peer assessment in a pivotal module in their BA in Public Relations. They show how peer assessment relates directly to their learning, teaching and assessment philosophy for the course. A group assignment, addressing a typical public relations scenario, was the most appropriate form of assessment, because it could simulate types of campaigns and working practices in the public relations industry. The authors introduced peer assessment of individual students' contributions to encourage cooperative working and to ensure fairness in marking. The authors also knew there were numerous objections to peer assessment, and that the principles and processes essential to making it acceptable to and successful with students required careful introduction, transparency and constant reinforcement. Used properly, peer assessment has proved valuable in rewarding appropriately individual students' and groups' contributions. It facilitates students' ownership of the assessment process and encourages them to take responsibility for their own learning. Informal and formal evaluations of the module show that students give it the highest rating of any core module in the degree. Although peer assessment does not remove all student objections to group work, it has proved effective in reduc-ing what they perceive as unfairness in group marks, and in encouraging careful reflection on individual and group contributions and performance.

Chapter 9, Group work and the Web: FINESSE and TAGS, by Rosa Michaelson, Christine Helliar, David Power and Donald Sinclair, Accountancy and Business Finance, University of Dundee, and Colin Allison, Computer Science, University of St Andrews

This is the story of FINESSE (Finance Education in a Scalable Software Environment) and, to a lesser extent, of TAGS (Tutor and Group Support), both examples of innovative Web-based learning environments. They provide a different kind of Web interface for group-based work from those virtual learn-ing environments (VLEs) currently used in higher and further education.

FINESSE is a Web-based portfolio management game for student groups, used in a final year honours course in an accountancy and business finance department. The game sits within the TAGS system. The software for TAGS provides easy-to-use administrative tools for lecturers administering group work: it allows for real-time data to be integrated with the totality of the Web interface; and goes beyond the typical multiple choice assessments currently available on the standard VLE. The project consortium for FINESSE consisted of finance lecturers and computing specialists, who worked together during 1996–98. This story first highlights the project's rationale and objectives; then it describes the educational context and how the students use the software. Next it describes development of the software, and discusses the resources that constitute the portfolio management game. It summarizes the evaluation methods used for the FINESSE project and offers an overview of TAGS. The final section explores lessons learnt by the team, and lists implications for collaborative software development in business education.

Chapter 10, Using learning technology resources in teaching management accounting, by Greg Stoner, Department of Accounting and Finance, University of Glasgow

The University of Glasgow has succeeded in integrating learning technology resources into the teaching of an innovative first-level management accounting undergraduate course. This story tells how the development evolved over seven years and the benefits it brought. It also reports on the evaluation and subsequent adaptation needed to enhance the students' learning experience. Finally, it attempts to draw lessons from experience, particularly about how different learning resources can be integrated into course design and later evaluated.

Chapter 11, Creating a Web site for studying strategic management, by Colin Clarke-Hill, University of Gloucestershire, and Ismo Kuhanen, formerly at Plymouth University

This story is about the efforts of two academics teaching strategic management, research methods and management ethics at different universities, who decided to create their own innovative Web site for students and colleagues (http://www.strategios.co.uk). They adapted the A T Kearney 3-C model to meet the students' needs. They describe the site and its design and explain how it expanded through links to other sites. They also give details of their students' evaluation of it. Finally, they discuss the use of Internet technology as a means of reducing costs and facilitating radical transformation of business and university systems, and argue for wider use of personal controlled learning Webs that are free to access and use, to further students' understanding of the subject area.

Chapter 12, The live consultancy case study, by Suzanne O'Hara, Steve Reeve and Stephen Flowers, University of Brighton

Some years ago the authors designed a 'live' consultancy case study, for use in a part-time MBA residential programme. Long experience of running this activity on more than 30 occasions led them to believe that it provides a rich learning experience for all those who take part. It brings together the essential elements of a Master's-level qualification: implementable solutions to 'real-world' problems, informed by academic concepts and analytical thinking. The story explains how and why the original process was conceived and goes on to outline its subsequent development. The authors believe that this case study exercise offers a vehicle for learning on any Master's-level, post-experience practitioner course.

Chapter 13, Building and maintaining distributed communities of practice: knowledge management in the OUBS MBA, by Stephen Little, Wendy Fowle and Paul Quintas, Open University

This story is about the development of a new Open University Business School course on knowledge management, now being taught to students at a distance using a wide range of media. In the course, technologies that support knowledge strategies are examined along with current best practice in knowledge management. A key feature is the use of established and state-of-the-art knowledge technologies in creating the distance learning environment. One aim is to build and maintain distributed communities of practice among tutors and students, despite the distances between them, through asynchronous text conferencing using FirstClass™, plus synchronous voice, text and graphics conferencing using Lyceum, a new software system.

Comparing the best stories with those excluded

Whatever happened to all the other innovations in learning and teaching identified during the Web-based national landscape survey? Why have they been excluded (so far)? Table 1.3 lists the main reasons why we picked particular innovations. Each innovation had to show at least several of the characteristics: be newsworthy and likely to be of interest to other business schools; be fully developed; be obviously transferable to other universities and colleges; be used by at least 25 students a year; be sustained financially by the university; be repeated more than once; be written up; and be evaluated, with success demonstrated. It also helped if the development of the innovation contained lessons for colleagues elsewhere, and if it had been used successfully in at least one other university or department.

As for the innovations that were rejected, they lacked the positive characteristics shown by the BEST stories, and in some cases had other drawbacks too, as Table

Table 1.3 *Comparing the BEST stories with those excluded*

BEST stories were selected because the:	Other innovations were rejected because the:
innovation was newsworthy, likely to be of interest to other business schools.	innovation was of limited interest and the papers reflected little or no innovation.
innovation had been fully developed.	innovation was still under development.
innovation was obviously transferable to other universities and colleges.	innovation was grounded in a single individual and not easily transferable.
innovation was used by at least 25 students a year.	number of students involved each year was small (fewer than 25).
funding was sustained by the university.	funding was short-lived and has ended.
innovation had been repeated more than once.	innovation had run only once.
innovation had been written up.	author(s) could not set aside time for writing it up.
innovation integrated ICT into learning and teaching.	hardware and/or software were innovative but methods of learning not.
innovation had been evaluated and success demonstrated.	
development of the innovation contained lessons for colleagues elsewhere.	author was under a non-disclosure agreement; rights to marketed innovation were held by a company.
innovation had been used successfully in at least one other university or department.	innovation had already been tested better elsewhere.
	innovation was too simple to make a story.
	innovation was only just approved.
	innovation was too vaguely defined.

1.3 shows. We were surprised to learn that some of these so-called successes that had been drawn to our attention by senior staff in UK business schools were of limited interest and the papers reflected little or no innovation. Others were still under development, or else grounded in a single individual and not easily transferable. A few innovations served fewer than 10 students a year, and did not look cost-effective. Some authors had little or no evaluative data, or their evaluative data indicated very little success. In one or two cases, the technology was new, but the learning and teaching were old: is putting your old lecture notes straight on to the Web newsworthy? Some innovations had been tried only once: we shall wait to see if they are repeated. And then there were those innovations that were so successful that the author was under a non-disclosure agreement, or the rights to the innovation were held by a company controlling it, as in the case of a novel teaching CD ROM under development in Scotland. Finally, just a few were too simple to make a story, or had only just been approved, or were really too vaguely defined to be describable as innovations, even though somebody senior thought they were!

Evidence of success in the BEST stories

In our search for evidence of success in innovative learning and teaching we developed criteria (see Table 1.3) to use in selecting 'stories' brought to our attention through the BEST survey or by other sources. We recognize that these are subjective criteria that may not satisfy critics who prefer to look at objective measures of performance. Politicians – and business school managers – like to ask two particular questions about innovations: does the innovation produce better results for the same cost, or does it cost less and produce just as good results as the old system or method? By 'results' they usually refer to the number and quality of passes achieved by students. If more pass than before, or the quality is higher, then the innovation must be worthwhile. Or if as many pass and the quality is as high as before, but the cost is lower, then again the innovation is worth disseminating.

Such comparisons, in our experience, prove extraordinarily hard to draw. The old and the new are different. Testing students' performance in the same way as before may not be at all appropriate. If comparisons based on testing are shaky, those based on costs are even more so. Suitable costing models are often simply unavailable for both the old and the new. Where models have been developed, their underlying assumptions can be questioned. The cost data are hard to obtain and must often be fudged.

These are reasons why we rejected the 'hard-nosed' cost-effectiveness approach of some evaluators of educational innovations. Instead, we looked for evidence that an innovation in learning and teaching had acquired something of a reputation for success, as judged by the innovators' academic peers and possibly their students (see Chapter 8, for instance). Mere popularity of an innovation among students is not a sufficient condition for its survival and dissemination. Respect for it among staff may sometimes be.

There is no clear definition of what it is for an innovation to be newsworthy and likely to be of interest to other business schools. In one sense, successful innovations do not fit the widely accepted view of the most saleable news being bad news. There are no disasters to report, dramas to portray or tragedies to mourn. Yet success stories command interest because their originators have solved problems with enthusiasm and energy. Written well, they convey the excitement of creativity and invention. They may inspire others to be innovative or at least to try using the innovation for themselves.

For an innovation to be fully developed, we think it should be well beyond the pilot stage, without necessarily being absolutely 'polished'. Perhaps the novelty has worn off a little, but no matter if the innovation has bedded down and is working well. In the case of the intranet for Brighton Business School (Chapter 3), we were pleased that the pilot system was used to assess whether this technology was wanted by both students and staff. By the time of the BEST 2000 survey, the full version had been released, and when the BEST story was written it had been in operation for quite a few months. Though the context shifted because of restructuring in the university, the change process went fairly smoothly despite constraints. Evaluation data showed that students' excitement had by then changed to acceptance but that their expectations of what staff would do in teaching with the new intranet were not yet entirely fulfilled. Staff said they were still uncertain about how to use it and why. By 2001/02, a cultural shift was occurring. The intranet was becoming part of the school's academic experience, almost institutionalized.

Innovations are transferable to other universities and colleges if they cover curriculum content that can be taught elsewhere, or if they employ methods that can be copied, or if they include software or teaching materials that can be made available to other institutions. Byzantium (Chapters 6 and 10) is an example. This software for teaching topics in financial and management accounting, after being externally funded in its development phase, was put to regular teaching use in universities in England and Scotland. Monopoly©, the trading game (Chapter 7), was first deployed to teach financial and management accounting in US undergraduate and postgraduate business education. Plymouth University introduced it into a business administration programme from where it migrated to three other programmes.

We applied an arbitrary figure in saying that an innovation should be used by at least 25 students a year. We did not think that anything used with a smaller group than that would command much respect. Indeed, we would prefer to disseminate innovations that are always scalable: that is to say, that can be applied to much larger numbers, preferably with a less-than-pro-rata increase in cost. The International Consultancy Assignment (Chapter 4) started small, with 18 students in 1998 from each of the two universities involved; yet it has built up a good deal since then. Some innovative methods, such as peer assessment (Chapter 8) or the live consultancy case study (Chapter 12), may still work with smaller numbers than 25, of course.

If an innovation is being sustained financially by the university, particularly for the second, third or fourth year running, then either it has an extraordinarily effective champion or it is seen to work. Universities and colleges have a reputation for being adaptive, but they are generally reluctant to commit their own funds, as opposed to somebody else's, to perpetuate anything innovative that is not clearly to their advantage. FINESSE, a Web-based portfolio management game involving group learning (Chapter 9), was started with support from the

Scottish Funding Council, as a joint project between Dundee and St Andrews, but is now built into the teaching at three universities.

If an innovation is repeated more than once, this repetition usually includes some sort of further development and problems in earlier rounds are ironed out. Quality improves. The International Consultancy Assignment (Chapter 4) required phenomenal effort and organization to get it started, and there were plenty of difficulties in the first year. It turned into a successful innovation as it built up over several years. At Glasgow University (Chapter 10) many changes were introduced following evaluation of students' use of Byzantium and Understand Management Accounting software, but the innovations have been repeated. Developing a Web site for teaching strategic management (Chapter 11) turned out to be a four-year project initially, but it continues to this day. The live consultancy case study (Chapter 12) was refined over several years.

Another arbitrary criterion we applied in selecting the BEST stories was that they should be written up already, if only as conference papers, but preferably for publication in print. In some cases (Chapters 3, 4, 5, 6 and 10, for instance), they had been written up from several angles. Our reasoning was that an innovation that was succeeding would not lie unnoticed. Usually the originators wrote it up, and we looked too for other written evidence from less involved observers.

Finally, we searched for evidence that the innovation had been evaluated, with success demonstrated. Evaluation takes many forms. Usually student and staff satisfaction are assessed by questionnaire and sometimes through interviews as well. Occasionally there is observation. Often the innovators mull over the whole process or system to find ways of improving it.

To take just one example, Ottewill and Wall (Chapter 2) evaluated their resource-based learning innovation using methods imposed by Sheffield Hallam University plus their own. The data enabled them to show that it was well received and greatly valued by students, relative to other units being taught at the same time. The questions ranged across clarity of learning outcomes; quality of the support materials; extent to which learning encounters were interesting and stimulating; helpfulness of feedback on assessment; and organization of the student experience. Other feedback led to ethical issues being made more explicit in the unit. From the tutors, evaluation data raised the problems of dependence and free riders in using resource-based learning.

It is clear from later chapters that none of the BEST stories meets all of the criteria we have discussed here. For example, Stephen Little and his colleagues write about innovations in teaching knowledge management in the Open University's MBA (Chapter 13): this particular story is, in our opinion, newsworthy and likely to be of interest to other business schools for several reasons. Its content is innovative, and so are the means of delivery. It is fully developed and used by several hundred students a year. It is sustained financially by the university and has been repeated more than once. It has been evaluated, with success demonstrated. It had not been written up, however, and as it stands the whole innovation cannot be transferred to other universities and colleges. Parts can be.

Evidence of failure from the BEST survey

The BEST surveys were not probing for evidence of failure of innovations in learning and teaching, or in assessment, but we think we found some, if our interpretations are correct. Without revealing the names of the business schools concerned, we can say we believe that it is quite common for apparently promising innovations to fail. The reasons are fairly well known: the champions leave, the original funding ends, the rules change, the course or module is dropped, demand falls away, the novelty fades, nobody wants to make the extra effort needed, and so on. Lessons are learnt, maybe. The fact is that failure is not easily talked about between competitors, particularly in the world of business.

Dissemination and diffusion of successful innovations is easy by comparison, through benchmarking clubs, good practice exchanges and other means that we discuss in Chapter 15. The chapters that follow are about successes in the new world of learning and teaching.

Reference

Business Education Support Team (BEST) (2002) *Managing Better: UK business schools today and tomorrow*, Business Education Support Team, Learning and Teaching Support Network, Open University Business School, Milton Keynes

Chapter 2

Resource-based learning in the business environment

Roger Ottewill and Ann Wall

Driven by the desire to enhance the quality of students' learning experience coupled with the pressure to secure efficiency gains, tutors responsible for a business environment unit of study at Sheffield Hallam University provide their students with a form of resource-based learning. Their students have access to four types of resource to support them in achieving learning outcomes. These are a unit learning scheme; learning support materials; a Web site; and timetabled weekly 'learning encounters' with tutors. Assessment of their performance is based on the principle of a seamless web of coursework and examination tasks with the former being both formative and summative. Evaluative evidence, gathered by a variety of means, shows that the unit is well received and greatly valued by students and that the delivery mode enables tutors to play to their strengths while ensuring equivalent experience for all students.

Objectives

In this chapter we focus on a first year unit of study at Sheffield Hallam University (SHU) designed to equip students with concepts and tools that they need to analyse the social and demographic environment of business and public sector organizations. Overall, our aim at SHU is to provide students with a rewarding, challenging and transparent learning experience. In pursuing this aim, resource-based learning has a pivotal role to play.

Since the mid-1990s, when the unit was introduced, SHU tutors responsible for it have developed and applied a resource-based learning (RBL) approach to learner support. The origins of the approach, which combines elements of open learning with more traditional methods of learning facilitation such as workshops (Jennings and Ottewill, 1996), lay in experiments with open learning materials to support campus-based students during the early 1990s (Ottewill, 1994).

In telling the story of RBL's contribution to delivery of the Social and Demographic Environment unit, we will elaborate on the context, explain the rationale for adopting RBL and highlight some of the tensions we experienced. We will describe and explain the purpose of the different types of resource provided for students, while commenting on the relationship between them and their links with the assessment strategy. Finally, we will evaluate the approach, discuss some issues raised and point to likely future developments. Throughout, our emphasis is on reflective practice.

Context

Social and Demographic Environment (SDE) is a 20-credit unit in the Business and Management undergraduate programme in the School of Business and Finance at SHU. It was introduced in 1995 as a compulsory unit for students on the Public Policy and Management degree route (Business and Public Policy since 2000) and on a BTEC HND route in Public Policy and Management. It has also been an option for students on the business degree routes (ie Business Studies, International Business with Languages and Business Systems Modelling) and, until 2001, the HNC/D in Business Studies. Each year, out of approximately 500 first year degree and BTEC students on the programme, between 150 and 200 have taken SDE. A few students from the combined studies and ERASMUS programmes have also opted for it.

The unit strongly emphasizes using knowledge about social and demographic components of the external environment of public sector and business organizations, and the development of transferable work-related skills. It is neither a pure sociology nor a pure demography unit. Table 2.1 gives the flavour of its subject matter, which is organized around four themes: the past in the present (1, 2 and 12); the demographic environment (3 and 4); societal culture and its transmission (5 to 8); and divisions in society (9 to 11).

The school wants students to use their knowledge of SDE later in their studies. Thus, for public policy students SDE serves as a foundation for second year units, such as Managing Welfare and Health Care Services and Policy (eg the growing appreciation of the impact of social class on health status). For business students, SDE underpins units in marketing and human resource management. At Level 3, Equal Opportunities is a popular option for both sets of students and has a very

Table 2.1 *Topics in the Social and Demographic Environment unit*

No.	Topic	No.	Topic
1	Key developments in British society pre-1945	6	The family
2	Key developments in British society post-1945	7	Education
		8	Media
3	Introduction to demography	9	Class divisions in British society
4	The census	10	Gender divisions in British society
5	Culture	11	Racial divisions in British society
		12	Continuity and change

direct link back to SDE. It enables students to study racial divisions and discrimination in greater depth.

Until 2001, SDE was taught in semesters of 15–16 weeks. The first 12 weeks were allocated to formal timetabled teaching and learner support and the remainder to revision and examinations. For 20-credit units like SDE, timetabled hours consisted of a one-hour weekly lecture for all students plus a two-hour weekly session for groups of 20–25 students. For RBL purposes, these weekly lectures and group sessions are called 'learning encounters'.

To supplement their formal timetabled sessions, students were expected to devote another 9–10 hours per week per unit to self-managed activities. These include coursework assignments (40 per cent weighting) and preparation for examinations (60 per cent weighting); groundwork for group sessions; and using paper-based and electronic resources to develop a broader awareness and appreciation of the unit's subject matter (Bannister, Hanson and Ottewill, 2002; Ottewill, 2002). The total learning time for SDE is 12–13 hours per week or 200 hours per semester.

Since 2001, a 'long thin' delivery mode has been in operation. Although the total amount of time formally allocated to learning encounters has not increased, it is now spread over two semesters instead of one, with a one-hour lecture every fortnight and a one-hour group session every week. This has the advantage of enabling students to spread what was previously one week's learning over two, with the time allocated to self-managed activities being adjusted accordingly thereby giving them a longer period to undertake assignments and reflect on feedback. As a result, we have been able to reduce the gradient of their learning curve. The change to a 'long thin' delivery mode also holds out the possibility of opting for what could be described as a 'lecture sandwich' pattern of delivery. This would be based on the following: a pre-lecture group session during which students would, amongst other things, pool their prior learning to prepare for the lecture; an interactive lecture; and a post-lecture session, which would serve as an opportunity for checking learning from the lecture and subsequent reflection on its content.

To assist students, we have set out their entitlements and responsibilities in a unit charter. Entitlements include provision of learning resources; access to guidance and support from tutors; return of, and feedback on, assessed coursework;

and investigation of any failure to secure an entitlement. Responsibilities relate to the learning process, such as being aware of entitlements and keeping abreast of any changes in the delivery arrangements; meeting assignment deadlines; managing one's own learning; and preparing for, attending and making contributions during group sessions. Having such a charter is by no means unproblematic since it has often proved easier for us to guarantee student entitlements than to enforce student responsibilities.

Rationale

Our development of an RBL approach has been prompted by five main considerations. First is the desire to make SDE a flagship unit in order to enhance its attractiveness in the eyes of students for whom it is an option. To this end, tutors have provided a supportive and reassuring, as well as high-quality, learning experience for students. With SDE being a first year unit, many students taking it are still adjusting to the demands of higher education, especially the very considerable increase in their self-managed learning time. Here, RBL has been seen as offering an effective way of supporting them, although, as discussed later, this has given rise to issues concerning the appropriate balance between tutor support and learner autonomy. That said, through preparing and selecting resources for their students, tutors can try to ensure that students use their time profitably and productively.

A second consideration has been the need to secure efficiency gains. This has been brought into sharper relief by increasing financial pressures on both tutors and students. Like other universities and colleges, SHU has had to find ways of coping with a declining unit of resource. For SDE, this has meant that only about 25 per cent of students' learning time involves face-to-face contact with tutors. There are now larger numbers of students in lectures and, more significantly, in 'small' (!) group sessions. In such a situation, RBL has been seen as a way of compensating for the relatively limited amount of face-to-face contact time and increased group sizes; of helping students to get the most from their self-managed time; and of enhancing the quality of learning encounters. The increasing financial pressure on students means that many have resorted to paid employment to support themselves. Consequently, in class they are often tired and cannot give of their best. RBL provides them with some flexibility regarding their self-managed time and, if well designed, the resources can enhance their efficiency as learners.

A third consideration is the undergraduate programme's explicitly vocational nature at SHU. For degree students this is symbolized by the work placement in Year 3. For HND students it is reflected in assessment through the medium of BTEC common skill outcomes. Vocationalism implies the need to balance a study of business and the public sector (ie context of employment) with a study for business and the public sector (ie content of employment) (Macfarlane, 1994). Units such as SDE are seen as primarily contextual, in contrast with more overtly vocational units such as Information and Data Handling and Introduction to Finance and Accountancy. In the past, contextual units have tended to betray their disciplinary roots with respect to both subject matter and pedagogy. Hence, there is often little to distinguish, say, an introductory unit in sociology on specialist sociology programmes from a social environment unit on vocationally orientated business and management programmes. As a result, students receive little assistance in appreciating the relevance for the world of work of what they are studying. Lectures, seminars, reading lists and essays remain central features of learning, teaching and assessment strategies. In our case, RBL has enabled the vocational relevance and the business dimension of topics to be elicited in a way that is rarely the case in standard textbooks. Moreover, it has freed up time for this purpose. For example, as mentioned earlier in considering gender and racial divisions in society, space is found for making links with the equal opportunities and equality of access policies currently being pursued by business organizations and public authorities, of which many students will have direct experience through part-time employment. Additionally, the time management and information-gathering skills fostered by RBL are of particular value in the workplace and essential for lifelong learning (Ottewill and Wall, 2000). Because demonstrating the material's relevance to the business and public services has been a particular challenge, we would argue that we have gone further in this respect than units where the subject matter is perceived as self-evidently vocational, and we are therefore in the vanguard.

A fourth consideration has been the teaching team. Because of the relatively large numbers of students, three or four tutors have been required. Through careful planning RBL has contributed to a high degree of consistency with respect to the student experience, while providing team members with space and opportunities for personalizing their contribution and playing to their strengths.

A fifth and final consideration has been the diversity of students taking SDE in terms of both their prior knowledge and experience and their route. While some have previously studied components of the unit's subject matter, others have only limited knowledge derived from direct experience of performing the roles of family member, school pupil, part-time employee and newspaper reader. It is rare, however, for any student to have reflected on the subject matter of SDE from a vocational perspective. In helping students do this, we have had to take account of route. Thus, for students on the public policy route, a more public service emphasis has been required (eg the pressure on social care services as a result of the increasing numbers of elderly people). For students on the business routes a more private sector orientation (eg the use of demographic data for market research purposes) has been needed. In these circumstances, RBL has given tutors room for fine tuning essential for capitalizing on the students' interests and aspirations.

Thus, RBL has played an important part in enabling tutors to respond positively and creatively to the demands placed upon them. It has also contributed to the robustness of the learning, teaching and assessment strategy.

Description

At the heart of the learning, teaching and assessment strategy for SDE are the learning outcomes, of which there are three main types: subject-based; personal transferable; and general academic (Allen, 1996). Over the years, the outcomes have been debated and subsequently modified to capture ever more closely changes in the knowledge, understanding and skills of students that tutors have sought to bring about through the learning process. The outcomes for 2002/03 are set out in Table 2.2. We draw a distinction now between essential outcomes (E), which are formally assessed, and useful outcomes (U), for which development opportunities only are provided. Useful outcomes are not formally assessed. To help students pursue and achieve these learning outcomes, we adopt what is called

Table 2.2 *Learning outcomes for 2002/03*

No.	Outcome	Type
E1	Define key terms and concepts associated with contemporary social and demographic issues.	subject-based
E2	Apply knowledge of social and demographic concepts and trends to business activities and public service provision.	subject-based
E3	Illustrate some of the basic ethical principles that inform business activity and public service provision.	subject-based
E4	Demonstrate a sense of history in describing the social and demographic structure of contemporary Britain.	subject-based general academic
E5	Use various theoretical perspectives to analyse different aspects of British society.	subject-based general academic
E6	Locate and utilize oral, paper-based and electronic sources of information about the social and demographic environment.	personal transferable
E7	Employ written communication skills in transmitting information and analyses concerning aspects of the social and demographic environment.	personal transferable
E8	Apply basic mathematical operations and statistical techniques to socio-demographic data.	personal transferable
E9	Evaluate own learning and performance and determine development needs.	personal transferable
U1	Explain how social and demographic factors affect employment opportunities and career choice.	personal transferable
U2	Collaborate with fellow students on a variety of tasks involving different aspects of the social and demographic environment.	personal transferable

elsewhere a 'maximalist' stance (Bannister, Hanson and Ottewill, 2002). This involves providing students with four main types of resource: a unit learning scheme; learning support materials; a Web site; and the timetabled weekly learning encounters with tutors.

The *unit learning scheme* serves as a map of the unit and a guide for the students on their journey through the SDE of business and public sector organizations. More specifically it:

- provides a commentary on each of the learning outcomes;
- shapes student expectations regarding their responsibilities as learners and those of tutors as learning facilitators, the delivery methods and the assessment arrangements;
- helps students maximize the potential of resources at their disposal;
- supports students through the four stages of the learning process: pre-lecture preparation, lecture, post-lecture tasks and group sessions (Ottewill and Jennings, 1998);
- encourages a more active and independent learning style;
- ensures that tutors operate within the same parameters; and
- explains the assessment arrangements and relates the assessment criteria to outcomes covered by a particular instrument of assessment (see later).

Underlying the unit learning scheme is the belief that tutors have some responsibility for the whole of each student's learning time and not simply that part that is in class.

The *learning support materials* have been specially prepared by tutors and provide students with the basic knowledge and conceptual underpinning they need. They are based on principles of open learning and include self-assessment activities, linked to one or more of the learning outcomes, such as:

- calculating birth and death rates and dependency ratios;
- identifying the implications for product design and marketing of the increased concern within society for health, convenience and lifelong learning;
- listing ways in which businesses and public services support and/or replace functions that were previously the sole preserve of families;
- relating personal experiences of learning and teaching to broader trends in education;
- suggesting reasons for the gender balance within the various categories of staff employed by SHU;
- identifying the ethnic groups to which they belong and some of their principal characteristics.

The materials are also designed to encourage deep, as opposed to surface, learning and students are expected to reflect on what they bring to the unit – their prior knowledge and experience of social and demographic trends.

By working through the materials in their self-managed time students can relatively painlessly arm themselves with sufficient knowledge and ideas to make a lively contribution to group sessions. They are also in a better position to appreciate the vocational significance of the unit's subject matter.

The main purpose of the *Web site*, which was set up in 1999, has been to add value to (not to replicate) the paper-based unit learning scheme and learning support materials. Thus, students are still provided with their own copy of these documents. The unit team is opposed to using the Web site as an electronic dumping ground for documents that are best suited to a paper-based format. Figure 2.1 illustrates the site's home page.

Key elements of the site are:

- the noticeboard, which serves as a channel of communication between the unit leader and students;
- weekly multiple choice questions for self-assessment purposes and to help students prepare for one element of the examination paper;
- weekly PowerPoint presentations, for students to revisit the lecture;
- links to sites of particular vocational relevance to the unit, such as the Office of National Statistics and Commission for Racial Equality (ie Learning Zone: Resources: Web).

Since 2001, the Web site has been in a Blackboard format to ensure consistency with other units. In one respect this has been a retrograde step since it has made the SDE site less distinctive. In another respect, however, it means that students are becoming more proficient e-learners.

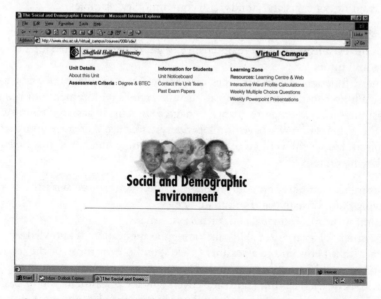

Figure 2.1   *Social and Democratic Environment Web site home page 1999–2001*

As we said earlier, for timetabling purposes *learning encounters with tutors* are formally designated lectures (one hour per week) and group sessions or seminars (two hours per week). However, we ought to stress that these encounters are not primarily about the dissemination of information. Lectures provide tutors with opportunities for exploring their interests and conveying their enthusiasm to students. The role of group sessions is to facilitate the learning process by providing students with opportunities for:

- contributing to the analysis of socio-demographic trends, such as the changing pattern of family life, and assessment of their relative importance for businesses and public sector agencies (eg undertaking a demographic audit of different types of organization, such as a sports centre, supermarket and university);
- pooling responses to the self-assessment activities in the learning support materials and the results of information-gathering exercises (eg on social trends);
- accessing, manipulating and interpreting demographic data in both paper-based and electronic formats;
- participating in a community of learning;
- working, either individually or collectively, on the application of socio-demographic concepts to business activities (eg the link between societal norms and values and advertising);
- receiving support in tackling tasks they find difficult;
- considering collective feedback on assignments, with a view to enhancing their performance in the examination;
- illustrating concepts and trends with contemporary examples.

Above all, the encounters are intended to demonstrate that effective learning requires the establishment and maintenance of a productive partnership between students and tutors.

A crucial function of all four types of resource is to facilitate the assessment process. Within constraints arising from the university's requirement of making a clear distinction between performance of degree students in assessed coursework and in the examination, we have developed a systematic and creative approach to assessing students' achievement of the essential learning outcomes. It is based on the following principles:

- a seamless web between coursework and the examination, with the former having both formative and summative roles;
- a combination of informal and formal assessment;
- assessment of a variety of skills, including the application of knowledge;
- direct links between the assessment task(s) and one or more of the learning outcomes of the unit;
- feedback on each learning outcome covered by the assessment, on the basis of predetermined criteria stated for students in the unit's learning scheme.

Over the years, one of the ongoing challenges has been to ensure that the assessment strategy remains compatible with the learning outcomes for SDE. How this challenge was met in 2000/01 is illustrated in Table 2.3, which should be read in conjunction with Table 2.2.

Thus, the assessment strategy blends more traditional elements, such as essays, which serve to enhance students' critical faculties, with the innovative, namely the ward profile/analysis.

To meet the demands of assessment, students receive guidance on the nature of the tasks involved and the assessment criteria in the unit learning scheme. There are self-assessment activities in the learning support materials, links to useful sites via the Web site, and workshops during the learning encounters. Thus, the learning resources play a crucial role in the assessment process.

Evaluation

The unit has been evaluated using methods imposed by SHU, but the unit team's commitment to innovation was behind the use of other methods, some of which we have written about (see Table 2.4). We want to ensure that both students' and tutors' voices are heard.

Feedback about RBL from students shows that they think its principal benefit for them has been the support and encouragement for experiential and self-managed learning, within a coherent and explicit framework of outcomes. We

Table 2.3 *Assessment strategy for 2002/03*

Coursework element (weighting)	(40%) Outcomes	Examination element (weighting)	(60%) Outcomes
(Electoral) Ward profile – formally assessed (20%)	E2, E6, E7, E8 and E9	(Electoral) Ward analysis (25%)	E2, E7 and E8
Fortnightly quizzes, Web site multiple choice questions – informally assessed	E1	12 short answer questions (10%)	E1 and E7
Essay – formally assessed (15%)	E1, E4, E5, E6 and E7	Essay (15%)	E1, E4, E5, E6 and E7
Week 5 exercises – informally assessed	E3 and E7	Ethical awareness task (10%)	E3 and E7
Preparation for, attendance at and participation in group sessions – formally assessed (5%)	E9	Not applicable	Not applicable

Table 2.4 *Methods of unit evaluation*

Year	Method
1995/96	Unit team 'away-day'.
1996/97	Unit-initiated student survey (Wall and Ottewill, 2000).
1997/98	Student focus group (Ottewill and Brown, 1999).
1998/99	Seminar 1: structured group feedback plus school-wide unit questionnaire. Seminar 2: peer support review with Functions of Business Unit Team (Bingham and Ottewill, 2001) plus school-wide unit questionnaire.
1999/2000	School-wide unit questionnaire plus team meeting, incorporating pilot of unit audit pro forma.
2000/01 and 2001/02	School-wide unit questionnaire plus team meeting.

think the framework, together with the wide range of resources at their disposal, has provided them with the security that they need during their first year at university. Some positive comments from students include:

The learning support material was a very good and useful idea.
Unit learning material is very helpful and improves my organization of notes.
I liked the inclusion of work boxes in the learning support. This made revision easy.
I believe the methods of teaching and learning support materials have been the most effective I have experienced [during my first year] in terms of being interesting, informative and reader friendly.

(Wall and Ottewill, 2000)

In addition, evidence from the school-wide unit questionnaire at the end of the semester indicates that, relative to other units, SDE is well received and greatly valued by students. Students consistently give it well-above-average mean scores in most areas covered. These include clarity of learning outcomes; quality of the support materials; extent to which learning encounters are interesting and stimulating; helpfulness of feedback on assessment; and organization of the student experience. This evidence does not mean that the RBL approach used for SDE is above criticism. Comments from a minority of students suggest that they find it a little patronizing and that it undermines their autonomy as learners.

For tutors, RBL has enabled the quality of the student learning experience to be maintained and even enhanced at a time when the resources available for face-to-face tuition are being spread ever more thinly. It has also facilitated more creative uses of tutor–student contact time by reducing the need to go over ground covered in the unit learning scheme, learning support materials and Web site. Each year, the evaluation process has highlighted where further improvements

Table 2.5 *Innovations and developments arising from the evaluation process*

Year	Innovations/Developments
1996/97	Revamping of learning support materials to ensure consistency of style and format. Introduction of short answer questions on examination paper.
1997/98	Revision of learning outcomes to emphasize vocational nature of unit. Preparation of alternative learning support materials for Week 8 on the theme of employment.
1998/99	Unit charter. Revision and enlargement of unit learning scheme to include assessment criteria and past examination paper. Development of resource bank for unit team members.
1999/2000	Development of Web site.
2000/01	Enlarged role of the Web site through addition of further interactive features. Refinement of assessment strategy to incorporate an ethical awareness task. Work on an ethical awareness e-learning resource.
2001/02	Division of ward profile assignment into two stages, with the first being purely formative.

could be made to the learning environment. Table 2.5 shows examples of innovations and developments arising from the evaluation process.

Arguably, of current developments the most significant are those arising from a decision taken in 2000 to strengthen and make more explicit the ethical dimension of the unit. This was in response to a growing recognition that, taking the Business and Management programme as a whole, ethical issues do not receive the attention they deserve. As a result, students tend to see business and even public services as value-free zones; hence, there is a need to begin the process of stimulating their ethical awareness at an early stage of their studies. However, because of the already crowded curriculum, it was decided to begin work on an e-learning resource to support students with this aspect of their personal and professional development (Ottewill and Wall, 2002).

Alongside these strengths and innovations must be set a couple of major tutor concerns about RBL. These are the reinforcement of a dependency culture – and free riders. We think there is a paradox: the better the learning resources, the more students expect to be spoon-fed by tutors and the less they are willing to read around a subject (Ottewill and Jennings, 1998). While considerable help and support can be justified, given that SDE is a first year unit, RBL can have unfortunate consequences for later years if it undermines efforts to move students towards a greater degree of independent learning. There are no easy answers to this concern, except to ensure that students are made aware of why they have been provided with a considerable amount of support and to encourage them to use the opportunities provided by units like SDE to begin the process of becoming more self-reliant in their learning. The latter can be encouraged, to some extent, by rewarding students whose assessed work reflects a willingness to use learning resources beyond those formally provided and/or prescribed by tutors.

Although 'free riding' is a term more often used in connection with group work, it is appropriate here since underlying RBL is the assumption that students will use the learning resources to prepare systematically and thoroughly for group sessions. For campus-based courses, the resources are not designed to enable students to study at a distance from tutors. On the contrary, their principal role is to enhance the quality of learning encounters, not to replace them. Unfortunately, some students use the provision of learning resources as an excuse for avoiding learning encounters and/or for coasting and cramming, with the result that they have little, if anything, to contribute when they do attend. Unlike more traditional methods of unit delivery, RBL can throw into starker relief lazy and poorly motivated students (Ottewill, 1994) and this form of free riding. Over the years, the question of how to deal with such students has caused more heart-searching amongst unit team members than anything else. Some favour a tough response, such as requiring anyone who has not used the resources in preparing for a group session to do so before they join the class discussion, so that the tutor can concentrate on those who have prepared. Others are more tender-hearted. As a compromise, since 2000/01 five per cent of the weighting for coursework is allocated to preparation for, attendance at, and participation in group sessions (see Table 2.3).

In keeping with the team's commitment to the principle of continuous quality improvement, evaluation and review will remain a key feature of the unit. We will continue to experiment and innovate, with respect to both delivery and content.

Discussion

In looking back over the past six years, we see that one of the biggest challenges has been to ensure that the RBL approach to delivering SDE has retained its cutting edge. We know that after the initial investment of time and energy in producing learning resources, there is a danger that the approach becomes stale and 'routinized', and tutors complacent, especially while feedback from students and colleagues remains favourable. To guard against this and keep the unit team members on their toes, most years have seen a substantial innovation resulting from critical thought and reflective practice on their part, as Table 2.5 illustrates. Every year time has been found to revise and update the unit learning scheme and, more importantly, the learning support materials, to ensure that they do not show their age. When embarking on an RBL approach, we think it is important to remember that the greater the range and variety of learning resources developed by tutors the greater the maintenance costs. At present, these amount to approximately 60 hours of staff time every summer. While this is substantial, the processes involved provide an opportunity for recharging batteries. This is important, given that there is often a gap between ideal and reality in teaching and learner support, yet 'hope springs eternal in every tutor's breast'! Moreover, RBL has enabled a degree of order to be imposed on what is essentially an open-ended and potentially frustrating enterprise.

As for student achievement, while it is the outcome of many influences, RBL has certainly ensured that there has been no deterioration despite increasing pressures on staff time. The marks and grades of students taking SDE cover the full range and compare favourably with those for other units, even though the breadth of skills and knowledge being assessed is often greater (see Table 2.3 for the complex format of the examination paper).

Our experience of RBL to date suggests that the approach is eminently transferable to other units of study and other institutions. Indeed, a number of colleagues within the School of Business and Finance have adopted a similar approach, with SDE serving as an exemplar. The circumstances we outlined under 'Rationale' above clearly have a much wider applicability than just SDE within SHU. Wherever they apply, the approach is worth serious consideration.

Having embraced RBL, members of the SDE unit team are well placed to take advantage of advances in educational technology, such as video streaming and multimedia applications, which can provide students with access to an ever wider variety of learning resources. The subject matter of SDE is such that there is no shortage of good-quality learning resources in every type of medium. For the unit team, the challenge is to evaluate these and harness the best in the support of student learning.

References

Allen, J (1996) Learning outcomes in higher education, *Studies in Higher Education*, **21** (1), pp 93–108

Bannister, P, Hanson, J and Ottewill, R (2002) From dependence to independence: issues concerning student self-managed learning time, *International Journal of Management Education*, **2** (3), pp 35–44

Bingham, R and Ottewill, R (2001) Whatever happened to peer review? Revitalising the contribution of tutors to course evaluation, *Quality Assurance in Education*, **9** (1), pp 32–39

Jennings, P and Ottewill, R (1996) Integrating open learning with face-to-face tuition, *Open Learning*, **11** (2), pp 13–19

Macfarlane, B (1994) Issues concerning the development of the undergraduate business studies curriculum in UK higher education, *Journal of European Business Education*, **4** (1), pp 1–14

Ottewill, R (1994) The contribution of open learning to the delivery of BTEC units: striking a balance between skill development and knowledge acquisition, Conference on the Implementation of Open Learning in Business Studies and Related Areas, Sheffield

Ottewill, R (2002) Student self-managed learning: cause for concern?, *On the Horizon*, **10** (1), pp 12–16

Ottewill, R and Brown, D (1999) Student participation in educational research: experimenting with a focus group, *Journal of Further and Higher Education*, **23** (3), pp 373–80

Ottewill, R and Jennings, P (1998) Open learning versus lecturing: creating and sustaining competitive advantage in business and management education, in *Innovation in Economics and Business III: Innovative practices in business education*, ed R Milter, J Stinson and W Gijselaers, Kluwer, Dordrecht

Ottewill, R and Wall, A (2000) Vocationalism and relevance in higher education: issues concerning the delivery of contextual material to first-year students on business and public sector courses, *Journal of Vocational Education and Training*, **52** (3), pp 521–34

Ottewill, R and Wall, A (2002) Ethical awareness and e-learning: a contradiction in terms, *Teaching Business Ethics*, **6** (3), pp 319–34

Wall, A and Ottewill, R (2000) Delivering contextual material on a vocational business and public sector programme, *Education and Training*, **42** (3), pp 150–59

Contacts

Joint unit leaders:
Ann Wall and Clive Woodman
School of Business and Finance
Sheffield Hallam University
Howard Street
Sheffield S1 1WB
E-mails: A.L.Wall@shu.ac.uk and C.L.Woodman@shu.ac.uk

Chapter 3

From leading edge to mainstream: the evolving Brighton Business School intranet

Becci Newton, Cameron Paine and Stephen Flowers

The term 'intranet' began to enter corporate vocabularies around 1995 (van der Linden, 1998). It is used to describe an 'in-house' computer network, normally based on Internet technology, which facilitates information and file sharing within a closed group of users, such as the employees of a company. We wanted to test whether an intranet could be used in an educational setting to enhance student access to the range of information relating to their studies. We developed a pilot intranet that was introduced to Brighton Business School in autumn 1997. After the pilot, we went on to develop a second version using industry-standard software that was released to the school in September 2000.

In this chapter we try to convey a sense of the impact that an intranet can have on staff and students. We describe the context into which the School's intranet was first released and compare it with the context in 2001. We trace changes in the system's conceptual design and the underlying technology. We examine student and staff reaction at the two release dates and the evaluation data gathered then. Finally, we discuss how such a project, in an established school with established learning and teaching methods, can be evaluated.

Objectives

Our aim for the intranet was to enhance the teaching and learning modes of the school by pulling together the many threads of information available to students in an electronic venue. Initially, we developed a pilot system to assess whether this technology was 'desirable' to both students and staff within the school. Response to the pilot was generally positive and we redeveloped the system, addressing the problems of the pilot, and the second version was released in September 2000.

Context

The University of Brighton is not at the forefront of learning technology development. It positioned itself as a 'fast follower'. In late 1996, when the intranet was proposed, the university's policy focus was on changing the structure of faculties, and on the large-scale implementation of modular programmes and database development for central records. There was, and remains, an understandably cautious view of learning technologies (Flowers and Reeve, 1998; Reeve and Flowers, 2000; Reid, 1999). Certainly in 1996 the university's preference was to keep a watching brief on experimentation within the faculties and externally.

By 2000/01, the year of the intranet's full implementation, the university had made a successful bid to HEFCE for funds to develop its Teaching and Learning Strategy. The aim of this project was to level up intranet provision across the university and to address issues of IT skilling among academics. By August 2001, the project had helped most schools to develop a presence on the central student intranet. The Computer Centre and the Learning Resources Department had been merged as an Information Services Department. Within this department a Learning Technologies Group had been created to continue development of the use of technology and to support and develop the existing student intranet.

Between the pilot intranet (1997/98) and full-scale release (2000/01) significant changes occurred within the Faculty of Business, as part of the university-wide restructuring process. Two undergraduate departments (Finance and Accountancy, and Business Management) merged with the postgraduate Centre for Management Development, to form Brighton Business School. From small departments of around 30 academic staff plus administrative and technical staff, one large school was created consisting of around 100 academic staff, 30 administrative staff and five technical staff. Due to its large size the school needed a new 'academic management' structure: formal subject groups were chosen as the management structure for syllabuses, double marking, peer review, etc.

The Faculty of Business as a whole, although innovative in learning and teaching through methods such as action learning, case study approaches and group projects, did not have a coherent vision for enhancing learning through the use of technology. Information technology was present in the curriculum but little use had been made of information and communication technologies (ICT) as a learning and teaching tool. The staff to whom the intranet was introduced were mostly novices in using learning technology: there were some 'pioneers' experimenting with technology but no collegiate vision. And after the faculty's structure had changed the majority of staff were still novices, as two of the three departments that formed Brighton Business School had little experience of the pilot project.

Description

Early in 1997 the concept for the business school intranet was proposed. The vision, which was inspired by commercial use of such technologies, was to provide an electronic venue where students would find a range of information relating to their educational experience. This would include materials already available in hard copy (eg handbooks and lecture notes) plus some that were not (eg guided Web links, student home pages and online system feedback mechanisms).

The first phase: planning the pilot

We were successful in bidding to the Faculty Management Group for funds to pay for the development of a pilot intranet. This system would test whether the technology could enhance learning and teaching in the school. We proposed to introduce it to one year of the largest undergraduate course in the faculty.

The funds paid for hardware and software we needed for technical and interface design and development. They also covered our time as the development team: an academic/concept developer, a technician/demonstrator and an administrator/graphic designer.

Prior to development, we consulted key stakeholders: school management, academic and administrative staff, and students, to develop a shared vision of what the intranet would provide and how it would interact with the various elements of the learning and teaching experience. These 'blue-sky' discussions resulted in the list below:

Level A – study-related resources (proposed by staff and students)
- online course noticeboards;
- links to generic business-related Web sites;
- student handbooks, university regulations, etc;
- course and examination timetables;
- module schedules and syllabuses;
- module materials including lecture slides, reading lists, Web sites and assessment outline;
- past examination papers;
- study support materials including Internet research tips and a guide to referencing style;
- links to library catalogues and databases;

- e-mail link to course administrator;
- bulletin boards;
- newsgroups;
- frequently asked questions (FAQs).

Level B – social (proposed by students)
- student home pages;
- weather;
- horoscopes;
- discussion boards;
- What did I do last night? discussion board;
- second-hand book exchange and social noticeboard.

The students were overwhelmingly positive and provided a number of ideas. Indeed, they had a vision that perhaps staff did not share: using bulletin board discussion groups, developing Web gateways and making lecture notes available. Academic staff, while in general supportive of the intranet proposal, feared its potential impact: if lecture notes were made available, would students attend lectures? Some also feared the technology's potential: providing academic materials over the intranet might lead to an attempt to automate the academic's role, perhaps leading to job losses.

Administrative staff told us they were keen to use the intranet to reduce face-to-face enquiries for fairly mundane information and standard materials. For this reason, they wanted to make available course handbooks and regulations, and saw the potential for developing FAQs associated with courses. School managers were concerned about achieving standards of information on the intranet, but in general supported the others' ideas.

We were already aware of the importance of carefully positioning the intranet but this was emphasized in our discussions with the stakeholders. As we have said, the aim of the intranet was not to replace the school's traditional teaching and learning modes, but to enhance them by pulling together information available to students. The discussions centred on the learning vision (Norris and Dolance, 1996) rather than the technology, and we were careful not to make grand promises (GSA, 1998) to any of its stakeholders of what the system might deliver.

With this shared vision, we began technical and interface development. When the pilot was launched, out-of-the-box software was not readily available; therefore a tailor-made system was designed, integrating standard HTML with Perl and Javascript. The framework for the pilot intranet was based on a course hierarchy, illustrated in Figure 3.1 (arrows indicate information flow).

Release of the pilot intranet

At the start of the academic year 1997/98, the pilot was released to the second year of the largest undergraduate course within the school, BA (Hons) Business

↓	Navigation screen	Courses; modules; home pages; Web links; library catalogue; social
↓	Navigation screens	List of courses; list of modules; list of home pages (not realized); Web sites by theme; library catalogue; list of social resources
Level A1 Administrative	Course navigation screen	Handbook; contact; timetable leading to list of modules by year of course and the module pages
Level A2 Academic	Module navigation screen	Syllabus; reading list; past exams; useful Web sites; discussion boards
Level B Social	A social area (requested by students). This included:	Discussion boards; horoscopes; weather; student home pages; social noticeboard

Figure 3.1 *The hierarchy of the pilot intranet*

Studies. This course year involved 11 modules (some shared by three other courses), 11 members of staff and around 250 students. There was also a partial release to the courses that shared modules with the BA, partial in that only the shared modules had materials available although all the course-level documentation (handbooks, timetables) was made available. Increased access to the intranet, and to the Internet, was provided through the introduction of a 'cyber-bar' in the undergraduate lounge.

The pilot project relied heavily on the technical member of the team to facilitate the migration of materials on to the system. With a staff base of approximately 50 academics and nine support staff in the Business Management Department it was clear that this reliance on only one member of staff would be problematic later, unless addressed, when school-wide release came.

One of the largest problems encountered was the matrix structure of modularization: that one module was shared by different courses and that any module could be taught by different members of staff in different semesters of the year. Not only that but, having made material available, academic staff wished it to remain for reference, while incoming tutors wished to differentiate their materials from colleagues'. Thus two iterations of the same module were required. The course hierarchy and coding structure used for the pilot project were unable to deal effectively with the complexities of this matrix.

While this complexity could be addressed by providing hyperlinks to different iterations of a module, it led to the replication of information. Administrative information (syllabus, past exam), the same for each module iteration, had to be loaded on to each iteration of the module to provide the information standards and the differentiation required by academic staff. Business Management (the department in which the BA Business Studies was located) offered 20 undergraduate courses, with over 250 modules that could be shared by different courses and/or taught in both semesters and/or led by different members of staff. A more elegant solution to this problem would be required for school-wide release.

The time lapse between concept and implementation meant that the students who had provided the vision for intranet resources were not the students who used the intranet. Even so, when student reaction was tested in the summer of 1998, feedback was generally positive: students were aware (100 per cent) of the intranet and were using it (92 per cent). In general, they were making greater use of the study-related levels than the social ones; for instance, the bulletin boards requested by the student focus group remained largely unused by the student user group, while lecture notes, closely followed by past exam papers, gained the highest number of 'hits'.

Staff reaction was generally positive, with key people who were not involved in the pilot project advocating use of the intranet. That 10 out of 11 modules on the pilot system had all their resources available online perhaps reflects staff reaction to the system.

Negative comments from both groups related to the speed of the system, which was hampered by the interface design. This problem was addressed for the pilot's second semester. Informal discussions indicated that the redesign had improved the speed. (See Flowers, Newton and Paine, 1998 for more on the pilot project's implementation.)

The pilot project provided us with a valuable opportunity to reflect. Any new version of the intranet must readily accommodate modular structure. It was becoming apparent to us that students associated their educational experience with individual staff members; therefore a means of navigating information in this way would probably be beneficial. The size of the staff base meant, however, that it would be impossible to upload learning materials on their behalf. Instead we felt that the intranet should empower staff to load and manage their own content, although recognizing the need for initial support in doing so.

Starting the second phase

We put a proposal to the university's Academic Development Fund Committee to obtain funding for the second phase, and it was granted in the autumn of 1998. Our project was aligned with other learning technology developments within the university, particularly with technical development of ICT systems in the Faculty of IT. Another project, in the Faculty of Education, was to investigate distance learning, initially in traditional paper-based form. Funding of these projects by the Academic Development Fund (ADF) perhaps illustrated the university's growing interest in using technology to support learning.

The three projects influenced each other. The Faculty of Education project moved into providing an online distance learning course and culminated in building an intranet to integrate learning technology developments in the faculty. All three shared the same technology (Lotus Domino) and benefited from the tools developed for the IT Faculty project. Our project provided an example of a framework for an intranet within a modular structure that was shared by the other projects.

The key areas we therefore addressed in the second phase of the intranet's development were:

1. developing a structure that could handle the complexity of modularization;
2. developing a structure whereby staff could 'upload and manage' their own materials without significant reskilling or new technology-based learning;
3. linking materials to people, to reflect better how students navigate the academic process.

To address the first issue we envisioned a matrix structure for information (see Figure 3.2), a move away from the course hierarchy of the pilot project.

The second problem was solved by the technology: Lotus Domino 5, released in early 1999, provided the flexibility to let us upload materials in native formats (Word, Excel, PowerPoint, HTML, Access, etc) and to serve these through the Web client for students to read on screen, download to disk or print. As a database

Courses
Handbooks
Timetables
Exam timetables
Student support information

Managed by
school administrators

Modules
Syllabus (admin)
Reading list (academic)
Past exam papers (admin),
Lecture notes/materials (academic)

info flows to individual staff pages

Web links
Generic Web links
Module-related Web links

Managed by academic staff

info flows to individual staff pages

Staff
Directory of e-mail addresses,
phone numbers, room number,
research interests etc

Managed by individual
members of staff

info flows to modules and Web links

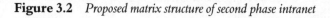

Figure 3.2 *Proposed matrix structure of second phase intranet*

structure it also enabled us to enter information in the document description that would distinguish between the different versions of modules (semester 1, semester 2) and the different staff teaching them. We designed automated information flows, facilitated by integration with the central university directory server, to provide multiple navigation structures linking people and materials.

A beta version of the new structure was released for testing in the autumn of 1999. We invited staff to test the system and introduce it to their students. After amendments to data fields and structure, the system was ready for full release in September 2000. Given the flexibility of the technology, further 'resource areas' evolved in the meantime. The structure that currently exists is described in Figure 3.3, which shows the information flow for documentation, based on the user identification of each member of staff central to the design.

Full-release implementation

The intranet is as much about a process of change as it is about a technology innovation. We did significant work, detailed above, during the pilot of the project to prepare the ground for change. During the redevelopment phase, there was less consultation because a shared conceptual vision had been achieved: the challenge was to provide a technical structure to enable it to progress. For school-wide implementation, the discussions that had formed so much a part of the pilot project had to be reinvigorated. In addition, the importance of achieving a minimum of provision on the system was recognized.

The system needed the support of school managers to lend it credibility. All staff, including the managers, needed to feel some ownership of it. Meetings in the spring of 2000 yielded agreement to provide support for implementation (see Table 3.1).

The researcher was to induct students, train staff in the loading of materials, foster learning technology developments and provide an enabling springboard for staff who wished to experiment in this arena, based on Collis's idea of supporting volunteers (1997). This focus was combined with evaluation of the system.

In September 2000 the intranet was released and the agreed information standards were achieved, mainly through the incentivized work of the administrative staff. For each of the 30 courses, handbooks and timetables were loaded. For each of the 500 modules, syllabuses and past examination papers were loaded. The intranet was introduced at student inductions during large group lectures about all the resources that were available to them. We took care to promise only the minimum of provision although the potential that lecturing staff could make use of it as a resource was raised.

Some 45 per cent of academic staff experimented with using the intranet, making five or more documents available, but sustained and extended usage was lower at around 30 per cent. Despite this it had become part of the school's vocabulary, the assumption being that everyone else was using it, even if some individuals were not participating.

Courses
Handbooks
Timetables
Exam timetables
Student support information

Managed by
school administrators

Web links
Generic Web links
Module-related Web links

Managed by academic staff

info flows to individual staff pages

Modules
Generic resources (study guides,
research tips, referencing guides)
Syllabus (admin)
Reading list (academic)
Past exam papers (admin)
Lecture notes/materials (academic)

info flows to individual staff pages

Subject groups
Generic resources related to
subject fields

All modules within subject area
All Web links within subject area

Managed by academic staff

info flows to individual staff
pages

Staff
Directory of e-mail addresses,
phone numbers, room numbers,
research interests etc
Individual's resources

Managed by individual
members of staff

info flows to modules and Web
links

Placements
Placements news
Placements opportunities
Placements resources

Managed by Placements Office

TeamRooms
Module discussion boards
Course discussion boards

Available to staff on request –
staff then take responsibility
for management of the
discussion boards

Figure 3.3   *Structure of the 2001 intranet*

Table 3.1 *Strategies for top-down approach to implementation*

Strategy	Status
Identification of two academic staff as intranet 'champions' (one Business, one Law, reflecting the then national LTSN/CTi structure).	Achieved.
Agreement for incentive funding of subject groups to encourage development of learning materials for the system.	Agreed in principle.
Agreement that a minimum standard of information would be provided (syllabuses, past exams, reading lists).	Achieved.
Agreement that administrative staff, in the first year of implementation, would receive a goodwill payment for loading all the required syllabuses, handbooks and past exam papers.	Achieved.
Appointment of a person to support staff in using and considering use of the intranet (post is funded through our project although the person is selected by school and faculty managers plus ourselves).	Achieved.

One module tutor made use of the 'PageOut' service provided by McGraw-Hill, with links from the intranet, and this was the students' sole source of access to his materials. Another, who had already introduced a support intranet for the marketing subject group, initiated a bulletin board in parallel with his seminars and the course work. A postgraduate part-time course used the intranet fully for lecture materials, with hard copy of all materials. In tandem, a bulletin board was introduced to provide a support base for students outside the face-to-face classes.

Some staff made all materials available for their modules from the start of term and developed an 'e-library' for students following discussions in seminar groups as the module progressed. Others provided a full set of materials at the end of a module to help with revision.

During Week 10 of the autumn term of 2000, the intranet was evaluated via a survey of four sample groups. The generally encouraging results were reported to the school board in February 2001. However, the survey revealed that the students were not using the resource to the level staff had assumed and this was a constraint that staff mentioned during informal discussions. This perceived underuse by students may be an expectation failure (Lyytinen and Hirschheim, 1987): that the students knew the amount of documentation that existed and knew that it wasn't being replicated on the intranet, leading to a reduction in their usage of it.

We discussed barriers to content provision during informal interviews with academic staff, which yielded a list of perceived constraints:

- No time to learn new technology – other priorities (eg research, QAA).
- Little use of electronic resources and concern that students should be independent in using such resources.
- No method of transfer for hard copy material to electronic format.
- Copyright issues – exposed.
- Ownership of the material once it's loaded.
- Students won't attend lectures.
- What's the benefit? It's easier to identify the non-benefits.
- Students don't use it.

Note that the initial fear of automation had disappeared as understanding of the technology had increased. These discussions with academics continued to be where most of these concerns could be addressed.

Evaluation

The intranet has been subject to a range of formal and informal evaluation since its inception. The formal elements have been mostly questionnaires, selected because with them we could contact large representative groups of students.

The different aims for each survey were reflected in the questionnaire design. For evaluation of the pilot intranet, we wanted to understand whether the intranet was seen as a 'desirable' resource and whether it would be valuable to extend the pilot to a school-wide release.

The survey of BA Business Studies second year students, the entire population for the pilot project, revealed that 92 per cent of respondents said they had used the *intranet*, with nobody claiming not to know what it was. However, only 7 per cent said they used it frequently, and 78 per cent used it only occasionally; 15 per cent had used it only once.

As for the *Internet*, 97 per cent of respondents had used it and 92 per cent claimed to use it to support their academic work. The key Internet facilities they identified for study were the World Wide Web (92 per cent) and e-mail (84 per cent), although they also used other facilities such as Telnet (51 per cent) and newsgroups (37 per cent).

When we asked them how useful the materials delivered to them over the intranet were, remembering that they received much as hard copy too, respondents marked a 1–7 scale where 1 was most useful and 7 least useful. The mean ratings were as shown in Table 3.2.

Students saw lecture materials as the most valuable resource. None of the resources achieved a 'very useful' rating, but none was viewed as entirely useless. This mild indifference cropped up again: half the respondents said the intranet was relatively unimportant to their studies.

When asked for ideas for further content, our respondents gave us replies that we classified as academic (69 per cent), general (16 per cent), maintenance (12 per

Table 3.2 *Students' ranking of usefulness of the materials on the intranet*

Rank	Document	Average
1	Lecture notes	2.7
2	Past exams	3.1
3	Assessments	3.8
4	Reading lists	4.3
5	Syllabus	4.4
6	Teaching programmes	4.6
7	Web sites	4.7

cent) and social (2 per cent). Most academic comments centred on lack of lecture materials in the system, closely followed by a desire for more past exam papers. General comments referred to access to hardware; the students wanted more pooled computer rooms. Maintenance comments were on reliability, speed of the system and ease of navigation to resources. Social comments were requests for notification about social events.

The 2000/01 survey was undertaken to provide a snapshot, for school staff and management, of student usage, rather than proving the concept. How had students used the provision open to them? Did they have ideas for further development? The survey sampled the views of undergraduate and postgraduate populations across course years. All students had handbooks, syllabus, teaching programmes, and past examination papers available on the intranet. Among the undergraduate samples, the first year module had a PageOut Web site with lecture notes, Web links, teaching programme, etc. The second year students had all their lecture notes on the intranet plus placement information (opportunities, news and templates such as CV structure). The third years had no additional materials. The postgraduates had all their module materials available, guided Web links, electronic database links and a bulletin board.

Results from the pilot evaluation influenced our design of the second questionnaire. For instance, *Internet* usage was assumed, but its role in their academic work was investigated: 72 per cent of the respondents said they used the Internet for academic purposes. Highest use was in the first year (80 per cent), dropping to 52 per cent in the third year.

From server records, we could assess the rate of change of documentation on the *intranet*. Staff members were using it in several ways: some loaded content once a week, some loaded all the materials at the start of a module and some made the materials available for revision only. We established that the intranet was not a fast-changing environment demanding a daily log-in to keep up to date. We felt that frequent usage might naturally mean weekly or less often. We added a 'Never used' option to test how far the intranet had become part of student life.

Of the respondents, 59 per cent classified themselves as frequent users, while only 6 per cent said they had never used the intranet. The occasional band gained

35 per cent agreement, although, if anything less than weekly usage is included in the occasional band rather than frequent, occasional rises to 56 per cent and frequent drops to 38 per cent.

We asked the frequent users about the value of materials, and what they liked best. The occasional users were asked what they had liked and what they would like more of (ie what would encourage them to make more use of the intranet). Those who replied 'Never used' were asked what they would hope to find on the intranet: we thought that possibly the questionnaire would make them more aware of the intranet.

As in the evaluation of the pilot project, lecture materials and past examinations were ranked highest. Again the guided Web links did not receive a high rating, leading us to question the role of these, as students appear confident in searching the Web for themselves.

Qualitative feedback was gathered for the areas in which students felt improvement was needed. We classified the replies: improved study-related resources (academic) 36 per cent; improved hardware access 17 per cent; improved technical structure and training/support (maintenance) 14 per cent; make it compulsory 8 per cent; and improved support resources (administrative) 4 per cent.

From their comments it was clear that, with the intranet provided to them, they felt that more staff should be making more material available. Their excitement about a new system had changed to acceptance of it but their expectations were not entirely fulfilled.

Navigation of the system was a problem for many students. We are adding more induction about the database's structure, but the Faculty of IT project has developed a tool that may make navigation more student-centric. Students may get a hyperlinked list of the modules they are registered for, based on integration with the university's central records database.

Our less formal evaluation, through discussion with school staff and informal interviews with stakeholders, suggests that most have encountered few difficulties since management of materials/content was passed on to staff. What remains less clear for staff is how to use the intranet and why. Not all staff members are confident in using electronic resources, and they have little time to investigate and experiment with them. Those who wish to go beyond the simple provision of lecture notes are likely to require professional development in producing content (Kirschner et al, 1998).

Discussion

We positioned the intranet carefully without making grand promises. We wanted to encourage experimentation while recognizing the existing organizational culture. Basing our ideas on Orlikowski and Hofman's (1997) improvisational model of change, we expected a long period of adaptation (emergent and opportunistic change) during which staff and students would develop their own sense of purpose for using the intranet. Compared with the call centre case outlined by Orlikowski and Hofman, educational establishments have much slower organizational rhythms: for example, most degrees take three years to complete. We think the intranet is still finding its niche within the school's learning and teaching.

Developments for the 2001/02 academic year included:

1. school funding for the Research Officer and Technical Developer posts, indicating further commitment on the part of the school;
2. integration of seminar-based bulletin boards to support the Personal Academic Skills/Personal Transferable Skills modules throughout the school;
3. the revalidation of IT311 (Electronic Commerce) to replace the traditional lecture–seminar model, with lectures supported by bulletin board discussion and information sharing;
4. in the Postgraduate Diploma in Law (CPE), reintroduction of a bulletin board to promote cross-year networking between attended elements;
5. reference to the intranet and how it is to be implemented on courses in all handbooks and school regulation documents;
6. funding for subject group development;
7. introduction of an open TeamRoom for students by the Law Subject Group and in the part-time ACCA programme;
8. assignment submission.

These show that the intranet is becoming part of the school's academic experience. Discussion is moving from provision of lecture notes to roles for ICTs. Proposals are coming from a 20-strong staff group. Around half the staff (50) continue their sustained usage of the system. Reporting, subject group discussions and meetings are all helping staff to review what their peers are doing and to consider for themselves what use they might make of technology in their teaching.

We analysed the advantages and disadvantages of the intranet for its stakeholders (see Table 3.3). Within current learning and teaching paradigms, academic staff, who control access to materials the students want, get few rewards for making content available. Some academics see only minor advantages like not having to carry spares of lecture notes usually already produced and photocopied in quantity. Others are concerned about poor attendance at lectures. Should they wish to integrate bulletin boards into their teaching, especially alongside lecture and seminar attendance, research indicates that they will spend more time on these and that benefits, such as building an archive of frequently asked questions for their module/subject, will only develop over time (Salmon, 1998).

There is a cultural shift within the school, however. More staff members wish to integrate bulletin boards into their teaching, suggesting a real interest in experimenting with technology. Staff attendance at courses (eg the Certificate in Learning and Teaching and the MA in Academic Practice) shows their interest in professional development. The challenge is to provide development opportunities that consider the pedagogies involved in the use of learning technology. Funds for subject groups may help more staff to benefit.

Table 3.3 *Stakeholder analysis of the intranet in Brighton Business School*

Stakeholder group	Advantages	Disadvantages
School and faculty managers	Tool for staff evaluation. Marketing opportunity if development successful.	Content holes exist – a clear strategy is required, for example, for QAA.
Administrative staff	Reduction of mundane work: eg past exam papers don't need to be photocopied or sold to students. Reduction of enquiries to office.	Additional work to load and manage content year on year.
Academic staff	No storing needed of spares of lecture materials. Opportunity to experiment with new methods.	Loss of control over delivery of materials. Additional work required. Concern over quality of students' educational experience.
Students	Material readily available. Other implementations, such as integration into teaching programme, may add flexibility to help enable part-time work.	Uneven computer provision (and ownership of personal computers).
Development team	Opportunity to experiment. Potential for career development (if intranet is successful).	Pressure to deliver. Personal career risk (if intranet is a failure).
University policy makers	Materials open for review. Marketing opportunity if the development is successful.	Content holes exist – a clear strategy is required, for example, for QAA.

The administrative staff members get fewer enquiries, particularly in the undergraduate office. Staff can point students to the intranet for the information they want, although postgraduate part-time students may not have computer access and much communication is still by letter, telephone and face-to-face enquiry.

Now that the intranet exists, school managers want at least the minimum level of provision to be achieved, as measured by external bodies such as the QAA. These standards have been met. The idea of using the intranet as an evaluation tool has proved less attractive, owing to the time required to evaluate the provision that staff make. There is an appreciation of the marketing opportunity offered by the system, and that enhanced learning resources can be referred to in the school's marketing materials (Alexander and McKenzie, 1998).

Students now want academic materials to be available. We need to study further the value to them of having lecture notes online. Jin (2001) argues that learning support materials play an important role in students' experience of a module, but their enjoyment depends more on the style of delivery and applicability of the content. We think that if staff continue discussing their roles they will overcome their fear of losing control over delivery of content, which is actually only a small part of students' educational experience. Subject groups, with their new power within the school structure, may discuss generic subject-based materials, which may provide the added value expected of the intranet.

Without doubt the intranet has stirred debate about the role of electronic resources in Brighton Business School and about learning and teaching strategies. The intranet's structure and content will evolve as stakeholders continue to engage with it and each other.

The events discussed in this chapter are an inside account of the kinds of challenges that face any group working at the leading edge of technology. The project was initiated at a time when the Internet had yet to move into the mainstream, when Internet browsers were still new and when the term 'e-commerce' (or e-anything, for that matter) had yet to be coined. As a result, the early stages of the project were as much concerned with educating potential users about the technology itself as with how such a technology could be used within an educational context. In the early stages of the project the enabling technologies were not yet stable, nor were user perceptions about the potential of an intranet within the specific context of Brighton Business School. How things have moved on!

The various intranet initiatives that sprang up within the University of Brighton were a classic example of the 'contagion' stage in organizational technology (Gibson and Nolan, 1974). Whilst some technologies may fail to achieve widespread acceptance and fall into the 'chasm' (Moore, 1991), it is clear that the intranet is not one of these. After the university had established its central Learning Technologies Group, a university-wide Managed Learning Environment (MLE) was launched in the 2002/03 academic year based on Blackboard. Within three months of the launch, over 500 active teaching modules were available on the system. The role of intranet technology within the University of Brighton has thus moved from being a leading-edge initiative to a mainstream application.

References

Alexander, S and McKenzie, J (1998) *An Evaluation of Information Technology Projects in University Education*, Australian Government Printing Service, Canberra

Collis, B (1997) Implementing ICT in the faculty: letting 1000 flowers bloom or managing change?, Keynote presentation for the conference, Studying in Digital Learning Environments at the University of Utrecht [Online] http://education2.edte.utwente.nl/teletophomepage.nsf/PapersNLViewForm?readform

Flowers, S, Newton, B and Paine, C (1998) Creating a faculty intranet: a case study in change, *Education and Training*, **40** (8), pp 340–46

Flowers, S and Reeve, S (1998) The shape of things to come: a discussion on the nature of the technologised higher education institution, Proceedings of the CTI-AFM conference, Brighton, http://www.mgt.uea.ac.uk/cti/conference/paperlst.html

General Services Administration (GSA) (1998) *An Evaluation of the Grand Design Approach to Developing Computer-Based Application Systems*, General Services Administration, Washington, DC

Gibson, C F and Nolan, R L (1974) Managing the four stages of EDP growth, *Harvard Business Review*, **52** (1), pp 76–88

Jin, Z (2001) The learning experience of students in Middlesex University Business School (MUBS): why do they enjoy some modules/lectures and dislike others?, *International Journal of Management Education*, **1** (1), pp 22–36

Kirschner, P *et al* (1998) An ICT competence-based environment for (re)training educators in educational innovation and technology, http://www.coe.un.edu/insite/elec_pub/HTML1998/ln_kirs.htm

Lyytinen, K and Hirschheim, R (1987) Information systems failure: a survey and classification of the empirical literature, *Oxford Surveys in Information Technology*, **4**, pp 257–309

Moore, G A (1991) *Crossing the Chasm: Marketing and selling high-tech products to mainstream customers*, HarperCollins, New York

Norris, D M and Dolance, M G (1996) IT leadership is the key to transformation, *Cause/Effect*, **19** (1), pp 12–20

Orlikowski, W J and Hofman, D J (1997) An improvisational model of change: the case of groupware technologies, http://ccs.mit.edu/papers/CCSWP191.html

Reeve, S and Flowers, S (2000) Positioning Web-based learning in the higher education portfolio: too much, too soon?, in *Teaching with Technology: Rethinking tradition*, ed L Lloyd, Rollins College Press, Winter Park, FL

Reid, I (1999) Online strategy in higher education, http://ausweb.scu.edu.au/aw99/papers/reid/paper.html

Salmon, G (1998) Developing learning through effective online moderation, *Active Learning*, **9**, pp 3–8, www.cti.ac.uk/pubs/actlea/al9.html

Van der Linden, P (1998) *Not Just Java*, Prentice Hall, Englewood Cliffs, NJ

Contacts

Becci Newton
Brighton Business School
Unversity of Brighton
Mithras House
Lewes Road
Brighton BN2 4AT
e-mail: b.newton@bton.ac.uk

Cameron Paine
Faculty of Information Technology
Same address
e-mail: carp@bton.ac.uk

Stephen Flowers
Centre for Research in Innovation Management
Same address
e-mail: s.h.flowers@bton.ac.uk

Chapter 4

The International Consultancy Assignment

David Edelshain and Carol Vielba

This chapter is about the development and introduction of a course taught jointly by City University Business School (CUBS, now renamed as the Sir John Cass Business School) and Fordham Business School in conjunction with Chase Manhattan Corporation. The course ran in 1998, 1999 and 2000, and is continuing in expanded form. Fordham Business School in late 1997 was exploring ways of developing international links with other schools and approached CUBS. At that time we were directing the MBA programme at CUBS and had been focusing on the development of international business as a prime feature of the MBA programme. The two schools agreed to set up a joint course, for students of both business schools, that would stress learning of knowledge and skills needed for international business.

CUBS agreed with Fordham that, to enable students from both schools to work together, it would be valuable if they could meet. Given the cost to students of staying in London and New York, visits would have to be short. Most of the students' activities would be from their domestic campuses. All of them, from both schools, would meet together at CUBS or Fordham to be briefed on a project. They would then work together electronically from their respective campuses, before meeting up again to present their work to each other. As this design developed it became clear that the students would need an assignment to work on. Given the choice of a desk assignment or a practical one for a business concern, the latter seemed far more appropriate. Through a Fordham alumnus in a senior position at Chase Manhattan Corporation, that corporation agreed to be the client for whom the students would work. CUBS staff recommended, and Chase Manhattan agreed, that the assignment topic for the first year (1998) should be the euro.

Once administrative arrangements had been set up, the course ran for 10 weeks, April–June. The same pattern was repeated in 1999 and 2000, except that a new topic, e-commerce, was agreed and the project's style shifted from research on behalf of a client to an international consultant's assignment.

For 1998 only 18 students from each school could be taken on to the programme and the number of applicants conveniently matched this number. In 1999 demand increased and there were 49 applicants, increasing in 2000 to 59 applicants, most but not all of whom were able to enrol. In 2001, such was the demand that a second client company had to be found and two different consultancy assignments arranged. We describe how these successful international consultancy assignments (ICAs) were organized and carried out, and discuss the pedagogical and academic issues that they raised.

Objective

The objective of this course is to provide students with a vehicle through which they can increase their skills and knowledge of international business.

We determined in 1997 that the changing nature of international business required changes in how it was taught and learnt in an MBA programme. Both CUBS and Fordham were seeking, and still are, to find the most effective ways of providing students with the knowledge and skills to succeed in an increasingly international business world.

The course is provided for full-time (one year) and part-time (two years) campus-based students, though we think there is no reason why it could not be offered to students following a distance learning MBA.

Rationale

At CUBS (and Fordham) most MBA teaching takes place in the classroom. Indeed, for part-time students, who can usually only study in the evenings or at weekends, there may be little alternative to this format. For the purposes of studying international business, classroom teaching is arguably suitable for providing frameworks for understanding the subject, analysing knowledge about foreign environments and discussing issues relating to international trade and investment. For example, students can gain some understanding of the nature of foreign exchange risk. But there is a limit to what can be achieved in the classroom, as the old adage, 'hear and forget, see and remember, do and understand', reminds us.

More than superficial understanding of international environments is likely to be achieved only by visiting them.

In recognition of this limitation many business schools, including CUBS, have instituted foreign visits. During these courses, known in CUBS as international teaching weeks (ITWs), students visit businesses, international, central and local government institutions and other bodies located in the country visited, and study the local environment. In 'seeing', students are more likely to remember their experiences. They are also able to practise skills of transacting international business that they cannot practise in their own country.

Some institutions, including CUBS, have gone further and have incorporated into these short foreign visits actual consultancy, by students, for the organizations they visit. This consultancy allows for an element of 'doing'. Of course, students who are not studying full time can rarely spend more than a week away from home and work, and in such a short period it is impossible to carry out anything more than a very modest consultancy. At CUBS, even full-time students have other courses running concurrently with the ICA one and cannot afford to be away for long. The ICA we discuss here has a structure that enables students to spend 10 weeks on a serious assignment while still limiting the time spent abroad to a week.

Context

We have identified two trends with implications for the teaching of international business. The first is pedagogical. Public concerns about the quality of higher education and accountability for the use of public funds by universities and colleges gave rise to an extensive system of quality assurance. At the heart of this system was the belief that higher education should be much more output-focused than it has been. In other words, educators should be concerned first with learning and second with teaching. The second trend stems from continued globalization of business. International business is less and less a special field of business and more and more a factor in all business decisions and processes. As a result, the study of international business has shifted from being either a contextual or technical subject to being in the mainstream of business and management knowledge and skills. The interaction of these two trends highlights the need for the teacher of international business to change teaching strategies in response to the changing requirements of the international business world.

Changes in the pattern of how international business is carried out are reflected in how managers are called upon to carry out their functions. The globalization of business means that skills associated with cross-border activity are no longer those of the specialist but of all managers and entrepreneurs. This means that all students of business and management need a much broader set of personal skills to be effective in the new global economy than when the ability to manage effectively across borders was the province of the international specialist.

This shift in educational needs is supported by research on what managers say are the most important and most difficult international issues they have to tackle in managing across borders. Two studies (Ricks and Czinkota, 1979; Blume, 1994) illustrate the differences produced by the changing nature of international business over the intervening 15 years.

Some years ago we undertook a survey (Vielba and Edelshain, 1995) that identified the knowledge and skills that managers considered necessary for managing across borders. The most important areas of knowledge identified related to the culture of the locality in which business was being undertaken. Parts of this knowledge and business competence can be acquired effectively in the classroom. For learning that requires practical application and, in some cases, contextualization outside the classroom, we think new methods are essential. Skills can best be acquired by practice, including those identified by Ronen (1989) as important for someone undertaking an expatriate assignment. Moreover, given cultural differences, arguably all of the international management competencies and skills are best acquired or improved in a foreign setting.

In the foreign environment, there is the added challenge of operating in unfamiliar surroundings, which encourages students to identify quickly what is different from their own culture and conventions. Such exposure makes students more aware of their self-reference criterion (SRC) and able to minimize the obstacles to doing business in other cultures (Cateora and Ghauri, 1999). The unfamiliarity makes students question the reasoning behind their own approach, leading to greater understanding that can then be applied when entering new situations. As Kobrin (1984) makes clear through his research, few managers believe that they can acquire international expertise in the classroom. Overwhelmingly, managers told us that overseas visits were both the most important and the most critical way of acquiring such expertise (Edelshain and Vielba, 1998, 1999).

Description

The ICA was introduced at CUBS after many years of including an ITW in the MBA (Edelshain and Vielba, 1998, 1999). How does the ICA differ from the ITW and why? The ICA offers students the opportunity to become consultants within an international team and do work for an actual client operating in a country different from that in which the managers are studying. In the story we are reporting, CUBS, together with Fordham Business School in central Manhattan, New York, designed and ran the ICA in three successive years, and it is still continuing. Each year, starting in 1998, MBA students from both business schools carried out a consultancy assignment with Chase Manhattan Corporation as client. In 1999 and 2000, the topic was changed from the euro to e-commerce, to reflect the client's priorities. In all three years, all the students, from both schools, met in London for four days where they received their brief from Chase London. They were organized into teams containing equal numbers from the City and Fordham schools.

Normally each team dealt with a different sub-topic, although in one year one team provided an integrating function. During the subsequent two months the London students worked principally with Chase London while their counterparts worked with Chase New York. The students in each team communicated with each other across the Atlantic using videoconferencing, e-mail, electronic conferencing, fax and sometimes telephone. In the last week, the groups came together again in New York for a further four or five days to coordinate their work and to prepare their written reports and presentations made to Chase New York management.

Staff in both institutions acted as group facilitators and gave or arranged classroom teaching on the euro and e-commerce. The client was involved, to reinforce the standards that were expected of students, in further classes on process skills, dealing with group work, the practice of consultancy, handling client relationships and making presentations.

The ICA thus offered some unique opportunities. First, students were actually working for a client, rather than visiting companies to see and hear. By working within the company they were given the chance to gain insights into the organization, which through reflection and discussion they would be able to generalize. In particular by working within a company in two different countries, and on issues that are international, they could learn about international business first-hand. The second opportunity students had was to work with other students who were themselves working and studying in a foreign environment. Many were nationals of a different country working and living in a different cultural context. The multinational teams, with 7–12 participants, in many cases included half a dozen different nationalities, and posed a learning challenge for the participants, as did the different knowledge frameworks that had been acquired in class at the two business schools.

The third opportunity students had was in experiencing the problems of cooperating and coordinating remotely. Students had to find out how to keep in touch. They had to build a virtual team as well as dealing with problems such as time zones. The ICA gave them the opportunity to acquire and practise international business skills and to enhance their management skills and personal competencies. These skills included communications, including use of English in its different forms, negotiating, listening, interpersonal and diplomacy skills, sensitivity to cultural differences, patience, flexibility and adaptability, open-mindedness, focus and tenacity. All of these skills are required for successful international business management (Vielba and Edelshain, 1995).

Evaluation

The innovative, experiential nature of the course enables students to pursue learning outcomes beyond the scope of classroom lectures, but its design and execution were not easy. There was potential for problems arising with partner institutions and the client. The course is resource-intensive and, however profound the learning experiences involved, many participants would like to find an easier way to a grade! Students find learning the toughest in managing themselves and their groups and in handling the client. Staff have to tread a fine line between pushing students to solve the problems for themselves and solving the problems for them. We kept a detailed record of issues raised in setting up, conducting and evaluating the entire exercise (Edelshain and Vielba, 1998, 1999). We summarize the main points below.

Setting up the assignment

Coordinating the activities of two business schools was the first issue faced by CUBS and Fordham in developing the course. Except when Fordham staff visited London, the five-hour time difference meant that staff could phone each other only in the afternoon London time. From 1998 the Internet proved invaluable, however, because e-mails sent from New York late in the day could be acted on the following morning in London and replies would await Fordham staff that afternoon. Nevertheless, the time for decision making was probably doubled by this international dimension.

Both schools found that they had different course and term structures, which required compromises. Our options were limited by the need for visits of Fordham students and staff to London, and of CUBS students and staff to New York, to be when reasonably priced accommodation was available. Timing was also complicated somewhat by the need to run the course when convenient to the client, whose staff had to brief the students, provide ongoing input and be an audience for student output at the end. Fortunately the client was very flexible in this respect.

To facilitate interaction with the client it was vital to have a substantial presence of client staff in London and New York. Any joint course must enable students from and in each location to have access to the client. CUBS and Fordham had to take into account Chase London as well as Chase New York. We found that our suggested topic, the euro, was of more interest to Chase London than to Chase New York. Vice versa, e-commerce was an initiative being led out of the New York office.

In setting up the ICA we also struck student-related issues not normally encountered even on ITWs. For example, some students worked for competitors of the client: we decided that the client ought to approve each applicant to the course. In the event Chase accepted all students who applied and indeed remarked that those who were familiar with its type of business would possibly provide different insights to those without such experience.

Decisions on fee supplements to cover travel and accommodation that are straightforward when only one academic institution is involved are complicated by different institutional policies in pricing elective courses. For example, Fordham incorporated the cost of all elective courses in the overall price of the programme, whereas CUBS did not and had to learn quickly how to manage student expectations in this regard.

Running the assignment

Running the assignment fell into three phases. From our perspective as CUBS staff, the first was the visit of Fordham staff and students to London to set up the assignment. The second phase was the work of CUBS and Fordham students in their respective home locations, coordinated among themselves, between them and the client, and between them and staff. In this phase, coordination was needed between the two groups of staff, and between staff and the client's New York and London offices. The third phase was in New York.

The course proper begins with the visit of Fordham students to London, the allocation of students from the two schools to five–eight groups and the division of the overall assignment among the groups. Although most administrative decisions at CUBS are made before the Fordham students arrive, the final composition of the visiting group is never entirely clear before they arrive. The same is true when the CUBS students visit New York. Apart from inevitable illnesses and failure to obtain visas, the odd part-time student invariably fails to secure time off work from his or her employer. So, despite considerable staff efforts to match student backgrounds to particular sub-topics, some rearrangement has always been necessary.

Given that both schools recruit full-time and part-time students on to the course, individual students may not even know a majority of those on the course from their own school. Only a short time is available for students to get to know each other face-to-face, and the storming phase of team formation was sometimes incomplete after only four to five days spent together in London. From 1999 onwards, in response to feedback from students, staff from Chase and the host university designed a session on team building, in a safe environment where groups could develop team-working relationships through exercises unrelated to the consultancy exercise that was to follow. At the same time students were given one or more sessions on the subject of professional consultancy and client management. As few students had prior experience of consultancy, this input was found to be, as anticipated, critical.

For the course to be a valuable 'doing' experience it is important that students get as much exposure to client staff as possible. The initial briefing day and further briefings of individual groups were arranged, whenever possible, at the client's offices, which fortuitously were only several hundred yards distant from the business school. For the first course several Saturday videoconferencing sessions were also arranged using Chase's London and New York facilities. However, for the second course, Chase had to hire costly accommodation for briefing from the second day onwards. For the third course, this factor resulted in all briefing beyond the first morning taking place in the business school.

Making sure that five to eight groups of students are able to access relevant client staff was likely to be problematic, and each group had a member of CUBS and Fordham staff to provide advice. Such large-scale consultancy is awkward and atypical of most consultancy assignments but is the price that has to be paid to enable sufficient numbers of students to participate and make the exercise economically practicable. For the first course, students had access to a relatively small team of Chase staff developing the company's response to the euro, in response to tight deadlines. Moreover, given that Chase London was taking the lead on the euro, finding client staff to work with in New York was never going to be easy. For the second course groups of students spent a whole morning in London being briefed by groups of managers working on different aspects of e-commerce development, managers with whom the CUBS students stayed in touch once the Fordham students had returned home. But for the Fordham students, access to New York staff was always going to be more difficult because it rarely proved possible to bring New York staff to London for the initial briefings. Again, perhaps because the same general topic was selected for the third course, it proved much harder to gain client staff involvement even in London. Most groups were briefed initially by a single individual, and subsequent access to client staff was controlled through a central access point, a helpful one.

Once Fordham students had returned to New York, communication was largely through the Internet. Videoconferencing was used too by those on the first course, but not taken up on subsequent ones. Some telephoning also occurred. An objective of the exercise was to give students experience of international communication and, given that over half the CUBS students and a minority of their Fordham counterparts were not local nationals, the scope was considerable for cultural and linguistic differences and consequent misunderstandings.

Frustrations inevitably developed on all three courses and staff had to remind students constantly that another objective of the exercise was not for staff to minimize these problems, but for students to develop their own ways of dealing with them. Nor were the frustrations merely reflections of two common peoples separated by a common language when it was the case of British and US natives trying to understand each other. In the first course CUBS students felt their Fordham counterparts were studying in an environment that paid too much attention to detail, and Fordham students felt the CUBS environment was one that encouraged a superficial level of analysis. Staff soul searching on this issue was interrupted when in the second course students in London and New York came to precisely the opposite conclusions! Students did become conscious of other differences in teaching styles, and all remarked on the tendency for Fordham students to seek and/or take a closer 'steer' from their staff on what to do than was the case at CUBS.

The third and final phase was centred on the visit of CUBS students to New York, with preparation of written and in particular oral presentations by all the students to Chase New York staff. Over half of this visit was inevitably taken up with group consolidation of findings and progressive rehearsals of the material to be presented. Staff were advisers and the audience for these rehearsals. Students were under considerable pressure to meet their looming deadlines and on occasion tempers became quite frayed.

On reflection, it is not surprising that CUBS and Fordham staff, wanting their schools' products to succeed in impressing the client, should drive their students hard and be less than diplomatic in their critiques. Nor is it surprising that students should regard staff on occasion as being overly harsh. For all three courses, however, it rarely proved possible for Chase London staff to attend the New York presentations and often the same was true for the more junior Chase New York staff who had worked with the New York students. In consequence, the Chase staff who did attend the presentations were largely an unknown quantity to all of the students; therefore a heightening of tension was unavoidable.

Nevertheless, the staff were unanimous in regarding the final oral presentations as unrecognizable when compared to first rehearsals. In each of the three courses, students prepared PowerPoint presentations and consistently kept to the tight time schedules demanded by the client.

Evaluating the assignment

We discuss four types of evaluation of the ICA. First is evaluation by and of students. Second is evaluation of the course as part of an MBA programme. Third is evaluation of staff, particularly regarding the role of staff and client employees in relation to the ICA. There is also the important question of the value of the exercise to the client. Fourth is evaluation of the management of feedback and its impact on the process of arranging further courses.

Feedback from CUBS students came from interim and post-course evaluation forms, and also from the examination for part-time MBAs, who knew in advance that they would be asked to assess the ICA process. Though there was potential for some bias, much of the comment was uncompromising enough to be considered valuable.

Evaluation of student performance was complicated by the different methods used at CUBS to evaluate part- and full-time MBA students, but more so by the different systems of evaluation used by the two schools. Fordham did not assess students taking elective courses by either coursework or examination, only on their oral presentations. Students were therefore concerned that motivation to perform well might become an issue though staff did not detect any problems in relation to the written or oral presentations. However, after the first course the deadline for the written reports was extended until after the return of CUBS students to London. It was CUBS students only who then finalized the reports and submitted them to Chase London and to Fordham, for onward transmission to Chase New York.

A particular difficulty proved to be the interpretation by students of the assignment given to them. In the first course the topics given to the different groups were highly interlinked and it was not clear how general or specific each group should be. Staff of the two schools found it difficult to agree, as the students perceived, and ambiguity lingered. On the second and third courses different groups were assigned tasks that were related to different departments within the client corporation and the problem did not recur. However, it was still found necessary to select representatives from each of the groups to create a new group responsible for providing the client with an overview.

All students were asked to complete a CUBS interim course evaluation questionnaire at the end of the London visit, and CUBS students completed standard course assessment forms at the end of the course. Fordham did not ask all students to evaluate the New York visit. All student course ratings were consistently within the range experienced for CUBS MBA courses. Fordham students, though they applauded all other aspects of their visit, did not like British sandwiches and British food generally. Frustrations in melding as teams and in dealings with client staff were sometimes articulated as criticisms of the course rather than as opportunities to master skills that would overcome common international business problems.

We formed the view that the role required of staff in organizing, running, reassessing and modifying the ICAs was different from that expected from staff operating in a more conventional domestic learning setting. The amount of preparatory administration was considerably greater, reflecting the fact that two business schools and two client offices were involved, and consensus had to be achieved before decisions could be confirmed. More effort than normal was needed in trying to align the teaching and learning styles of the two schools, whose views on the generalist versus specialist nature of MBA programmes were never fully reconciled. This difference reflected, in the view of the staff responsible for consultancy training, different consultancy styles, the United States favouring specialization and the United Kingdom favouring a more generalist approach.

Once the course began staff needed to embrace the role of facilitator rather than subject expert except in the case of teachers of consulting, presentation skills and other staff brought in because of their knowledge of, for example, e-commerce or the euro.

Feedback from the client was overtly positive. The fact that Chase was happy to participate on both a second and a third occasion is prima facie evidence that they found the exercise of value. More detailed feedback on the written reports was rarely forthcoming and more needs to be done in this regard. Also, the opportunity to use the ICA to recruit MBA students was only sporadically grasped, given the efforts that some students expended in enquiring into available positions within Chase.

In their turn, staff of both business schools took the opportunity to review the course and begin to plan for its next presentation whilst together in New York. Provisional dates were agreed. Few changes were in fact made to the second and third courses, though Chase New York's aversion to attending presentations on either the first or last day of the week was taken into account. After the third course, it became clear that it would probably only be possible to involve a particular client company for two or three years. Chase as the first client had been no less prone to reorganizations, mergers and acquisitions that any multinational.

Staff gradually perceived that, despite the fact that the client received 4,000 to 5,000 hours of 'free' consultancy in return for probably no more than 500 manager/staff hours of their own involvement, being the client was a growing burden.

Discussion

To address new types of learning outcomes in innovative ways, we think teachers of international business will need a wider repertoire of pedagogic skills than in the past. The shift in learning outcomes will require lecturers to have facilitation skills as well as traditional lecturing abilities. They will also need to be highly skilled in course design, for example in using simulation where teaching in context is not possible. Furthermore they will have to explore their own self-reference criteria and acquire a high degree of cultural sensitivity. Where lecturers have not had the opportunity for personal experience of managing across borders, they need to acquire this awareness in other ways through training.

Such shifts in teaching style also pose problems for educational institutions. Students also need to acquire new learning skills to be effective independent learners and to learn from experience and observation. Without these skills, students on the type of innovative course described above flounder and have unrealistic expectations of what they can achieve and how they should work, as well as of the role of the lecturer. Innovative courses and skills-based courses in general tend to be resource-intensive, which may be a problem for cash-strapped institutions. Finally, institutions also need to recognize that a lecturer who is responsible for an element of students' learning may be legitimately engaged in the process but not standing at the front of a lecture theatre imparting knowledge in a conventional manner.

We conclude that the learning outcomes associated with teaching international business are changing from being contextual and technical to being about the application of a broader set of mainly softer areas of knowledge and skills in varied international settings. As a result lecturers need to consider innovative course models and move away from conventional classroom teaching to achieve these objectives. Our paper outlines one example of innovation but many others could be cited, such as use of role-playing, simulations, multi-site degrees and more. To teach in such ways requires international business lecturers to widen their repertoire of teaching skills through training and for lecturers to be given more support by their institution to do so.

The structure of the International Consultancy Assignment has proved to be robust. By 2002, the original course leaders had moved on and another lecturer had taken over. Chase Manhattan was unable to continue hosting the project as a result of changes stemming from mergers and reorganization. A new company, in the information sector, was brought on board and a new overseas location, Spain, became involved. Maintaining the partnership with Fordham has not been easy as individuals there moved to other positions. Despite all these changes the course is still able to offer the students a practical way to learn consulting skills in an international setting. The successes and problems have not changed much. It seems clear that the International Consultancy Assignment as an innovation can be adapted to capitalize on opportunities and match the circumstances.

References

Blume, Y (1994) An investigation of issues considered important to and difficult for international managers, Unpublished MBA thesis, City University Business School, London

Cateora, P R and Ghauri, P N (1999) *International Marketing*, European edn, McGraw-Hill, London

Edelshain, D J and Vielba, C A (1998) Intercontinental joint ventures in international business education, Working paper for EIBA Annual Conference, Jerusalem

Edelshain, D J and Vielba, C A (1999) The International Consultancy Assignment revisited, Working paper for EIBA Annual Conference, Manchester

Kobrin, S J (1984) *International Expertise in American Business*, Institute of International Education, New York

Ricks, D A and Czinkota, M R (1979) International business: an examination of the corporate viewpoint, *Journal of International Business Studies*, **10**, Fall, pp 97–100

Ronen, S (1989) Training the international assignee, in *Training and Career Development*, ed I Goldstein, Jossey Bass, San Francisco

Vielba, C A and Edelshain, D J (1995) Teaching international business management effectively, *Journal of Management Development*, **14** (10), pp 32–47

Contacts

David J Edelshain and Carol A Vielba
Sir John Cass Business School
106 Bunhill Row
London EC1Y 8TZ
e-mail: d.edelshain@city.ac.uk and c.a.vielba@city.ac.uk

Chapter 5

Introducing action learning into a business school

Tom Bourner and John Lawson

This chapter reports on action learning in the business school at the University of Brighton. First, we review the story of how action learning began, and, following its successful introduction, its spread throughout the school and beyond. We highlight the subsequent development and application of self-managed action learning. We reflect on the worst and best aspects of its introduction, and what we might have done differently to ensure its wide adoption in the business school. Finally, we consider what helped and hindered the overall establishment of action learning.

How it all began

The story of action learning in the Business Faculty of the University of Brighton started with a restructuring of the university in 1987 that shifted departments between faculties. As a result, the Business Faculty became the largest of the university's faculties but, paradoxically, it had the smallest number of research degree students. This created a discomfort in the faculty that prompted a desire to develop a research degree programme in the field of business management that was distinct from the more general research degree programme of the university as a whole.

It became apparent at an early stage in the development that we were unlikely to attract many full-time research degree students, so the programme would have to focus on part-time students. In order to develop such a programme, the question arose: 'What would attract people to register for a research degree in the field of business management on a part-time basis?' Our answer was a programme that focused on research that would make a difference within potential students' organizations. The programme would aim to develop each candidate's capacity to make a significant difference to his or her employing organization through research.

We intended that the programme would be about both researcher development and management development. We hoped that the candidates' employers would realize tangible benefits in terms of both 1) the research-based resolution of some significant issue within their organizations and 2) the development of managers enrolled on the programme.

In order to practise what we would be preaching, we decided to underpin the development of the programme by research. That underpinning took the form of a literature review on research degrees and research degree students as well as a programme of interviews with people who had completed research degrees on the basis of part-time study and some who had failed to complete such part-time research degrees.

Again and again we encountered the phrase 'the social and intellectual isolation of the part-time research degree student' (ABRC, 1982). We needed to consider how to reduce this 'social and intellectual isolation'.

In seeking a resolution we encountered action learning. We first met the term 'action learning' in a book entitled *More than Management Development* (Casey and Pearce, 1977), which was an account of the first large-scale use of action learning across an organization. It suggested a learning process (action learning) involving groups of people coming together on a regular basis to share the difficulties in addressing work-based challenges.

We felt we were on the track of something that would perfectly meet the needs of the new programme. We pursued the scent to two volumes of writings on action learning: *The Origins and Growth of Action Learning* by Reg Revans (1992) and *Action Learning in Practice*, edited by Mike Pedler (1983). The former is a collection of writings by the father figure of action learning, which contains an account of the use of action learning with managers registered on a PhD programme in Belgium. The Pedler work, a collection of articles on action learning, particularly influenced us, as it included an account of the use of action learning at other HE institutions in the UK.

Rather than simply writing action learning into our emerging research degree programme, we decided to test out the ideas in action. We formed an action learning set with some Business Faculty colleagues. Each member of this action learning set was working on a work-related issue, from the completion of a PhD to the revalidation of an HND programme.

Our experience of this first, practical encounter with action learning proved such a positive experience for most of the members of the action learning set that four of the five members formed 'satellite' sets with other colleagues, whilst continuing to remain members of the original set. We wrote up the story of the set and published it in a leading management development journal (Segal-Horn *et al*, 1987). We decided to build the research degree programme around action learning, supplemented by workshops on themes in research methods and management development.

The original conception of the projected research programme was that, in the first year, the participants would research a live business problem within their own organizations and end with a research report containing their conclusions and recommendations. At this point, the candidates would be awarded a Postgraduate Diploma in Business Research Methods. In the second and third year they would test out their conclusions in action by attempting to implement the main recommendations and in the fourth and final year they would reflect on the outcomes and write up their experience in the form of a dissertation. The programme was validated and recruitment was successful. After operating the programme for five years we noticed a decreasing number of managers staying with their employing organizations long enough to complete the programme. It became apparent that, within a four-year period in the early 1990s, most of the managers we recruited either left their employer or changed their work role within their organization. While this was often the pleasing outcome of the personal and professional development that the course was striving to encourage, the inevitable and, for us, worrying by-product of such changes meant that our candidates' original projects became a much lower priority to them.

We responded to this growing awareness by redeveloping the programme into a two-year MA in Change Management. The first year was focused on the use of research methods in the diagnosis of change and still led to a Postgraduate Diploma in Business Research Methods. The second year was focused on the implementation of change and did not need to be based on the recommendations arrived at by the end of the first year, or indeed be within the same organization. Most importantly, action learning remained at the heart of both years of the programme.

Action learning was seen as the most successful element of the programme. Feedback from the participants about the action learning was very positive (Bourner and Frost, 1996a, 1996b). Action learning effectively provided participants with their own personal 'think tank', a group of personal consultants with whom to work on the issues they were finding most challenging at work. For participants, the action learning set provided:

1.   a sounding board for other managers to test out their ideas;
2.   support and encouragement, particularly important when they encountered obstacles, setbacks and pitfalls;
3.   motivation to take the action needed to move forward past barriers to business development and growth;

4. a forum for reflective learning from the outcomes of previous actions;
5. vicarious learning from observation of how the other members of their set were dealing with the challenges that they were experiencing;
6. the confidence associated with offering ideas or asking relevant and searching questions to managers across different employment sectors.

Action learning spreads in the business school

Action learning spread to other courses for students who were part-time, post-graduate and post-experience. These programmes had obvious work-based aspects that were natural vehicles for action learning. Beyond these courses, action learning was used as a means of staff development. For several years, a member of staff facilitated an induction programme for new staff members, and, for about a decade, a self-facilitated action learning set for staff, focused on their research, had a continuous life.

There was some attempt to introduce action learning into undergraduate programmes. It was used for some years as a form of learning support for students preparing final year dissertations on a BA Business Studies (part-time) degree course. For a couple of years action learning was also used to support sandwich placement students on an undergraduate Business Studies degree course (Bourner and Ellerker, 1998a, 1998b).

These ventures however seemed to depend on the initiative of a few enthusiasts for action learning within the faculty. It is worth noting that these enthusiasts were at least as committed to the process of learning *per se* as to a specific subject discipline, ie they were more student-centred than subject-centred. This made them a fairly rare breed in the faculty. Staff members who were more subject-centred were much less enthusiastic about action learning. For these people, action learning could be threatening, as it challenged subject disciplines to prove their worth in helping to resolve live work-based problems.

Eventually, the staff whose primary commitment was to learning and development formed a new unit called the Centre for Management Development (CMD). A majority of the courses in the centre were based upon action learning. It was from this base that some university-wide initiatives emerged.

First, a member of the CMD, Liz Beaty, was seconded on a half-time basis to develop a Certificate in Learning and Teaching for the preparation and development of teachers across the university. She took with her the concept of action learning but adapted it to meet the needs of her new brief. As originally conceived, action learning is a form of management development that requires each manager to bring to the learning set a problematic situation they wish to change (Revans, 1998). There was much in the action learning literature about what constitutes an appropriate 'problem' as the basis for action learning (eg Weinstein, 1995). Beaty, however, adapted the action learning process to provide learning support for the creation of professional development portfolios. This bears some similarity to the use of action learning sets to support learning contracts elsewhere (Cunningham, 1994).

The other university-wide development that occurred at the same time (that is, in the early 1990s) was the development of a Certificate in Research Methods. This programme, which included action learning sets, was designed to provide training in research methods for new research degree students across the university.

Both these university-wide courses included workshops alongside the action learning set meetings. Both of them introduced action learning to members of other faculties across the university.

The result of these developments was that, by 1999, courses based on action learning could be found in all the faculties of the university. By the end of the decade there were 27 courses claiming to use action learning across the university (Bourner, Cooper and France, 2000). That alone might testify to the success of the action learning process within the Business Faculty and beyond, but there were a couple of other significant developments with action learning at their roots.

The Management Development Research Unit

In 1996 the Business Faculty established a Management Development Research Unit (MDRU). This unit is at least as interested in research through innovation as it is in research through discovery. It is particularly interested in research into the process of action learning. It has sought to apply the questioning approach inherent within action learning (Lawrence, 1986) to action learning itself (Bourner *et al*, 1996). We started as a group of experienced action learning facilitators coming together to share our worst experiences of action learning, ie the times when action learning has worked least well for them – with a view to establishing the limitations and boundaries of the domains of applicability of action learning. The resulting set of four papers firmly set the foundations of MDRU.

The vision of the MDRU is:

> To be a centre of excellence in management development research. It intends to be internationally known and respected for its research and practice in action learning. It intends also to have a strong reputation for developing innovative approaches to management development.
>
> Its research will be informed by, and give direction to, management practice. It will be valued and used by managers and contribute to the success and development of themselves and their organisations. The Unit's members will apply their research to their own teaching and learning practice within the University and the wider community.

Most recently, the MDRU has sought to explore the conditions under which self-facilitated action learning is possible. We know that self-facilitated action learning can work. Indeed, our own first experience of action learning was in the form of a self-facilitated action learning set. However, the record of self-facilitated sets suggests that 'external' facilitation significantly increases the likelihood of success. Moreover, influential writers on action learning such as Weinstein and Pedler have claimed that the quality of facilitation is a key factor in the success or otherwise of action learning.

Our reflections on what enables an action learning set to self-facilitate led us to the preliminary conclusion that it depends on whether or not the set happens to contain members with skills in group facilitation. This led us to the conclusion that we could enable self-facilitating sets by providing a preliminary programme to develop the skills of group facilitation.

When the opportunity came to develop such a programme, our reflections deepened and we came to the following conclusions:

1. The skills required for facilitating an action learning set are a subset of the skills required for group facilitation more generally.
2. The most valuable part of what a so-called 'facilitator' brings to an action learning set is not so much group facilitation *per se* as set management.
3. Developing the skills of effective set participation is a substitute for developing the skills for set facilitation. If all the set members were highly skilled set participants then ongoing set facilitation would be unnecessary. Moreover, members of the MDRU had studied the necessary conditions for effective set participation (Bourner, Frost and Beaty, 1997).

Self-managed action learning

Reeve (1994: 3) has defined the work of managers as follows:

> Managers basically have to do two overlapping things: They have to keep the existing show on the road – that is to say manage the routine or recurring activities for which they are responsible. They also have to innovate and make improvements – that is to say change the way things are done or which things are done.

Reeve's two items are precisely the key aspects of the work of the so-called action learning set facilitator: they keep the show on the road, ie make sure the set meetings happen and achieve their purpose, and they help the set to find improvements to its processes. These conclusions provided the basis of a programme of what we termed 'self-managed action learning' (SMAL). Past experience indicated that the high cost of facilitating action learning sets was a barrier to their extensive use in organizations. Indeed, when a health board in Ireland asked the MDRU to undertake a change and management development programme for around 400 of its managers, an inexpensive way of undertaking the programme with set facilitation was required. SMAL was adopted.

The process developed for the health board was that the first two sets in the programme were facilitated by an experienced set adviser who modelled good practice. Thereafter, set members took turns in taking responsibility for ensuring that set meetings occurred as planned and achieved their purpose. Adopting the name 'self-managed action learning' was intended to communicate to managers that they already had skills relevant to ensuring a successful meeting.

To avoid a feeling of isolation, and simultaneously provide a means for review and evaluation, each set was given a 'set process adviser' (Set PA), a role taken by members of the health board's own team. Set PAs attended the whole of the first two facilitated meetings. Subsequently, they joined the set for the final 30 minutes of the meeting to conduct a review of learning, including learning about self-management for the set. As well as keeping the set focused, this process was intended to support the self-management process, ensuring that set members felt that there was always help if needed.

As far as the health board is concerned, SMAL has been seen to work: 390 managers, from a broad range of professional backgrounds and disciplines, have completed the programme or are at various stages within it. Participant feedback has been constantly positive. In total, over 65 self-managed action learning sets have been engaged in ensuring that the change projects around the health board have been successfully undertaken. No set has failed to complete its 12-month span. Almost all the set members have achieved their project goals. An independent evaluation by a member of the Institute for Employment Studies has confirmed the success of this programme.

The other significant development around the same time as MDRU was formed was the unofficial formation of another self-managed action learning set. There was a dearth of formal support for people undertaking work such as an MPhil, a PhD or even a research paper. An informal action set was formed, to provide support and challenge to a number of people who found themselves floating in such a situation. This version of self-management saw the set members decide to meet approximately every six weeks at the university and to run the set unaided, facilitated by themselves. There was no rotation of managers in this model, as was found in the Irish health board set. Indeed, no manager role was identified.

The formation and management of the set were informally conceived, with no obligation on members to attend all or indeed any of the set meetings. In practice, most of the members have attended most of the meetings most of the time. The fact that the set is still operating nearly six years after its conception is testament to its success. That it has developed and maintained its presence and significance beyond its original membership suggests that such an informal set can be viable in the long term. As long as the set is satisfying the requirements of its members, it will continue. Members come and go as its usefulness to them ebbs and flows and there are always people wanting to join. Its successful self-management is possibly a function of most set members having had previous action learning experience.

While most of the set members are undertaking research degrees at Brighton University, the set also includes someone researching for a PhD at another university. A learning community is being encouraged, similar to that which was so eagerly sought during the CMD days. This adds richness to the set members' experience that would otherwise be denied.

Reflections and conclusions

A device we sometimes use to facilitate reflection is to identify 'three worst aspects and three best aspects' of the experience in question. We use this approach here.

What were the three worst aspects?

First, the relatively high staff:student ratio when action learning is applied to higher education limits the extent of its adoption. As an alternative to conventional one-to-one supervision it is an efficient option, but that would restrict its use within HE to research degrees, dissertation support at Master's level and dissertation and sandwich placement support at undergraduate level. This ratio would not permit its application to mainstream undergraduate programmes where the decline in the unit of resource over the last decade has made classes with student:staff ratios in single figures uneconomical.

Second, because of the perceived success of action learning across the university, there has been a tendency to use the term 'action learning' to describe activities that bear little resemblance to purer notions of action learning. According to Revans (1998), action learning is not project work, it is not case studies, business games and other simulations and it is not group dynamics.

The tendency to abuse the term in higher education has been noted before by Brockbank and McGill (1998: 228): 'We have known sets to be used as a means of "sending students off" into small groups to discuss an issue or progress their projects. These are then given the title "learning sets". The result is often a travesty of action learning.' On the other hand, Easterby-Smith (1996: 46) argues against purism and for innovation:

> In my view this kind of definitional purity is unhelpful. The labels we use are based on agreed meanings; they are always subject to challenge and redefinition. No one has the right to impose meaning on others – this is a liberal and relativistic position that I hold with some passion! Attempts to restrict the usage of terms such as self-managed learning and action learning are dangerous because they inhibit experimentation and learning; they privilege the ideas of the past and downgrade experience.

Cunningham (1996: 42) forcefully puts the contrary view: 'If any tired old course puts a bit of project work in it and calls itself "action learning", and if we don't challenge that, we are colluding with unacceptable practice.' Whether such practices constitute 'innovation' or 'dilution' of action learning is open to debate.

Third, the conservatism of Brighton University has, at times, been frustrating. For example, in the early days when we were developing the research degree programme orientated towards managers in full-time employment, the university's Research Degrees Committee decided that our students could not register for a research degree until they had completed the Postgraduate Diploma in Business Research Methods. Moreover, they could not use the work completed for their diploma as part of their research degree. The Research Degrees Committee had a choice between the principle that students could not use the same work for more than one award and the principle of intermediate awards that was applied elsewhere in the university. It chose to privilege the first principle over the second by classifying the Postgraduate Diploma as a qualifying award rather than an intermediate award. The reasons for this decision were probably a combination of institutional conservatism at Research Degrees Committee level, and reluctance to let one part of the university develop its own 'customized' research degree programme. There was also concern about an initiative by the Business Faculty, which, at that time, did not have a strong reputation for research – evidenced, ironically, by the relatively low number of research degree registrations in the faculty. It felt like 'catch-22'. The Business Faculty was trapped in a vicious circle of low numbers of research degree students, which prevented it from effecting the changes needed to raise their numbers!

The result of this decision was to undermine the philosophy of the programme and, more practically, to lengthen it by one year, which was a critical factor in view of the consequences of employment instability referred to earlier in this chapter, and it was damaging to completion rates. The conservatism that lay behind this decision contributed in no small measure to the redevelopment of the programme to a Master's-level course.

What were the three best aspects?

First, it is clear from our experience that action learning can work in an academic context and not just within management development in a business school. This is not to deny that there are challenges in adopting action learning in the context of higher education. For example, it can raise issues at the point of programme validation since much of higher education is based on didactic teaching and 'programmed' learning rather than learning from questioning, action and reflection, which are at the heart of action learning. For this reason, in the context of higher education it is best to see action learning as supporting learning rather than as a direct challenge to higher education's traditional orientation towards subject-centred learning. What we have discovered is that action learning can thrive even in an environment dominated by didactic forms of instruction.

The second positive aspect is that action learning provided a focus for the work of a group of staff with views that were and are out of step with those of many others.

For example, many academics see the primary purpose of learning as the pursuit of knowledge for its own sake, whereas those attracted to action learning are more inclined to think that the purpose of learning is to make a difference or bring about change. Action learning has provided a beacon for those of the latter inclination.

Third, the development of action learning in the Business Faculty paved the way for the development of self-managed action learning (SMAL). We believe that the development of SMAL is our most significant innovation to date. One reason why action learning is not used more extensively in businesses is that fully facilitated action learning sets are expensive; they require that an expert facilitator be present during the whole of the time that an action learning set, comprising only four to seven people, is in session. This is a relatively high staff:participant ratio and is one reason why we introduced action learning into the university at research degree level – because this is the level where the staff:student ratio is highest. With the development of SMAL we have found a way of enabling action learning to be used much more widely in both business and higher education, ie a relatively heavy investment in skills development at the start of a programme reduces the need for ongoing facilitation involvement throughout the programme. We have yet to find ways of convincing business and higher education that SMAL works, and the significant upfront investment in skills development remains a significant deterrent.

What, with hindsight, would we have done differently?

We would have established a research agenda for action learning within the MDRU. It is clear that the people who are associated with this unit have an interest in action learning as a learning process and as a means of supporting other forms of learning. This interest has been the stimulus for many of our studies in the field of action learning and has found expression in our articulated vision (quoted above). However, at no time have we set out to identify an agenda for research into action learning, and such an agenda would have provided direction and inspiration for further studies into action learning as a learning process in higher education.

With hindsight, we would have been more politically astute. In 1998 the university had another reorganization. Departments were merged into a smaller number of schools. In one such merger the Centre for Management Development, mainly concerned with teaching postgraduate, post-experience and part-time students, was merged with two much larger departments that had a strong undergraduate perspective: the Department of Business Management and the Department of Finance and Accountancy. The ethos of the resulting Brighton Business School is very undergraduate-focused and it is a much less hospitable environment for action learning. For example, facilitating action learning has been reclassified from 'teaching', which attracts an allowance for 'teaching-related activities' on staff timetables, to 'supervision', which does not. The result is that the class contact of staff involved in the facilitation of action learning sets has increased and this has raised the class contact component on their timetables, leaving less time for research. The staff most involved with action learning had established a symbiotic relationship between teaching and research (into management development) and that relationship is now under threat. With hindsight, the staff members most involved with action learning realize that they allowed themselves to be led rather than engaging in the micro-politics needed to protect the relationship between facilitating action learning and research. The result is that they must now work in a colder climate for both activities. This experience has probably contributed to their interest in self-management, which is being reflected in the current direction of their work.

We have inclined more to Easterby-Smith's 'liberal' view of the concept of action learning (see above) than Cunningham's more restrictive position (also above). We have, after all, been in the business of innovating in the field of action learning ourselves. We could have been more effective guardians of the spirit of action learning within our institution. Where we have seen the dilution of action learning, we have tended to turn a blind eye, to focus on our own current interests. For example, when our university's Certificate in Research Methods was implemented, the number of action learning set meetings in which a participant would take part was reduced from one each month as in the validated programme to just four meetings of the action learning set over the whole year-long programme. It takes at least two or three meetings for members of a group to get to know each other well enough to be willing to disclose the work issues they are most anxious about. We knew therefore that just four meetings would lead to an impoverished experience of action learning.

For contrast we can look to the Revans Centre for Action Learning and Research at the University of Salford, which has set itself the task of being a beacon for action learning as conceived by Reg Revans. With hindsight, we would have been more inclined to follow the Revans Centre's lead and challenge unacceptable practice.

Again with hindsight, so much of our work has focused on action learning that we might reasonably have put 'Action Learning' into the name of our unit to signal that fact. We are currently interested in expanding the scope of the Management Development Research Unit into a Management Development Research Formatted Centre and this would open up the opportunity to include an Action Learning Research Unit as a part of such a centre. It is important that our name sends out accurate signals for where we wish to place most of our energies.

What helped or hindered adoption of action learning?

This question can be answered at national and local (institutional) levels. Nationally, there has been a growing acceptance of reflective practice within courses of study allied to professional practice. The works of Schön (1983) and Kolb (1984) have been particularly influential in providing a theoretical underpinning for this acceptance. Action learning is a way of realizing reflective practice. Nationally, too, there has been a growth in the acceptability of work-based learning at university (eg Brennan and Little, 1996), and action learning resonates powerfully with that development. Moreover, the last two decades have seen a broadening of the higher education curriculum as the dominance of the Humboldtian ideal has waned. Universities have been asked to do more than transmit the latest knowledge of each discipline and develop the critical faculties of students. There has been greater parity in the three historic missions of the university (research, teaching and service), and this is now reflected in three separate funding streams. It is also reflected in the broadening of the university curriculum and the fact that greater breadth has allowed space for action learning to find its place.

At the institutional level, the main factors that helped to disseminate the practice of action learning were introducing it at research degree level and its adoption by institution-wide courses.

Introducing action learning at research degree level gave it a credibility that would have been lacking if we had introduced it at undergraduate level. Despite the decline in the Humboldtian notion that the dominant purpose of the university is to contribute to knowledge, there is a hierarchy of esteem within most universities associated with the level of award, such that research degrees remain highest in the pecking order. It is no coincidence that student:staff ratios are lowest for research degrees (usually one:one for research degree supervision), higher on Master's courses, higher still on the final years of undergraduate programmes and highest of all at first year undergraduate level. By adopting action learning at research degree level it acquired credibility by association.

Of the two institution-wide courses that adopted action learning, the Certificate in Learning and Teaching and the Certificate in Research Methodology, there is no doubt that it was the former that did most for its dissemination across the institution. The Certificate in Learning and Teaching has been taken primarily by two groups of staff: 1) those who are new to the institution and 2) those who have an interest in learning and teaching. The former are staff who are relatively open-minded about methods of learning and teaching and enthusiastic to apply what they have learnt by example. The latter tends to consist of staff who are recognized as excellent teachers and are, therefore, relatively influential in terms of the learning and teaching methods used in the university.

Significant national and institutional factors have hindered the adoption of action learning across the university. The biggest national factor has been the falling unit of resource for teaching: it is currently about half of what it was in the 1980s. Action learning can seem to be an expensive form of facilitating learning as it normally involves groups of seven or fewer. The biggest institutional factor was the occasional attempt to put action learning facilitation into the timetables of those who are more subject-centred than student-centred in their approach to teaching. We can think of no case where this has been successful. Thankfully, it has not often been attempted.

Barnett (1997) tried to reconcile the Humboldtian ideal of the advancement of knowledge with the ideal of student development, and a recognition of the broadening curriculum, in the notion of 'critical being'. He emphasized critical reason, critical self-reflection and critical action. His thinking is summarized in Table 5.1.

Table 5.1 *Barnett's levels and domains of critical being*

Levels of criticality	Domains Knowledge	Self	Action on the world
4. Transformatory critique	Knowledge-critique: reconstruction of knowledge	Self-critique: reconstruction of self	Critique-in-action: collective reconstruction of the world
3. Refashioning of traditions	Development of subject within traditions	Development of self within traditions	Development of traditions
2. Reflexivity	Critical thinking: reflection on one's understanding	Self-reflection: reflection on one's own projects	Reflective practice
1. Critical skills	Discipline-specific critical thinking skills	Self-monitoring to given standards and norms	Problem solving (means–ends instrumentalism)

Source: Barnett (1997)

As the table shows, Barnett conceptualized the broadening of the domains of the curriculum for higher education in terms of knowledge, self and action on the world. Whereas the aspirations of the Humboldtian agenda lie only in the column headed 'knowledge', universities are expected nowadays to offer students a higher education than this, minimally encompassing a range of transferable skills. Action learning offers a path into the other domains. We hope that the experience that we have reported and discussed in this chapter offers ideas for a path into action learning in the fields of business, management and accounting.

References

ABRC (1982) *Report of the Working Party on Post-graduate Education* (Swinnerton-Dyer Report), CMND 8537, HMSO, London

Barnett, R (1997) *Higher Education: A critical business*, Open University Press, Milton Keynes

Bourner, T, Cooper, A and France, L (2000) Action learning across the university community, *Innovation in Education and Training International*, **37** (1), pp 2–9

Bourner, T and Ellerker, M (1998a) Sandwich placements: improving the learning experience – part 1, *Education and Training*, **40** (6/7), pp 283–87

Bourner, T and Ellerker, M (1998b) Sandwich placements: improving the learning experience – part 2, *Education and Training*, **40** (6/7), pp 288–95

Bourner, T and Frost P (1996a) In their own words: action learning in higher education, *Education and Training*, **38** (8), pp 22–31

Bourner, T and Frost, P (1996b) Experiencing action learning, *Employee Counselling Today: The Journal of Workplace Learning*, **8** (6), pp 11–18

Bourner, T, Frost, P and Beaty, L (1997) Participating in action learning, in *Action Learning in Practice*, 3rd edn, ed M Pedler, Gower, Aldershot

Bourner, T *et al* (1996) Action learning comes of age, part 1: questioning action learning, *Education and Training*, **38** (8), pp 32–35

Brennan, J and Little, B (1996) *A Review of Work-Based Learning in Higher Education*, Department for Education and Employment, London

Brockbank, A and McGill, I (1998) *Facilitating Reflective Learning in Higher Education*, Open University Press, Milton Keynes

Casey, D and Pearce, D (1977) *More than Management Development: Action learning at GEC*, Gower, Aldershot

Cunningham, I (1994) *The Wisdom of Strategic Learning*, McGraw-Hill, London

Cunningham, I (1996) Extending knowledge in management development: the case of self-managed learning, *Organisations and People*, **3** (2), pp 41–45

Easterby-Smith, M (1996) Rejoinder to Ian Cunningham, *Organisations and People*, **3** (2), pp 45–47

Kolb, D (1984) *Experiential Learning as the Science of Learning and Development*, Prentice-Hall, Englewood Cliffs, NJ

Lawrence, J (1986) Action learning: a questioning approach, in *Handbook of Management Development*, 2nd edn, ed A Mumford, Gower, Aldershot

Pedler, M (ed) (1983) *Action Learning in Practice*, Gower, Aldershot

Reeve, T (1994) *Managing Effectively*, Butterworth-Heinemann, London

Revans, R (1992) *The Origins and Growth of Action Learning*, Chartwell-Bratt, Bromley

Revans, R (1998) *ABC of Action Learning*, Lemos and Crane, London

Schön, D (1983) *The Reflective Practitioner*, Jossey Bass, San Francisco

Segal-Horn, S *et al* (1987) Non-facilitated action learning, *Management Education and Development*, **18** (4), pp 277–86

Weinstein, K (1995) *Action Learning*, HarperCollins, London

Contacts

Tom Bourner and John Lawson
Brighton Business School
Mithras House
Lewes Road
Brighton
East Sussex BN2 4AT
e-mail: t.bourner@bton.ac.uk and j.j.lawson@bton.ac.uk

Chapter 6

Byzantium for learning accounting in English business schools

Ashok Patel, Anne Cook and Tudor Spencer

This chapter describes Byzantium's design, development and evaluation, and discusses how students and staff can use the software. It includes details of its use in two English business schools, at Liverpool John Moores University and the University of Hertfordshire.

Byzantium is interactive computer-aided learning software for introductory topics in financial and management accounting for business school students. It seeks to emulate a human tutor and provides students with opportunities to learn, practise and test their skills.

After prototype development at De Montfort University (1990–93), Byzantium was developed by a consortium of six universities within the Teaching and Learning Technology Programme of the Higher Education Funding Councils of the United Kingdom (1993–97). It is now distributed by Blackwell Publishers.

Objectives

Prototype software for interactive learning in marginal costing was developed at De Montfort University in 1990–93, supported by a seedcorn grant from the

Chartered Institute of Certified Accountants. This software was well received at conferences and was shown to be fairly effective and favoured by students at several universities and colleges.

One aim in this pre-Byzantium period was to make specific (and therefore verifiable) the objectives in using computer-aided learning, which were identified as to:

1. enhance the quality, speed and thoroughness of student learning;
2. make more efficient use of teaching resources, particularly the staff time deployed within formal teaching time and for correcting student work and feeding back;
3. make numeric disciplines more accessible to non-specialists;
4. encourage IT awareness and integrate IT into courses;
5. improve access to educational opportunities by promoting learning tools suitable for flexible and distance learning delivery methods;
6. develop and evaluate the outcomes of the Byzantium prototype.

The overall aims for Byzantium were to develop and implement human-tutor-emulating software for teaching introductory financial and management accounting.

Rationale

We realized that, to achieve the first three objectives, the Byzantium software would have to be considerably more intelligent and interactive than an 'electronic page turner'. Indeed, if students and staff were to adopt it, Byzantium would have to emulate the methods human tutors use to guide students when teaching numeric business topics.

We identified performance standards for computer-aided learning software aimed at emulating a human tutor teaching introductory accounting. Byzantium had to:

1. require no fixed sequence of data entry and accept and evaluate any suitable data;
2. call for solving any entered problem for itself, rather than reproducing a solution held on a 'provide answers' file;
3. record how the solution is arrived at and offer the student help in working towards the solution;
4. recognize when the student takes a valid but different route to a solution and help the student along that different route, like a human tutor;
5. generate numerical examples based on random but meaningful values so that students can practise on their own, thus ensuring they understand the technique being studied;

6. operate in a test or examination mode where no guidance is offered to the student and mistakes are allowed, and record against a computed correct solution the students' answers submitted via disk or network;
7. automatically read and record students' results in the test mode and reliably mark randomly generated examples, without any need for specialized staff input;
8. accept input as a result of students interpreting a narrative-type question typically set in a paper-based examination and allow them to enter the solution, given these input values;
9. graphically represent numeric relationships involved in the technique under study and provide full printing facilities for numerical and graphical data involved in the question;
10. incorporate necessary utilities such as calculators, key-stroke reduction systems (eg hot keys) and a common interface between a given suite of programs for handling and saving, and require no significant prior knowledge of computing.

Further, if Byzantium was to use the scarce and expensive specialist staff resources, it would have to focus on the widest potential student audience. In accounting, classes are largest at the introductory stages because students from several disciplines need a basic appreciation of accounting. Each lecturer has to run 'machine-like' repetitive tutorials four, five or six times a week! We thought we could therefore improve lecturers' morale and use teaching resources well if we were to develop software that helped in understanding the basic principles. We also knew that interactions at this level of learning were less complex and more easily handled by the software.

Context

Byzantium started as part of the Teaching and Learning Technology Programme of the Higher Education Funding Councils of the United Kingdom. The project was undertaken in 1993–97 by a consortium of six universities:

1. De Montfort University – Gregory Wilkinson-Riddle (chair) and Ashok Patel (software director);
2. Liverpool John Moores University – Anne Cook and Sheila Grant;
3. University of Huddersfield – Denise Gallagher;
4. University of Middlesex – Mary Simpson;
5. University of Plymouth – Lindsey Lindley;
6. University of Teesside – Alyson Tonge.

Liverpool John Moores University developed the student manuals, Teesside and Huddersfield universities the academic papers and pedagogic tests. Middlesex

University did the large-scale testing. Plymouth University took on network installation testing and use in open learning. All five contributed to design aspects and selection of accounting content, but the hub was at the Computer Aided Learning Research and Development Laboratory at De Montfort University. Ashok Patel led a programming team of Kinshuk, Jamie Hunter and Navjeet Megh in developing software for financial accounting and management accounting, plus common code used in both, and for the Byzantium Marker.

By 1997 the consortium had available:

- *management accounting*: absorption costing, marginal costing, standard costing and capital investment appraisal;
- *financial accounting*: introduction to the profit and loss account and balance sheet, recording transactions in the books of account, trial balance and trial balance adjustments and construction of final accounts;
- *the Automatic Marker program*: this program marks work from all the above programs, producing fully exportable student performance data and enabling students to access feedback indicating correct and incorrect work and to compare their answers with a fully correct solution.

The decision to code the software in a programming language was crucial because it enabled us to combine common utilities (such as calculator, control buttons and saving routines) into the content logic structures, which were individually very different. We were also trying to keep up with technology. The speed with which the Windows platform was adopted in the early 1990s surprised many. Its arrival made obsolete most of the coding approach used for the prototype. We switched to Visual C++, the most effective and flexible language available, consistent with the need to produce a very substantial set of programs to a definite timetable. More advanced versions of Visual C++ appeared throughout the consortium's lifetime. We underestimated the amount of time and effort required for testing our software. Probably only 20 per cent went into the initial coding and 80 per cent into testing and debugging. Our first implementation was delayed, and this limited the enhancements we could make later.

We had to change operating system too, from the 16-bit Windows 3.1 to the 32-bit Windows 95 and Windows NT. The tutoring software is written in the 16-bit version and can run in Windows 3.1 and all subsequent versions of Windows until support for the 16-bit version is no longer provided by Microsoft. The Marker is written in the 32-bit version, as institutions were very quickly switching over to Windows NT networking: doing this enabled lecturers to mark work saved on a network.

None of the authoring packages had what we wanted. Instead, we had to design and code a 'software engine' that could randomly generate meaningful questions and provide feedback to the students about their attempts to answer these.

Description

When students and staff use a Byzantium program to learn accounting they see throughout a standard screen framework with standard areas for control buttons, feedback messages, utilities and, most importantly, one or more work screens. Within each work screen, topic-specific program applications address a specific part of learning the overall topic. For readers interested, we describe below the design principles underlying the software architecture.

Each tutoring program, which we call an 'intelligent tutoring tool' (ITT), is designed around a software engine that stores and processes content-specific knowledge rules. Figure 6.1 shows the main features.

The *knowledge base* contains the conceptual rules and processing information. It consists of two sections that together embed common didactic knowledge and domain didactic knowledge.

The *student model* records each student's progress towards a complete solution. It contains four items:

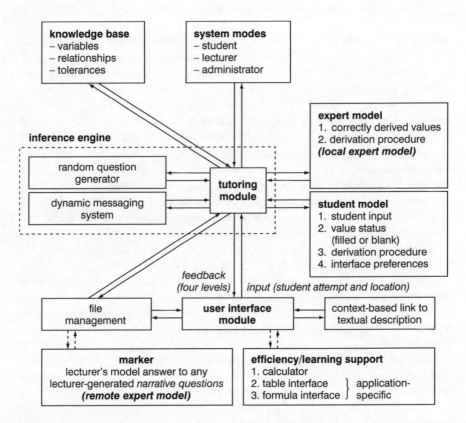

Figure 6.1 *Main features of an 'intelligent tutoring tool'*

1. values entered by a student;
2. value status: for example, differentiating a zero value because of a blank variable, calculated zero or data not processed due to an infinity condition;
3. status of the edit fields filled in by students, such as blank or intrinsically dependent (to begin with) and an independent or dependent variable when filled;
4. user preferences for generative aspects of the interface, for example in the Capital Investment Appraisal ITT, students can choose whether the discount factors are given by the system, filled by using a 'Table' or calculated using a formula.

The *expert model* links to the knowledge rules. It derives correct outcomes and records how they are derived. In the case of a narrative question, the local expert model is based on a student's interpretation of data, while the remote expert model in the Marker software provides the correct interpretation. Their combination enables the Marker to assign a partial score for an answer based on a correct method but an incorrect interpretation of given data, thus demonstrating emergence of a higher degree of overall intelligence through the connection to the Marker of the rudimentary intelligence of an ITT.

The *tutoring module* links students to various parts of the engine through its user interface and gives advice based on the work done so far. It allows a student to adopt a different route to the solution than the one provided by the expert model.

The *user interface module* provides for interaction between a user (a student or staff member) and various parts of an ITT.

The *level selector* determines the functionality that is made available to a user through the interface:

1. The students' level allows them use of the ITTs for learning but cannot create examples for others to use.
2. The lecturers' level enables them to create examples or templates for their students and to save model answers used by the Marker. Marking of students' assignment work is also possible at this level. An 'auto-solve' option is provided that solves whatever it can as each independent variable is inputted, to enable adjusting of inputs with the aim of obtaining a desired scenario.
3. The administrators' level makes possible management of marking schemes and students' data. This functionality was later taken out of individual ITTs and centralized in the Marker to provide summarized results over several ITTs.

Enhanced features are embedded in the software: for example, a random question generator randomly picks variables and assigns random values within specified bounds and then derives the solution by applying its own knowledge rules. Thus, an ITT need not contain any data bank yet all students can get individual questions, though, if so desired, a lecturer can create a bank of questions to be used by all the students. There is also a dynamic feedback system that generates feedback messages based on the information received from a tutoring module. Byzantium's advice to a student is based on work already done by that student and what the student should best do next.

Each ITT can operate in interactive or assignment modes. In interactive mode, the software will not let a student enter a wrong value and it provides immediate feedback, as found in a student modelling technique known as 'model tracing' – the difference being that a student's outcome is monitored rather than the process (rule) employed. Such dynamic feedback goes well with formative assessment as it can prevent at source the results of any incorrect mental associations being made by students, saving them from gross errors.

In assignment or test mode there is no immediate feedback and the software allows students to enter any values. Feedback on their correctness is given only after the work is marked. This static feedback is perhaps less obtrusive and better suited to summative assessment.

Each ITT is designed with high visibility, logical decomposition and visible dependencies in mind. It does not provide immediate ready solutions and waits for a student to execute an action before providing a hint. It can also provide support for students not confident about using a formula: for example, they can call up a formula interface in the Capital Investment Appraisal module, which has the formula broken down into its various constituents. A student can obtain expert help in filling each of the constituents and can work in stages to derive a result of that formula, within the context of the data to which the formula is to be applied. Readers interested in our screen design should go to http://ifets.ieee.org/periodical/vol_1_2000/patel.html.

Interface design is essentially the same across all the programs and includes various features such as context-sensitive help links to textual descriptions of topics, file-saving routines and print management. The user interface is mouse-driven and, to make the interaction as simple and instinctive as possible, employs only push buttons, scrollbars and edit controls. A push button is also activated by a key-stroke of the letter highlighted on its label. All data entry is done through an edit control, suitably masked to prevent entry of illegal data. The interface also reserves a certain area on the screen for interactive feedback, so users do not have to search the whole screen for information that they require. As students prefer lecturers to use diagrams and pictures, graphical representation of data is provided wherever possible and the on-screen tutorial text is augmented with illustrations and replicas of screens.

Evaluation

Summative evaluation in a real environment over longer periods is better than formative evaluation, which may fail to capture all the dimensions of learning and retention, perhaps even blurring the difference between concept acquisition and cognitive skill acquisition. For all that, we think formative evaluations are vital for identifying key design issues and for improving our understanding of pedagogical issues surrounding ITTs.

Formative evaluation of the ITT design began as early as 1995, when students at one university studied capital investment appraisal in two groups. The control group had classroom-based tutorials led by an experienced teacher whereas the computer-aided learning (CAL) group used the ITT in a computer laboratory. Results of pre- and post-tests showed the ITT was effective, and observations and questionnaire feedback from the CAL group validated the interface design.

Further evaluation took place, after some design changes, at the six universities, but this time with three ITTs: Capital Investment Appraisal, Absorption Costing and Marginal Costing. Another control versus CAL group trial at two universities for the Capital Investment Appraisal ITT showed there was no statistically significant difference between the performance of the two groups.

At the other universities, we tested all three ITTs with a random sample of about 40 students. Questionnaires easily and quickly elicited information and opinions from the students, through structured and open-ended questions. One of us, together with a staff member at each university, also observed students at work to augment the questionnaire responses and to capture students' initial reactions.

Through these evaluations we gained valuable understanding of students' feelings about navigational procedures, screen layouts and other human–computer interaction issues. Readers interested in these evaluations – and their limitations – should go to http//ifets.ieee.org/periodical/vol_1_2000/patel.html.

Over the last three years at De Montfort University, for modules that use Byzantium ITTs, around 70 per cent of the respondents to a summative feedback questionnaire made favourable observations about Byzantium. The most favoured features are a) they can practise when they like, b) they can practise as many examples as they like and c) it helps them understand concepts that they could not follow in the lecture. Fewer than 10 per cent of the students made negative comments about computer-aided learning. Indeed, the negative comments were all about availability of the computers.

We also observed some De Montfort students taking notes to cram the numeric relationships rather than internalize them through practice and reflection with an ITT. We noticed that lack of hardware and the pressure of the semester system make it difficult for weaker students to find time for practice.

Our story continues at Liverpool John Moores University and the University of Hertfordshire, where Byzantium is now in routine use by large numbers of students (see also Chapter 10).

Byzantium at Liverpool John Moores University

In the 1997/98 academic year, Anne Cook and Sheila Grant integrated Byzantium into their teaching of accounting for the Business Studies degree at Liverpool John Moores University's Liverpool Business School. They used the Financial

Accounting ITT on a Level 1 module (250 students), and the Management Accounting ITT on a Level 2 module (over 300 students). Most class contact sessions for the Level 1 module and all those for the Level 2 module were in a brand-new state-of-the-art IT suite, and the ITTs ran over a new computer network.

Anne Cook comments:

Byzantium enables students to study at times suited to them. It provides progressive feedback like a human tutor: it will patiently generate an infinite number of questions on each topic, which enables self-assessment of progress throughout a module and is invaluable for revision purposes. The ITTs give students control over their pace and style of learning.

Sheila Grant and I felt at first that the software might lead to a radical change from a didactic approach to a completely student-centred approach to learning. We found, however, that most undergraduate students are not yet ready to take ownership of their own learning, especially at Level 1. The modules are currently delivered in highly structured workshop sessions (20–30 students) by a combination of formal input, CAL and directed reading, with learning materials designed to be compatible with the Byzantium approach. Using the IT suite for all the Level 2 module workshops brought the added bonus of spreadsheet facilities being available for each student when delivering the budget preparation aspects of the module. We decided to use the software for teaching purposes only for one year and, if this was successful, to introduce computer-based assessment the following year.

We felt that the new network and the software were sufficiently robust to introduce computer-based assessment for 1998/99, with 30 per cent of marks going to it for the Level 2 Management Accounting module. Our main aim was to motivate students to acquire the necessary numerical skills on a continuous basis throughout the semester. This spreads the student workload over the semester and is preferable to the approach adopted by many students who rely on last-minute cramming before end-of-semester examinations.

The large numbers of students in the business school made continuous assessment costly in terms of staff resources. Byzantium, however, which can generate an individual test for each student with automatic marking, makes viable regular assessment. Computer-based assessment takes place during scheduled workshops, under examination regulations, using Byzantium's assignment mode. Two staff members invigilate each session.

Students' work is saved on to disk and automatically marked at the assessment sessions. Feedback is immediate as, after marking, the disks are returned so the students can use the software to 'View Marked Work'. Students have to keep the disks in a safe place for the external examiner if required. Most are highly motivated from the outset by the assessment process, which provides them with clearly defined short-term goals. As a result, students take charge of their own learning process early in the semester, striving for the excellent results that they perceive as attainable. Students' motivation is increased by the immediate feedback, and Byzantium engenders a spirit of competitiveness.

We also find that the computer-based assessment enables us to identify early those students who are weak in the subject area, and to take appropriate remedial action. We spotted several students with examination phobias and counselled them individually. As a result, they performed better on all modules.

We did not use computer-based assessment on the Level 1 module, taken in the first semester mainly by non-specialist students, many of whom enrol late for various reasons. Few of the learning outcomes could be assessed by Byzantium therefore we could not justify the resources required.

We were keenly aware that computer-based assessment of over 300 students under examination conditions in a short period has potential for disaster. We invested much time in setting up procedures and avoided the worst pitfalls.

We recognized that involving other staff in Byzantium would be a major challenge. It would not be sufficient merely to circulate an e-mail message announcing its availability! Instead, we held seminars and demonstrations of Byzantium for our colleagues who expressed interest in using the software. Some encouraged students on their own modules to use it, and some asked us to demonstrate the software to their students. Byzantium has not been integrated into other modules as yet.

In 1999 Sheila Grant retired. From the 1999/2000 academic year other staff had to become involved in teaching the modules using Byzantium, for which Anne Cook continued as module leader. Most had not used computers in their teaching programmes before, but all the new members of the module teams quickly overcame their understandable apprehension about the different delivery style.

Byzantium has made a valuable contribution to the teaching of accounting, a discipline that is best learnt through active participation, impossible in enormous lecture groups. Students must develop computational skills to understand and apply accounting techniques. Byzantium gives them opportunities to acquire these skills at their own pace with immediate feedback. The Financial Accounting ITT is probably best suited to Liverpool John Moores Accounting and Finance degree programme and to its professional accounting students. The software will be used more extensively on these programmes as a result of more staff being involved in teaching the business studies modules. Byzantium brings about high attendances, improved motivation and confidence, all leading to better progression rates, important in a numerical subject taught to general business studies students, many of whom fear such subjects.

Those teaching the modules before and after the introduction of Byzantium have commented very favourably on improvements due to its use. At present, Byzantium software is only available on the university's own networked computers, although students may buy a copy for themselves. In future, Byzantium may be integrated into part-time and distance learning, with students downloading the software via the Internet. Byzantium should continue to be an important feature of Business Studies Accounting, and will be integrated into more modules as staff become familiar with the software.

Byzantium at the University of Hertfordshire

A challenge faced by everyone lecturing on accounting degrees is how to get students to work steadily on their own throughout each module. If possible, students will try to study in groups; which is fine in most circumstances but not where one is trying to build up basic accounting skills in the first year. With large groups of students the number of written examples lecturers can take in and mark is limited. To address these problems the University of Hertfordshire's business school introduced Byzantium during the academic year 1998/99.

Tudor Spencer writes:

> Our objectives were to improve first year pass rates and provide a better skills base for subsequent years. We thought Byzantium would help to achieve these objectives by encouraging students to practise examples, giving them feedback week by week throughout the course.
>
> All our business school students must take a one-semester module in accounting and finance during their first year. About 150 students specializing in accounting, or who wish to study the subject further, in the second semester take Accounting Practice, into which we brought Byzantium. This course builds up skills in both financial and management accounting as a firm basis for the more empirically based and conceptual work in the second year. We assess students' performance three times during the module, with a two-hour examination at the end. The first assessment is based on Byzantium's marginal, absorption and standard costing examples, the second on Byzantium trial accounts and final accounts examples. We do not use the Capital Investment Appraisal ITT. The Byzantium assessment requires students to answer two randomly generated questions on each of the three management accounting modules and on the two financial accounting modules.
>
> The Byzantium software is loaded on the university network and is accessible by all students in the learning resource centre. Students can if they wish buy the software disks but very few choose to do so. Generally, students have been very positive about using the software. Our experience is that they can pick up how to use the system from the manual. They quickly find out about the few oddities and work round them. A handful of students need more support: we run a voluntary workshop each week for them.
>
> We encourage students to use the software to build up their accounting skills and to go into assessment mode only when they are confident they have a reasonable mastery of the techniques. Byzantium is used throughout in tandem with paper-based examples and we stress to students that the final exam tests their ability to tackle paper-based examples.
>
> Students answer the Byzantium questions in the learning resource centre and save to floppy disk for the lecturer to mark on a laptop after the main lecture or during the voluntary workshop. Most students who submit answers get high marks.
>
> We notice that marking Byzantium answers is very quick. Normally disks for nearly all the 150 students can be marked in under 30 minutes. The few students

who have used a faulty disk or used wrong identification numbers then take another 30 minutes or so to sort out.

We think the main strength of Byzantium is that we can have students submit a total of 10 questions for automatic marking in addition to the paper-based coursework test. The system works well and even provides feedback to the students – provided they have not write-protected their floppy disks!

We find there's a lot of work keeping track of student marks. Byzantium's database of marks helps but we do have to maintain a spreadsheet of all the marks and check it every week. We can then export the database reports in Excel format.

Overall, on the plus side, our students find Byzantium user-friendly and it operates well from the lecturers' viewpoint. Using unlimited new examples, students can practise accounting techniques at their own pace in a relaxed environment. We think Byzantium is best used in conjunction with other teaching and learning techniques but it does provide a welcome contrast in approach.

On the minus side, Byzantium does not seem to encourage students to work at a steady pace throughout a course. Self-disciplined students use Byzantium to extend their understanding and for this the software serves a useful function. But little learning occurs for students who treat assessment exercises merely as a hurdle to jump if they are to pass the course.

Discussion

We recognize the implementing teacher as a very important partner in implementing Byzantium. We believe that the only way to encourage widespread use of learning resources like Byzantium is to enable the implementing teacher to contribute through configuring the learning space, and to add to and restructure the scope and functionality of learning components. Byzantium was developed in an era that did not facilitate such features. Adaptations are now possible with standardized Web browsers and the communications capability of the Internet.

Byzantium represents successful application of a methodology that was first developed and tested through a single prototype. It is amongst the 7 per cent of Teaching and Learning Technology Programme projects that have been adopted and distributed commercially.

Further reading

Journal papers

Kinshuk, Hong Hong and Patel, A (2002) Adaptivity through the use of mobile agents in Web-based student modelling, *AACE International Journal of E-Learning*, **1** (3), pp 55–64

Kinshuk, Patel, A and Russell, D (1999) HyperITS: A Web-based architecture for evolving a configurable learning environment, *Staff and Educational Development International Journal*, **3** (3), pp 265–80

Kinshuk, Patel, A and Russell, D (2000) A multi-institutional evaluation of intelligent tutoring tools in numeric disciplines, *Educational Technology & Society*, **3** (4), pp 66–74

Kinshuk, Patel, A and Russell, D (2001) Achieving enhanced learning, greater re-usability and wider acceptance for multimedia learning environments, *Campus-wide Information Systems*, **18** (3), pp 110–19

Patel, A and Kinshuk (1997) Intelligent tutoring tools in a computer integrated learning environment for introductory numeric disciplines, *Innovations in Education and Training International*, **34** (3), pp 200–07

Patel, A, Kinshuk and Russell, D (1998) Accounting education and computer based learning, *Account: Journal of CTI Accounting, Finance and Management*, **10** (1), pp 21–26

Patel, A, Kinshuk and Russell, D (1998) A computer based intelligent assessment system for numeric disciplines, *Information Services and Use*, **18** (1–2), pp 53–63

Patel, A, Kinshuk and Russell, D (2000) Intelligent tutoring tools for cognitive skill acquisition in life long learning, *Educational Technology & Society*, **3** (1), pp 32–40

Patel, A, Kinshuk and Russell, D (2002) Cognitive skill acquisition and computer based intelligent tutoring tools, *Interactive Learning Environments*, **10** (2), pp 139–55

Patel, A, Scott, B and Kinshuk (2001) Intelligent tutoring: from SAKI to Byzantium, *KYBERNETES: International Journal of Systems & Cybernetics*, **30** (5/6), pp 807–18

Book chapters

Kinshuk and Patel, A (2001) Critical issues in Web-based training, in *Web-based Training*, ed E B Khan, pp 375–80, Educational Technology Publications, Englewood Cliffs, NJ

Kinshuk, Patel, A and Russell, D (2002) Intelligent and adaptive systems, in *Handbook on Information Technologies for Education and Training*, ed B Collis, H H Adelsberger and J Pawlowski, pp 79–92, Springer, Berlin

Patel, A, Kinshuk and Russell, D (2003) Cognitive apprenticeship learning: ensuring far transfer of knowledge through computer-based assessment, in *Learning and Teaching with Technology: Principles and practices*, ed S Naidu, pp 233–46, Kogan Page, London

Patel, A, Russell, D and Kinshuk (1999) Assessment in a cognitive apprenticeship based learning environment: potential and pitfalls, in *Computer-Assisted Assessment in Higher Education*, ed S Brown, P Race and J Bull, pp 139–47, Kogan Page, London

Conference papers

Han, B, Kinshuk and Patel, A (2001) A student model for Web-based intelligent educational system, in *Proceedings of EdMedia 2001*, ed C Montgomerie and V Jarmo, pp 656–57, June, Tampere, Finland, AACE, Norfolk, VA

Hong, H *et al* (2001) Adaptivity in a Web-based educational system, in *Tenth International World Wide Web Conference Poster Proceedings*, pp 100–01, May, Hong Kong, Chinese University of Hong Kong, Hong Kong

Hong, H *et al* (2001) Application of mobile agents in Web-based learning environments, in *Proceedings of EdMedia 2001*, ed C Montgomerie and V Jarmo, pp 778–83, June, Tampere, Finland, AACE, Norfolk, VA

Kinshuk, Hong Hong and Patel, A (2001) Extended ITS framework with human teacher model, in *Proceedings of the International Conference on Computers in Education/SchoolNet 2001*, ed C H Lee *et al*, 12–15 November, Seoul, Korea, **3**, pp 1259–62

Kinshuk, Nikov, A and Patel, A (2001) Adaptive tutoring in business education using fuzzy back propagation approach, in *Usability Evaluation and Interface Design: Cognitive engineering, intelligent agents and virtual reality*, ed M J Smith *et al*, pp 465–68, Proceedings of the 9th International Conference on Human–Computer Interaction, 5–10 August, New Orleans, Lawrence Erlbaum, NJ

Kinshuk, Patel, A and Russell, D (1999) A multi-institutional evaluation of intelligent tutoring tools in numeric disciplines, in *The Evaluation of Learning Technology Conference Proceedings*, ed M Oliver, pp 38–40, University of North London, London

Kinshuk, Patel, A and Russell, D (2001) Intelligent tutoring of domain skills: the need and a solution, in *Proceedings of 2001 Informing Science Conference*, ed A Harriger, pp 292–300, June, Cracow University of Economics, Cracow

Kinshuk *et al* (2000) Human teachers' role in emerging internet based intelligent tutoring, in *Supporting the Learner through Open, Flexible and Distance Strategies: Issues for Pacific Rim countries*, pp 209–17, Proceedings of the Distance Education Association of New Zealand, Wellington

Patel, A, Kinshuk and Russell, D (1999) Cognitive apprenticeship based learning environment in numeric domains, in *Human Computer Interaction: Communication, cooperation, and application design*, ed H-J Bullinger and J Ziegler, pp 637–41, Lawrence Erlbaum, NJ

Patel, A, Kinshuk and Russell, D (2000) Increasing usability and reusability through a configurable, incremental and re-structurable contributive learning environments (CIRCLE) architecture, in *Proceedings of the International Congress on Intelligent Systems and Applications*, ed F Naghdy *et al*, pp 645–51, 11–15 December, University of Wollongong, Australia, ICSC Academic Press, Switzerland

Patel, A and Russell, D (1999) Tools of trade or tutoring tools: the hard software choice in accounting education, in *Selected Proceedings of the 10th Annual CTI-AFM Conference*, ed K Fletcher and A H S Nicholson, pp 121–27, CTI Accounting, Finance and Management, Norwich

Patel, A, Russell, D and Kinshuk (2002) Implementing cognitive apprenticeship and conversation theory in interactive web-based learning systems, Sixth Multi-Conference on Systemics, Cybernetics and Informatics: SCI2002, 14–18 July, Orlando, FL

Patel, A *et al* (2001) Intelligent tutoring systems: confluence of information science and cognitive science, in *Proceedings of 2001 Informing Science Conference*, ed A Harriger, pp 392–97, June, Cracow University of Economics, Cracow

Contacts

Ashok Patel
School of Business
De Montfort University
Leicester LE1 9BH
e-mail: apatel@dmu.ac.uk

Anne Cook
The Liverpool Business School
Liverpool John Moores University
John Foster Building
98 Mount Pleasant
Liverpool L3 5UZ
e-mail: a.m.cook@livjm.ac.uk

Tudor Spencer
Business School
University of Hertfordshire
Mangrove Road
Hertford SG13 8QF
e-mail: t.g.spencer@herts.ac.uk

Chapter 7

Using Monopoly© as an introduction to financial accounting

Graham Clayton

Playing the board game Monopoly© enables students to run their own property businesses and, thereby, create their own financial transactions. The students are actively involved. Theory and practice meet. As a result basic financial accounting techniques are assimilated very effectively and students develop as autonomous learners.

We have used Monopoly© since 1998 as the key teaching method for the initial stages of a first-level financial accounting module. The module leader's main role is to plan and administer the exercise. The students, to a large extent, run each session themselves.

The students prepare balance sheets and profit and loss accounts for four trading periods. In addition, the exercise demands that they can interpret, at a basic level, their own and their peers' financial statements. In playing the game, they develop a range of personal skills.

Our students have greeted Monopoly© with much enthusiasm and feedback has been very positive. They enjoy being actively involved. Creating and recording their own financial transactions is an effective way of developing an understanding of how to draft simple financial statements. We have also found that adding a 'betting' element helps to develop the students' skills in interpreting financial statements.

Because of the success of this approach, Monopoly© is now also used on other modules at both undergraduate and postgraduate level. Again the impact on, and feedback from, students has been positive.

Objectives

Our objectives in setting up the original trial within the business school's BA Business Administration (BABA) programme were clear. We wanted to use Monopoly© to introduce parts of the syllabus because we thought it would help our students to develop as autonomous learners, and make them more active and engaged. The parts we had in mind were particularly the balance sheet, the profit and loss account, cash flow statements and the analysis and interpretation of financial statements.

Context

In September 1997 the first cohort of students registered for the BABA programme at the Plymouth Business School (PBS). Autonomous learning is at the heart of delivery of the programme. We expect students to 1) organize and take responsibility for their own learning, 2) be active and motivated, and 3) do so with adequate tutorial support.

In each year of the programme the students study six modules (three per semester). The Business Finance 1 module, which introduces students to financial and management accounting, is one of three taken in Year 1, Semester 2. Its syllabus is: *financial accounting* – the balance sheet, the profit and loss account, limited companies, cash flow statements, the analysis and interpretation of financial statements; and *management accounting* – cost–volume–profit analysis, full costing, budgeting, capital investment decisions, working capital, financing the business.

Students are assessed in this module via coursework (30 per cent weighting) and a three-hour examination (70 per cent) at the end of Semester 2. We decided to allocate one-third of the coursework mark to the Monopoly© exercise. The remaining coursework assessment is through individual tests and group work.

Rationale

Using Monopoly© to introduce fundamental aspects of financial accounting has been successful in US undergraduate and postgraduate business education. Knechel (1989) states the key reason for employing Monopoly© in preference to 'practice sets' (ie traditional accounting questions/exercises and solutions): 'Practice sets are relatively sterile. The students are presented with a set of facts and transactions that are generated without their active participation. As a consequence, the students may not appreciate the economic implications of some of the events that are described in the case.' Albrecht (1995: 128) lists advantages of using simulation exercises such as Monopoly©. He says that they:

- motivate students to participate in educational activities to a greater degree;
- enhance cognitive growth with increased recall and improved problem-solving skills;
- enhance effective learning because students attribute greater value to accounting information in the decision-making process;
- give students intensive practice in verbal and written communication;
- require flexibility in thinking and an adaptive response to a dynamic environment;
- can be repeated with the same participants and additional learning will take place;
- allow students to play at their own levels.

Knechel's criticisms of practice sets and Albrecht's positive views on using simulations were a real encouragement to us to experiment with Monopoly©. These US authors suggested that the board game is a good stimulus for autonomous learning. We used their experience as a guide.

We also knew that most students would be already aware of how to play Monopoly© and that most would enjoy it. We felt that if they were enjoying themselves then their learning would probably be more effective because they were active and engaged.

Description

Monopoly©'s place in the module schedule

The BABA Monopoly© sessions are offered for the first four weeks (of 12) of the module in place of the traditional tutorials. Each Monopoly©-playing student's formal contact time with staff over these four weeks consists of:

- two one-hour lectures per week;
- a weekly one-hour Monopoly© session;
- daily 'accounting surgeries' available for those who want them;
- a 45-minute fortnightly test, again voluntary.

The first assignment is based on the Monopoly© exercise.

Organizing the Monopoly© sessions

About 100 students take the first year of the BABA programme. These are split into two groups of 50 (Group A and Group B), each of which has a one-hour tutor-led Monopoly© session per week. Four students play in each game. Each student runs his/her own business based on Monopoly© transactions. Each business (player) has an alphanumeric code: for example, in Game 1, the four businesses were C1, C2, C3 and C4 (see Table 7.1).

Each of the four weeks of the exercise counts as one trading year for the student businesses. So Week 1 is used to create the financial transactions for Year 1, Week 2 for Year 2 and so on. Students follow this weekly cycle of events:

- *Day 1:*
  - Student teams play Monopoly© for approximately 25 minutes and record all financial transactions for their business.
  - During these sessions the module leader can halt play at any time and introduce/explain particular accounting issues, eg the meaning of 'capital', the creation of a profit and loss account, the difference between cash and profit, borrowings, depreciation, purchase/sale of fixed assets. The practical nature of the exercise should enhance students' understanding. (See 'The module leader's involvement' below.)
- *By end of Day 3:*
  - Teams submit (on maximum of two sides of A4 paper) the most recent financial statements (profit and loss account and balance sheet) for all four businesses in their game, ie half a page of A4 per business.
- *By end of Day 4:*
  - Financial statements for all businesses/games with the same letter code (ie C, D, E, etc) are stapled together by the module leader and held for collection by students.
- *By end of Day 5:*
  - Individual students study the financial statements of each game in their letter code and consider the likely future success of each business.
  - Students place 'bets' (maximum £10 per game) on each of the three games in their letter code.
  - The team representative submits team members' betting forms.
- *By end of Day 6:*
  - A spreadsheet copy of consolidated results of betting (see Appendix 7.1) is prepared by the module leader and then posted on the student noticeboard.
  Note that the mechanism chosen for student investment is the *pari mutuel* auction used by Albrecht (1995).
- *Day 8:*
  - Second Monopoly© session.
  - Individual students receive a copy of the consolidated betting results (see Day 6). Taking 'market' scores into account each student places another bet (maximum £10) on each of the three games in his/her alphabetical group (ie those with the same letter code).

Table 7.1 *Monopoly®, sessions 1 and 2*

Session 1, Group A (c. 50 students)

Game 1	Game 2	Game 3	Game 4	Game 5	Game 6	Game 7	Game 8	Game 9	Game 10	Game 11	Game 12
(C1 to C4)	(C5 to C8)	(C9 to C12)	(D1 to D4)	(D5 to D8)	(D9 to D12)	(E1 to E4)	(E5 to E8)	(E9 to E12)	(F1 to F4)	(F5 to F8)	(F9 to F12)

Session 2, Group B (c. 50 students)

Game 13	Game 14	Game 15	Game 16	Game 17	Game 18	Game 19	Game 20	Game 21	Game 22	Game 23	Game 24
(G1 to G4)	(G5 to G8)	(G9 to G12)	(H1 to H4)	(H5 to H8)	(H9 to H12)	(J1 to J4)	(J5 to J8)	(J9 to J12)	(K1 to K4)	(K5 to K8)	(K9 to K12)

–   Year 2 of Monopoly© is played (approximately 25 minutes). Cycle continues for this week and two more.

Note that at the conclusion of Year 4 it is a straightforward task for the module leader to establish who is the most successful 'punter' in each alphabetical group. He/she merely establishes the winning business in each game (ie that which has the highest capital figure) and multiplies each student's investment in that business by the odds for that business (see Appendix 7.1).

The module leader's involvement

The module leader's key roles are to ensure that each session runs smoothly and that students understand what is required of them. Beyond that, however, it is important to realize that different financial accounting topics can be explained and introduced into the exercise in stages, week by week, according to their degree of difficulty. Week-by-week stages are:

● *Week 1*:
  –   The basic balance sheet.
  –   Does actual cash equal 'book' cash?
  –   The accounting equation.
  –   Capital.
  –   Profit as a balancing figure.
● *Week 2*:
  –   Calculation of profit.
  –   The profit and loss account.
  –   Students can borrow money – leading to payment of interest charges.
● *Week 3*:
  –   Depreciation of fixed assets (properties and houses/hotels).
● *Week 4*:
  –   Students can trade properties.
  –   Students allowed to owe money to other players (concept of debtors and creditors).

The most successful business in each game is the one with the highest 'capital' figure.

This 'staged' approach works well and means that students avoid being either bored because of excessive repetition of tasks or overwhelmed by too much new information introduced too quickly.

The assignment exercise

As stated earlier, this exercise forms the basis of the module's first assignment, normally worth one-third of the coursework mark (ie 10 per cent of the total module mark). The key elements of the assignment are shown below:

- *Part 1* (70 per cent)
  Each team makes a 10-minute presentation, followed by approximately five minutes of questions. The presentation is a verbal summary of the four years of business trading of their game. Typical areas covered are:
  - Which businesses did well and why?
  - What were the key trading figures?
  - How easily did the Monopoly© simulation fit in with 'normal' financial transactions?
  - How did the team work together?
  - Were deadlines met easily?
- *Part 2* (30 per cent)
  After the team presentations all students submit individual pieces of work. These are personal summaries of the betting policies that students adopted during the exercise and include conclusions as to why they were successful or unsuccessful with their betting. Points to cover might be:
  - How successful were they compared to their team and their grouping?
  - What factors did they take into account when assessing which businesses would be, in their opinion, successful?
  - Did this policy alter throughout the exercise?
  - How much was their betting affected by the opinions of other students in their team or tutorial group?
  - Was it more difficult betting on those games in which they weren't involved?

Evaluation

We distributed Likert-type questionnaires to the BABA students each year after the simulation. We added two extra questions in 1999 and 2000, and changed the questions slightly in 2001. These questionnaires became part of a longitudinal study of using Monopoly© to develop personal skills. Tables 7.2 and 7.3 summarize the results and Appendix 7.2 lists individual student comments.

It is clear that the students were very positive about their experience. The questionnaire responses in 1998–2000 showed that our students agreed that the preparation and understanding of balance sheets (91 per cent) and profit and loss accounts (81 per cent) were made easier by playing Monopoly©. Further, 71 per cent felt that the exercise made it easier for them to link theory and practice, and 76 per cent saw the exercise as preferable to the traditional lecture.

Many students stated that Monopoly© was 'fun'. There were also many comments about the positive social impact of the exercise (88 per cent approval rating) and in at least one case it helped to reduce or remove the student's fear of studying financial accounting.

Some students also said that being active and creating (ie 'owning') their businesses' transactions made Monopoly© an effective way for them to learn.

Table 7.2 *BABA 1 student responses in 1998–2000 to the questionnaire*

	Agree %	Neutral %	Disagree %
1. The exercise was an effective way of learning how to prepare balance sheets (n = 192)	91	6	3
2. The exercise was an effective way of learning how to prepare profit and loss accounts (n = 192).	81	15	4
3. The exercise made it easy for me to link theory and practice (n = 132).	71	27	2
4. I would have preferred lectures instead of the exercise (n = 192).	6	18	76
5. The supporting materials handed out were easy to use and effective (n = 133).	76	22	2
6. The module was run efficiently by the module lecturer (n = 192).	96	4	0
7. I enjoyed the social aspects of the exercise (n = 192).	88	9	3
8. I didn't take the exercise seriously because it was a game (n = 190).	8	15	76
9. The deadlines for submission of work were too tight (n = 188).	13	20	67
10. The betting element of the exercise was a good way of developing my interpretative skills (n = 187).	49	33	18
11. This exercise should be used in the same way on this module next year (n = 188).	79	15	6

However, some respondents were unhappy with the betting element of the exercise and found it confusing. Others would have liked more time with the module leader to discuss the drafting and accuracy of their financial statements. Overall the exercise got very high ratings from the students over the four years: 79 per cent agreed that it should be used in the same way in the future whilst only 7 per cent disagreed with this.

Using Monopoly© for other modules

Certificate in Management Studies (CMS)

As the Monopoly© simulation had very positive feedback from the BABA undergraduate students we decided to use it from 2000 in a shorter (non-assessed and

Table 7.3 *BABA 1 student responses (n = 42) in 2001 to the questionnaire*

	Agree %	Neutral %	Disagree %
1. The exercise was an effective way of learning how to prepare balance sheets.	76	17	7
2. The exercise was an effective way of learning how to prepare profit and loss accounts.	74	14	12
3. The exercise was an effective way of getting to understand the concept of assets.	79	16	5
4. The exercise was an effective way of getting to understand the concept of liabilities.	69	24	7
5. The exercise was an effective way of getting to understand the difference between the cash and profit figure calculations.	64	31	5
6. The exercise was a relatively painless and speedy way of learning how to prepare balance sheets.	74	9	17
7. The exercise was a relatively painless and speedy way of learning how to prepare profit and loss accounts.	71	10	19
8. The exercise was a relatively painless and speedy way of getting to understand the concept of assets.	74	16	10
9. The exercise was a relatively painless and speedy way of getting to understand the concept of liabilities.	71	22	7
10. The exercise was a relatively painless and speedy way of getting to understand the difference between the cash and profit figure calculations.	57	41	2

without the betting) version in the Accounting Planning and Control module for the faculty's postgraduate Certificate in Management Studies (CMS) cohort. This is played for two weeks only and, as with the BABA exercise, was introduced right at the start of the module. Most of the 30 or so CMS students each year have little or no prior understanding of financial accounting.

Again the students' reactions were very positive (see Table 7.4 and Appendix 7.3): 86 per cent said that preparing and understanding balance sheets was made easier by playing Monopoly©, though only 46 per cent said the same about preparing and understanding profit and loss accounts. This may well have been due to the students having only two sessions rather than four. No fewer than 90 per cent of the students felt that the exercise made it easier for them to link theory and practice, and 83 per cent saw the exercise as preferable to the traditional lecture.

Table 7.4 *CMS student responses (n = 29) in 2000 to the questionnaire*

	Agree %	Neutral %	Disagree %
1. The exercise was an effective way of learning how to prepare balance sheets.	86	7	7
2. The exercise was an effective way of learning how to prepare profit and loss accounts.	46	43	11
3. The exercise made it easy for me to link theory and practice.	90	7	3
4. I would have preferred lectures instead of the exercise.	10	7	83
5. The supporting materials handed out were easy to use and effective.	93	7	0
6. The module was run efficiently by the module lecturer.	83	17	0
7. I enjoyed the social aspects of the exercise.	90	10	0
8. I didn't take the exercise seriously because it was a game.	0	11	89
9. This exercise should be used in the same way on this module next year.	85	11	4

Again, many students stated that it was 'fun'. There were several comments about the positive social impact of the exercise (90 per cent approval rating).

Overall, the exercise again got very high ratings: 85 per cent of the students agreed that it should be used in the same way in the future whilst only 4 per cent disagreed with this.

BA in Accounting and Finance, Year I

Monopoly© was introduced into Basic Financial Accounting within the BA in Accounting and Finance programme in the academic year 2000/01. The approach adopted by the module leader was different in that she used the exercise for three one-hour sessions in Semester 2 of this year-long module. Thus the students work through the simulation after they have learnt (via lectures and tutorials) the basics of financial accounting in the first semester. Monopoly© is used to investigate some of the more technical aspects of introductory financial accounting – such as double-entry bookkeeping, the calculation of depreciation and the valuation of fixed assets. There is a substantial assessment (one-half of the total coursework mark) to complete at the end of Semester 2. Informal feedback from the students has been good, and Monopoly© will continue to be used in this module for the foreseeable future.

Master's in Business Management

This programme was launched in September 2000 and a modified version of the BABA Monopoly© simulation was used (with both cohorts) in the first session of the Managerial Accounting and Finance module, as a two-hour introductory exercise. It was well received by the students, and the module leader continues to use it in this modified format.

Conclusions and future developments

Clearly, the simulation is very popular with students. They run their own 'business', create financial transactions for it and prepare its financial statements. They may also be asked to interpret the performance of their business and those of their peers. Their ownership and involvement make the learning more relevant to them. In addition, we think that the students' commitment is increased. Attendance rates (estimated to be at least 90 per cent) are much higher than for lectures. There is a tremendous level of activity at the Monopoly© sessions – the students are generally very competitive – with plenty of discussion and argument. The students enjoy the social aspects of the exercise.

For the module leader, once the exercise is organized and the sessions are adequately planned, the sessions are very enjoyable because he or she acts as a facilitator and adviser and can see the students getting real enjoyment from their studies. It is worth noting in Table 7.2 that 76 per cent of students took the simulation seriously, whilst only 8 per cent didn't.

Having 'physical' assets available (ie cards for property or fixed assets, and actual cash) eases the demonstration of certain technical points, such as: distinguishing between capital and revenue expenditure; reconciling profit and cash; being required to make a book (rather than cash) adjustment for depreciation.

The students also have to reconcile their Monopoly© experience and practice with the underpinning theory by using the module text and through attending lectures and (where available) surgeries.

However, the module leader will probably spend more time using this approach than with traditional methods. Preparing the betting spreadsheets (see Appendix 7.1) is particularly time-consuming. As a result, some parts of the exercise might not receive adequate coverage, such as checking through the accuracy of individuals' or teams' weekly financial statements and spending more time on the interpretation and betting aspects.

To date all the cohorts have welcomed and enjoyed the simulation. We are certain it has enhanced the delivery of course content and that it can develop personal skills such as problem solving, analysis, team working, communication and time management. We are glad to say that a longitudinal survey of the impact of Monopoly© on the personal skills of the BABA students started in spring 2001.

Working on the premise that students' learning is enhanced when they are proactive, a computerized accounting simulation was introduced into the Business Finance 1 module in March 2001. Students worked in teams in a competitive environment (ie trading against each other) over eight trading periods. Additional elements of the module syllabus (in particular management accounting) were studied through this mode. The feedback was yet again very positive and many of the favourable comments made about Monopoly© were repeated.

So, the experiment with Monopoly© has proved very successful. It is transferable – other members of staff have adopted it in various guises (and at different degrees of difficulty) for their modules. We have been encouraged to seek or develop other simulations that will also enhance the students' learning experience.

References

Albrecht, W D (1995) A financial accounting and investment simulation game, *Issues in Accounting Education*, **10** (1), pp 127–142

Knechel, R K (1989) Using a business simulation game as a substitute for a practice set, *Issues in Accounting Education*, **4** (2), pp 411–24

Contact

Graham Clayton
University of Plymouth Business School
Drake Circus
Plymouth PL4 8AA
e-mail: g.clayton@pbs.plym.ac.uk

Appendix 7.1a Student betting, Year 1, Round 1 (extract from working spreadsheets)

Game number	Business code	Year 1 Round 1	Game 4					Game 5					Game 6				
			D1	D2	D3	D4	Total	D5	D6	D7	D8	Total	D9	D10	D11	D12	Total
4	D1	Student A					0					0					0
4	D2	Student B	1	2	4	3	10	0	1	1	8	10	8	1	1	0	10
4	D3	Student C	5	5	0	0	10	0	0	0	10	10	5	5	0	0	10
4	D4	Student D	4	0	0	6	10	1	1	8	0	10	8	0	0	2	10
5	D5	Student E					0					0					0
5	D6	Student F					0					0					0
5	D7	Student G					0					0					0
5	D8	Student H	0	10	0	0	10	0	0	0	10	10	10	0	0	0	10
6	D9	Student J	10	0	0	0	10	0	0	0	10	10	10	0	0	0	10
6	D10	Student K	4	3	2	1	10	0	3	3	4	10	4	1	3	2	10
6	D11	Student L	3	3	3	1	10	0	2	2	6	10	4	3	2	1	10
6	D12	Student M	5	5	0	0	10	0	3	2	5	10	10	0	0	0	10
		Total	32	28	9	11	80	1	10	16	53	80	59	10	6	5	80
		Odds (to 1)	2.5	2.9	8.9	7.3		80.0	8.0	5.0	1.5		1.4	8.0	13.3	16.0	

Consider Student C above: S/he has £10 to bet on each of the three games (Games 4 to 6) in his/her alphabetical grouping (ie D). S/he will use the up-to-date financial statements for each of the businesses and decide which of them is the most likely to 'succeed'. So in this first round for Game 4, s/he feels that Businesses D1 and D2 are worth backing and the £10 is split evenly. For Game 5, however, all of the £10 is invested in Business D8, whilst Game 6 sees an even split between D9 and D10.

Student D, however, plumps for D1 and his/her own business D4 as the likely 'winners' of Game 4. In Games 5 and 6 this student puts sizeable bets on two other businesses – D7 and D9 respectively.

Betting on the games in which C and D are not involved (ie Games 5 and 6) should prove more difficult as they have only got the financial statements to work with. The lecturer could lead a discussion on the concept of 'insider dealing' here. Students' betting should be more successful in the games that they are playing.

Appendix 7.1b Student betting, Year 1, Round 2 (extract from working spreadsheets)

Game number	Business code	Year 1 Round 2	Game 4					Game 5					Game 6				
			D1	D2	D3	D4	Total	D5	D6	D7	D8	Total	D9	D10	D11	D12	Total
4	D1	Student A	5	3	1	1	10	1	1	1	7	10	0	5	5	0	10
4	D2	Student B					0					0					0
4	D3	Student C	5	0	5	0	10	0	0	3	7	10	7	3	0	0	10
4	D4	Student D	2	0	2	6	10	0	0	5	5	10	1	4	4	1	10
5	D5	Student E	5	5	0	0	10	6	0	0	4	10	8	2	0	0	10
5	D6	Student F	7	1	1	1	10	1	1	0	8	10	10	0	0	0	10
5	D7	Student G	10	0	0	0	10	0	0	0	10	10	10	0	0	0	10
5	D8	Student H	10	0	0	0	10	0	0	0	10	10	10	0	0	0	10
6	D9	Student J	10	0	0	0	10	0	0	0	10	10	10	0	0	0	10
6	D10	Student K	4	3	2	1	10	0	2	2	6	10	4	3	2	1	10
6	D11	Student L	4	3	2	1	10	7	2	1	0	10	5	3	2	0	10
6	D12	Student M	5	5	0	0	10	0	1	2	7	10	7	2	1	0	10
		Total	67	20	13	10	110	15	7	14	74	110	72	22	14	2	110
		Odds (to 1)	1.6	5.5	8.5	11.0		7.3	15.7	7.9	1.5		1.5	5.0	7.9	55.0	

These figures show the second round of betting on the Year 1 financial statements. The students will have seen how their peers are betting (ie how the 'market' rates the progress of the various businesses). So they might be influenced by the 'market' and change their policy accordingly.

Appendix 7.1c Student betting, final round – before Year 4 trading (extract from working spreadsheets)

Game number	Business code	Year 1 Round 2	Game 4					Game 5					Game 6				
			D1	D2	D3	D4	Total	D5	D6	D7	D8	Total	D9	D10	D11	D12	Total
4	D1	Student A	16	3	1	20	40	3	12	3	12	30	6	9	11	4	30
4	D2	Student B	7	2	4	17	30	2	13	3	12	30	13	3	9	5	30
4	D3	Student C	10	5	5	30	50	0	0	5	35	40	21	13	3	3	40
4	D4	Student D	11	0	2	27	40	1	6	13	10	30	11	6	6	7	30
5	D5	Student E	17	5	4	4	30	27	0	1	12	40	19	2	0	9	30
5	D6	Student F	17	1	1	1	20	6	1	3	20	30	20	0	0	0	20
5	D7	Student G	10	10	0	0	20	0	0	15	15	30	10	0	10	0	20
5	D8	Student H	25	10	0	5	40	1	3	3	43	50	30	0	0	0	30
6	D9	Student J	30	0	0	10	40	0	8	0	32	40	20	0	5	15	40
6	D10	Student K	17	8	10	5	40	0	14	5	21	40	14	7	10	9	40
6	D11	Student L	16	11	6	7	40	9	8	9	14	40	16	12	8	14	50
6	D12	Student M	16	16	2	6	40	3	8	7	22	40	22	8	6	14	50
		Total	192	71	35	132	430	52	73	67	248	440	202	60	68	80	410
		Odds (to 1)	2.2	6.1	12.3	3.3		8.5	6.0	6.6	1.8		2.0	6.8	6.0	5.1	

Only five rounds of betting were possible with this cohort. The last bets were made before the final year of trading (Year 4) was enacted on the Monopoly© board. The table shows the total amount invested by each student in the 12 businesses operating in Games 4 to 6.

For example, Student C has clearly changed his/her policy in Game 4 and has backed business D4 heavily (£30 out of £50 total). In Game 5 practically all of his/her money was placed on D8 whilst D9 and D10 were favoured in Game 6.

For the record, the three most successful businesses at the end of Year 4 were actually D4, D5 and D12. None of these businesses was the 'market favourite' (ie the one with the lowest odds) before the last trading year.

Appendix 7.2 BABA 1 student comments 1998–2001 from the questionnaire

Positive comments

'It's more effective when linking learning and practice.'
'Easier than learning from lectures.'
'More interesting than lectures.'
'Nice change from just sitting in lecture halls.'
'Easier to understand than just juggling numbers on a balance sheet.'
'You could see where the money was moving.'
'Fun way of learning. I felt I learnt a lot as we were taking an active part.'
'During lectures you can lose concentration, whereas using this exercise you are always focused.'
'Lectures not so involving. Rely on the lecturer too much.'
'Helped by using real data.'
'We had to do it and work for ourselves.'
'It involved a lot of interaction. It created a relaxed atmosphere.'
'Fun – it made people want to turn up.'
'I was very worried about accounts, but now I'm more comfortable.'
'Excellent idea, well executed over the weeks.'
'I met new people from the course.'
'Allowed us to mix fun with work.'

Negative comments

'The module leader should check balance sheets and profit and loss accounts each week.'
'It could be slower.'
'I found the betting confusing.'
'Four years [of trading] is too long.'
'I am still unable to fully understand this area [profit and loss account] as well as I can the balance sheet.'
'Would have liked a cash flow statement as well.'
'The Monopoly© profit and loss account was very basic compared to that in the text.'
'The exercise spent too much time on the basics and not enough on the more difficult aspects.'

Appendix 7.3 CMS 2000 student comments from the questionnaire

Positive comments

'A good "fun" way into a subject that may initially be intimidating for individuals with a non-finance background.'

'I enjoyed this and thought it as worth while.'

'Good example of the first principles of accounting – long may it continue.'

'[The exercise] could be developed further. This could be done if extra time was allowed.'

'Very good early in the syllabus.'

'A basic introduction was needed and this provided it.'

'Much better than expected. Facilitated good exchange with colleagues.'

'I have undertaken various accounting courses in the past, yet found this a valuable tool in aiding teaching – well done! It's the clearest method. I've even understood it! The fun element only enhanced understanding.'

'Monopoly© was a very useful exercise – enjoyable, fun whilst giving the opportunity to learn the foundation of this subject.'

Negative comments

'[Would prefer] not quite so much time devoted to it.'

'Perhaps too early in the programme.'

'Some groundwork is required prior to the exercise, ie how to lay out the balance sheet.'

Chapter 8

Peer assessment and enhancing students' learning

Anne Gregory, Liz Yeomans and Joanne Powell

We describe in this chapter how we use peer assessment in a pivotal module in our BA in Public Relations and we show how it relates directly to our learning, teaching and assessment philosophy for the course.

Our story begins in 1992 when Anne Gregory, then the leader of the Public Relations Planning and Management module, decided that a group assignment, addressing a typical public relations scenario, was the most appropriate form of assessment, because it could simulate types of campaigns and working practices in the public relations industry.

We introduced peer assessment of individual students' contributions to encourage cooperative working and to ensure fairness in marking. We knew there were numerous objections to peer assessment. We knew too that the principles and processes required to make it acceptable to and successful with students required careful introduction, transparency and constant reinforcement. Used properly, it has proved a valuable tool in rewarding appropriately individual students' and groups' contributions. Furthermore, it facilitates students' ownership of the assessment process and encourages them to take responsibility for their own learning.

Our informal and formal evaluations of the module show that students give it the highest rating of any core module in the degree. Although peer assessment does not remove all student objections to group work, it has proved effective in reducing what they perceive as unfairness in group marks, and in encouraging careful reflection on individual and group contributions and performance.

Objectives

Our objectives in setting up peer assessment for our students were to:

- use a form of assessment appropriate to the work being assessed;
- encourage cooperative group working among the students;
- facilitate student ownership of the process;
- reward students for taking responsibility for their own learning;
- ensure fairness in marking.

Rationale

Peer assessment is assessment by students of other students. It is generally used where students are working on a group project or oral presentation. The assessment is usually criterion-based, in that students assess each other on a range of criteria applied to the students' contributions to the project. It is common practice, according to Lejk and Wyvill (2001), to weight each criterion: then the weighted scores add up to give an overall score for each member of the group. Peer assessment thus provides a means of differentiating between individual students' contributions.

When setting up the project, we became aware of several reasons for trying non-traditional assessment (including peer assessment) in business education. Business schools teach skills such as communication, problem solving and team building, all to increase students' employability. They do so through small group work and active learning. Brown and Knight (1994) and Boud (1995) argue that students are more motivated when they are directly involved in the whole learning process. Indeed, the code of practice on assessment of students, recently issued by the Quality Assurance Agency (QAA), welcomes non-traditional methods of assessment (http://www.qaa.ac.uk/public).

Although peer assessment has been tried in different academic locations, it is still regarded by some as being 'risky' and open to serious challenges by students, with the spectre looming of academic appeals. A law lecturer told one of us during a peer assessment workshop that her students would simply refuse to assess each other!

Educationalists say that peer assessment is open to abuse, and warn tutors against the temptation, where there are large numbers, to 'dump the work onto the students' (Brown and Knight, 1994: 58). A single group mark that is awarded to all students is regarded as unfair when some have worked harder than others. Hard-working students feel that lazy students are holding them back, yet being rewarded for work they have not done. Peer assessment does have its own dangers. Students can use the system to settle old scores, reward friends or collude in awarding high marks to each other. Students who do badly, for whatever reason, may be 'carried' by the group, because its members do not want to confront difficult issues or because they sympathize with their colleagues' situation. From our own experience, we know that peer assessment is not an easy option. Conducted properly, however, it has considerable benefits for the tutor and the learners.

Context

A University of Applied Learning

Our university, Leeds Metropolitan, bills itself as a University of Applied Learning. The sentiment behind this billing is that many of its courses are vocational and that its learning, teaching and assessment philosophy encourages students to learn through application. 'Learning by doing' encapsulates its approach. This philosophy has been articulated by Leeds Business School (LBS), one of the four faculties of the university, through the concept of 'progressive problem solving', first adopted in 1989. It helps to characterize the educational nature of the school's provision, facilitates coherence in the curriculum and enables the university's mission to be served through the aims and objectives of the school's courses and modules.

With progressive problem solving, LBS seeks to provide a learning environment in which attention is given to personal as well as intellectual development. Staff emphasize the acquisition and effective use of business-related knowledge and skills, as well as greater independence in learning.

The implications of progressive problem solving for course curriculum design and learning strategies are that students should be given opportunities to:

- acquire and develop a range of intellectual and personal skills, as they advance in their studies;
- develop their skills through practice in problem solving, their advance being reflected as they move from simple closed problems to more complex open-ended ones all requiring mastery of increasingly complex concepts and techniques;
- take more responsibility for their learning, shifting from dependence to inter-dependence and independence.

To help embed progressive problem solving in its courses, the school and the university funded several initiatives. In the early 1990s staff devoted considerable time and effort to a review of teaching, learning and assessment. Although this review was partly stimulated by increases in student numbers, with the objective of maintaining the quality of students' learning in the face of the challenges of mass higher education, it was also regarded as the correct pedagogical approach for this particular module.

LBS supported the production of learning materials such as student workbooks, and fostered staff development in how to teach and manage large student groups or teams. There was also some development of group work and assessment, as these became features of the assessment strategy. A model for peer assessment was produced by an LBS member, Tom Burden, who published a guide for colleagues with support from the Enterprise in Higher Education Initiative (Burden, 1989).

The Public Relations BA (Hons)

The BA (Hons) in Public Relations was launched in 1990. It has been updated and reviewed over the years, but the aims of the course have always been to provide: 1) an intellectually and academically challenging study of the concepts, methods, environment and social and ethical constraints of effective public relations practice and theory; and 2) graduates of the level of competent junior executive with an academic grounding that equips them with the potential for development.

The course, which is modular, encourages students to develop an analytical and progressive problem-solving approach, and the teaching and learning strategy helps them to become independent learners. The course is intended to equip graduates with a general business education as well as a vocational specialism. It is approved by the Institute of Public Relations and has an industry advisory board: both influence curriculum content and delivery, and the assessment strategy, which is designed to assist students directly in their careers. For example, students compile a portfolio of public relations artefacts gained from work experiences during their course. The portfolio is assessed and students use it to demonstrate competence to potential employers. Employment of graduates is high (averaging more than 80 per cent) and evidence from employers is that graduates are well prepared for their jobs.

An explicit learning objective for several modules of the course is to develop team skills, which are regarded as particularly important, indeed essential, in the public relations (PR) industry. The backbone of PR consultancy is the 'account team', and in-house departments are usually small, interdisciplinary and highly interdependent. The nature of PR work is that it is public: individuals work in exposed situations, often under pressure, for example with the media, managing crises and events, and practitioners must be capable of working reliably in groups.

The Public Relations Planning and Management module

Public Relations Planning and Management (PRPM) is a second-level module regarded by the BA Public Relations course team as the pivotal one. It has a sound theoretical framework drawn from both management and communication disciplines, but the central aim is that students should be able to plan a well-founded PR campaign and understand the management process involved in making it successful. They are not expected to implement the programme, but the module does provide a simulated precursor to the Level 3 module in which they undertake a communication audit for an actual client.

We wanted to devise an assessment for this module that would: 1) be academically rigorous and require students to demonstrate and apply their theoretical and practical knowledge; and 2) simulate as realistically as possible how the planning and management process is actually undertaken. We thought that a PR campaign proposal, for a realistic scenario, was an obvious vehicle for assessment, lending itself to group work because such proposals are usually prepared by account teams or in-house teams rather than by individuals.

Description

Early considerations

From the start, we had to bear in mind our students' limited knowledge and experience. From the student perspective, the assessment was potentially quite daunting, particularly as it was the only one for the module and the largest and most sophisticated that our students had met on the course to date.

Success in this assignment would depend on group members pooling knowledge and experience (from their studies and work experience), dividing up sensibly the tasks and working cooperatively to present a single proposal. We therefore chose peer assessment because only the students themselves would know the proportion and quality of contribution made by each group member. We were also keen to provide an incentive for group members to work together, though we knew of students' concerns about fairness in the allocation of marks.

Peer assessment did fit with the assessment regime being developed in LBS and students were prepared for it. At Level 1 students had a modest peer review exercise: they were invited to provide feedback to their peers on a presentation (see Box 8.1). This exercise encouraged critical reflection on their own and their peers' work. They did not award scores. Tutors did that, taking the students' comments into account.

Box 8.1

BA (Hons) Public Relation Year 1

Introduction to public relations theory and practice

Group presentations: peer assessment

Please take into account the following when assessing the presentation. You can indicate with a tick what you think is a satisfactory performance in a category. If you have any constructive advice to give the presenters, there is space to do that also:

- preparation
- content

- structure
- delivery
- timing
- visual aids
- summary
- responding to questions
- personal qualities
- confidence
- impact
- manner
- non-verbal communication

We felt that peer assessment would also be appropriate in terms of progressive problem solving: at Level 2 students were progressing from a simple, closed business problem to a more open-ended one in which several solutions were available for each scenario. However, the scenarios were not too complex. Relatively straightforward PR problems were posed and students worked on scenarios, not live projects.

To help students move towards independence and interdependence, our Level 2 peer assessment would require full participation in group working, with each student taking some responsibility for his or her own learning – within clearly defined parameters. At Level 1 students reflected on their own and their group's contributions, but at Level 2, for their module, they would allocate a score against set criteria. At Level 3 students would also be encouraged to examine the assessment criteria, negotiate changes to these with their peers and then agree them with their tutor. We ought to emphasize that the criteria against which scores would be awarded by students were *not* for content, but for contribution. Furthermore, we decided that students would not allocate marks as such, but would decide on the proportion of marks that should be awarded for the contribution made.

How the peer assessment is implemented

As we said, PRPM has a single, group assessment. Each group is given a different scenario, but we check very carefully to make sure the scenarios are equally demanding. The PR campaign proposal is marked out of 100, with up to 50 marks awarded by the tutor on content, and up to 50 based on the tutor's mark weighted according to scores awarded by peers for individuals' contributions. For an example of a scenario, with marking criteria, see Box 8.2.

Box 8.2

Name of module: Public Relations Planning and Management

Level: Year 2, Semester 1

Scenario 19

You are a 'Friend' of the 400-bed Bradley General Hospital charged with fund-raising and welfare activities. Your committee has decided to begin a hospital radio service, staffed by volunteer broadcasters. However, many people, internal and external, think the money would be better spent on more baby incubators.

Submit a written, costed public relations proposal giving a detailed plan to cover the launch and continued support of the station, which is to be funded entirely by voluntary contributions.

Your plan should include:

- evidence of the research undertaken;
- issues identification;
- target publics;
- objectives;
- messages;
- strategy;
- tactics;
- timetable;
- resources;
- project management;
- evaluation.

Theoretical models and concepts should be used where appropriate.

This project accounts for 100% of the assessment in Public Relations Planning and Management.

Marks will be awarded for:

- initial assignment proposal (to be presented in class) (10%);
- evidence and use of research (20%);
- breadth and depth (25%);
- linking of theory to practice (15%);
- evidence and use of analysis (15%);
- presentation and clarity (10%);
- post-submission group meeting (5%).

If a tutor gives 60/100 to the group's campaign proposal, then the tutor allocates 30 as a base mark to each student. If the group decides to allocate the same score (30/100) to each member for his/her contribution, peer assessment results in the tutor giving another 30/100 to each member of the group, all getting 60/100 in the end.

Box 8.3 shows the score sheet, though not a facsimile. The tutor has entered the scores awarded by the students to their peers A–E, who were in Groups 1–5: in this example, peer scoring yielded different scores for individual students' contributions. The tutor gave a mark of 50/100 for the proposal; therefore each student received 25 marks as a base. In the eyes of their peers, students A and B contributed more than other members of the group, with a final mark of 56 per cent. Student E contributed much less and actually failed the assignment (and the module), with a final mark of 37.5 per cent. The formula for calculating the marks is as follows:

$$\frac{i \times \text{assignment mark}}{2 \times m} + \frac{\text{assignment mark}}{2}$$

where

i = individual student's score from the group
n = number in group
m = sum of all student scores

In the example in Box 8.3, Student A and B each get:

$$\frac{20 \times 5 \times 50}{2 \times 80} + \frac{50}{2} = 56\%$$

Student E gets:

$$\frac{8 \times 5 \times 50}{2 \times 80} + \frac{50}{2} = 37.5\%$$

Box 8.3

Leeds Metropolitan University, Faculty of Business

BA (Hons) Public Relations

Public Relations Planning and Management

Student contribution assessment form

After your group has completed your project, *each of you* should complete this assessment form. Then the group should collate the marks on a single *summary sheet* (giving the average mark for each individual to one decimal point).

Assess under the headings given. The assessment should reflect the level of contribution *each of your colleagues and yourself* have made while undertaking the project.

Score using 1 to 6:

1 means little contribution
6 means an outstanding contribution
0 should be given only in exceptional circumstances for no contribution

Names of students	A	B	C	D	E
Was he/she regularly at group meetings and available for discussions, planning and action?	5	6	5	5	2
Did he/she contribute to the needs of the group, eg produce ideas, listen to others, provide leadership/direction, help the group function well as a team?	5	4	4	4	2
Did he/she do what was agreed to be done at meetings?	5	5	3	4	2
Did he/she take a fair share of the work?	5	5	3	4	2
Total from peers	20	20	15	17	8
Tutor's mark	50	50	50	50	50
Overall mark	56	56	48.4	51.6	37.5

Once again it is important to note that students do not allocate marks. Their scores determine the proportion of the remaining marks allocated to each group member. This is a vital distinction: if they were awarding marks, students might agree to award each other maximum marks, especially since this module contributes to the final degree classification.

How students are introduced to the peer assessment

We are well aware that peer assessment must be introduced carefully and clearly to students. The process also needs reinforcement and opportunities for discussion during the module. We therefore break it up into four clear stages: the formal introduction; preparation, presentation and feedback of an outline proposal; the pre-assessment review; and the post-assessment meeting.

The formal introduction

The whole module, including the assessment, is introduced during the first tutorial. Students receive a module handbook, which tells them:

- the role of the module within the Public Relations degree;
- links back and forward to other modules on the course;
- its importance as a topic;
- expected learning outcomes;
- our teaching and learning approach;
- the assessment;
- the marking scheme;
- how marks and peer scores are allocated.

During the introduction we allocate students randomly to groups of four or less. For example, if there are 20 in the tutorial, the tutor counts from one to five along the rows and all those allocated 'one' form Group 1 and so on. We know that other methods have been used to select the groups, such as self-selection by students, or a predetermined mix ensuring a balance of gender, ethnicity, ERASMUS students and so on. However, the randomness, transparency and apparent fairness of the current system have proved most acceptable and rational to students and have led to least objection.

Students can negotiate with the tutor, outside the tutorial, a move to another group for genuine reasons. Reasons accepted have been a mature student with childcare responsibility living remote from the campus moving to a group whose other timetable and personal commitments meant she could do group tasks with them during the day when she was on campus.

Students then move around to sit in these groups for the rest of the tutorial. The assignments are numbered. The tutor asks which group would like first choice and the groups in turn choose an assignment number. Immediately after they have chosen a number the tutor reads out that assignment to the whole tutorial class. Each group receives its assessment scenario (one copy for each student plus one extra).

This method of allocation has again proved acceptable. Although students may feel they would have preferred to work on another scenario, they appreciate that they have been given a choice and that the distribution has been random and transparent. We have had no requests from students wanting a move to another group because of the scenario allocated. There is a 'spare' scenario so that the last group has a genuine choice too.

The reading of the scenarios is important. Students can compare the parity of the tasks and they also begin to appreciate the range of public relations activities in which a practitioner may be involved.

Students and tutors then discuss information sources and approaches to the task. Examples of past assignments are made available. They discuss the assessment, starting with the marking criteria, based on the handout (see Box 8.2). We explain peer assessment in detail with worked examples of how marks are eventually allocated. At this stage students are apprehensive; therefore we stress that:

- peer assessment is designed to ensure group marks are allocated fairly;
- we want the group to work effectively and there is an incentive: they will get equal marks if they make equal inputs;
- tutors can intervene in the process to ensure that the peer marking system is not being abused through favouritism or bullying;
- students do not mark content, which is the tutor's job, but they give scores for the quality of each other's contribution to the task;
- students don't deal with mitigation: if a student's score is reduced because of limited contribution due to mitigating circumstances, tutors deal with that.

We tell the students that the key to fair peer assessment is accurate and quantified record keeping, after which allocating scores becomes almost a mechanical process. We advise the group to set up early a timetable for meetings and milestones and to agree the allocation of tasks. The sort of records they should keep are attendance of members at meetings (for criterion 1); minutes of meetings with action points against named individuals help for criterion 3, and for making informed judgements for criterion 4.

We provide our students with support material on how to run and contribute to meetings (reinforcing learning already undertaken). We encourage them to analyse the effectiveness of each meeting so that they can learn as they progress and monitor their own and other group members' performance against criterion 2. They also receive practical guidance notes on task allocation.

We do not explain to students beforehand our policy on what happens if a student drops out. If it happens before the outline proposal is presented (see below), the group size is reduced by deleting the dropout. If a student drops out after the proposal is written, his/her contribution is scored by the other students in the group and the dropout's score divided equally between the group members to recognize that they will have had to make an extra contribution with little notice.

Apart from the assignment and the peer assessment sheet, we expect students to submit a group self-assessment sheet, which is designed to encourage serious reflection on the work they have submitted and a judgement of its worth, ie a suggested mark, with notes of areas on which specific feedback is requested.

We show students the very detailed feedback sheet that they will receive, with feedback on the marking criteria and on the elements of the PR campaign proposal, plus overall comments.

Preparation, presentation and feedback of a proposal outline

Because of the size and complexity of the assessment, we require students to present in Week 5 an outline of their approach and their initial thoughts on their scenario. Groups have to make a formal presentation to their peers supported by a written proposal outline, which is assessed by tutors.

The purposes of the exercise are to:

- identify any early problems with the task and/or the group;
- ensure that students begin work on the assessment early;
- provide formative feedback so that they can complete the assessment with a level of knowledge and confidence.

We give students written feedback within a week and explore general issues with them in the Week 6 tutorial. Each tutor again discusses peer assessment and encourages students to use this milestone to reflect on the group's performance, seizing the opportunity to practise peer assessment if they wish. They do not attempt formal peer assessment of the outline proposal and a group mark is allocated.

The pre-assessment review

During the module, each group can negotiate one meeting with the tutor to review progress. This usually takes place shortly after the initial proposal outline has been assessed and when students are beginning to encounter the real issues arising from their scenario. The tutor discusses content and process with them. The group is encouraged to share any issues arising from group working. The tutor checks that there is clear understanding of the peer assessment process and asks questions about record keeping, but, in keeping with the philosophy of increasing independence, allows the group to establish their own procedures. The tutor's main concern is that the process is being applied fairly.

The post-assessment meeting

After the assessment has been submitted and following initial marking but before a mark is finally allocated, each group has to attend a meeting with the tutor. At least 24 hours before the meeting, the group receives a short list of questions from the tutor so that further information/clarification can be obtained. At the meeting these issues are discussed. However, a key objective for the tutor is to obtain confirmation from the group that the peer assessment scores allocated are agreed and fair.

The tutor uses the rest of the meeting to comment to students on their work, especially regarding those areas where comments were specifically requested. The student group self-assessment sheet is used as a guide for this. This includes consideration of the suggested mark and the tutor indicates at this stage whether it is broadly in range. Given the discussion, this is not usually contested, as students appreciate the strengths and flaws in their work.

After the meeting the tutor allocates a final mark to the assessment, taking into account the additional information provided and makes the peer assessment calculation. Students receive their mark and the detailed feedback sheet within four weeks.

Evaluation

We evaluated PRPM in December 1999 by asking students to complete a brief questionnaire about module objectives and learning outcomes, lectures and tutorials, and assessment. We wanted to know whether our students thought peer assessment was a useful way to assess individual contributions. We obtained responses from 26 students, 22 per cent of the cohort by the end of the year, not as many as we wished. Most respondents agreed with the statement 'Peer assessment is a good way of recognizing individual contribution to group work'; only seven disagreed.

The university also carries out a standardized annual module evaluation where less module-specific questions are asked of every student via questionnaire. Table 8.1 shows evaluation scores for the last three years, comparing the module evaluation score for PRPM with the average score for all modules on the course, for the four questions shown, all of them important. The higher the score, the more positive the responses. The highest score possible is 10.

Besides their responses to the four questions shown in Table 8.1, the students' responses to the other questions were in similar vein and the comparative scores show similar superiority of PRPM over the average for all modules. We recognize that there are no specific questions on peer assessment, but on the basis of Table 8.1 we think students are on the whole happy with this module.

Student comments on the PRPM module are usually very positive with emphasis being placed on its usefulness and relevance. They state that it is 'hard work' and 'challenging', but 'worthwhile'. Although they have no specific comments on peer assessment, there are some negative comments about group work. We draw the conclusion that, while students can appreciate the principles of fairness, take responsibility for their assessment and increase their independence

Table 8.1 *Evaluation scores for PRPM and all modules*

Question	1999/2000		2000/01		2001/02	
	PRPM module score	Average for all modules	PRPM module score	Average for all modules	PRPM module score	Average for all modules
Recommend module to others?	7.92	6.86	8.15	6.67	8.63	7.07
Content relevant to module?	8.42	7.34	9.15	7.09	9.11	7.32
Feedback received sufficiently informative?	6.50	6.10	7.45	6.19	7.50	6.51
Final assessment reflected content and skills developed on module?	7.29	6.52	8.25	6.81	8.63	7.47

in the peer assessment process, they still have a fundamental dislike of group work if they find themselves with others who do not make a full contribution. Peer assessment helps to redress the injustice of a group mark that does not recognize the differing amounts of work put in by individual group members.

The module leader carried out a stand-alone evaluation of the module in January 2002, using a brief questionnaire designed to elicit opinions about the most useful and least useful lectures and tutorials, and the quality of teaching. One objective was to investigate students' perceptions of peer assessment.

All respondents commented favourably. When asked 'What is your opinion of peer assessment?' they expressed views such as:

- 'Good as it is fairer.'
- 'People get the fairest mark; if you don't work you don't get a good mark.'
- '[I] think it is good – makes you want to do your best so you don't get marked down.'
- 'Good idea.'
- 'Think it's a good idea if everyone is honest.'
- 'Not too sure if a true reflection of final result, but at least there is the chance for individual input to be assessed.'
- 'Good idea – you can mark down people who do not get involved.'

Apart from these evaluations, we elicit feedback via other routes. Students' presentations of their outline proposals enable tutors to ask about group working and to reinforce peer assessment. The meetings between tutors and groups part-way through and at the end of the module also provide opportunities to explore the effectiveness of the process.

Student meetings confirm that several students have found peer assessment to be a positive reinforcement to group working. Knowing that they will judge each other has engendered determination to play a full part in the group and a sense of responsibility towards each other. Where the group has not worked very effectively, the peer scoring has at least rewarded those making a greater input. On occasion, the tutor has required reassurance that victimization or favouritism has not been a factor in the scoring and has demanded that students show evidence to back up their scoring allocations. Students confirm that good record keeping has aided their objectivity.

Tutors also meet immediately after the final marks have been agreed and moderated to review the progress of the module and to feed back their own and students' suggestions for improvements. Out of these meetings we have made adjustments to the types of scenarios used. At one, we agreed to assess the proposal outline; previously it had not been assessed.

With regard to peer review, we have tried to improve processes. For example, we tested other ways of allocating groups, but the one we describe here is the most satisfactory. In 1999 we tried to conduct a peer assessment 'rehearsal' during a tutorial midway through the module: when asked about it in the questionnaire, students regarded this as the 'least useful' tutorial.

Finally, under the faculty's module review policy each module leader has to produce a report on its health and an action plan for improvements. At all stages of review, peer assessment has been favourably commented on. Not surprisingly, the model we use in this module is being adopted elsewhere in the faculty, for example in the marketing module on the Master's in Business Studies.

Discussion

While our informal and formal evaluations are generally positive towards the module, with students agreeing with the principle of peer assessment, the literature highlights students' problems in using it in other settings. Greenan, Humphreys and McIlveen (1997) found that postgraduate students were uncomfortable with peer assessment as an objective evaluation of individual contributions. Brindley and Scoffield (1998) found that students had difficulty in assigning marks to each other, particularly where students were in their third year of study together. The difficulties focused on two issues that, while separate, are also linked. First, by Year 3, students know each other reasonably well. They may have worked in groups together before and they will have heard comments, both favourable and unfavourable, from fellow students about the group work contribution that their peers have made. Personal friendships or animosities can be well developed, clouding students' ability to make objective judgements. Second, because Year 3 work is taken into account in the final degree classification, students are understandably nervous about judging their peers, especially their friends.

Objectivity and students' overfamiliarity do not appear to be issues in the PRPM module and do not arise in the module survey responses. This is partly because it is a Year 2, Semester 1 module, with up to 140 students. The chances that individuals will have worked with the same group members in Year 1 are low. ERASMUS exchange students and direct entrants at Level 2 help to create a different cohort in Year 2. Finally, the random selection procedure we use is effective in splitting up friends who usually sit together and reassures the students that groups are not being constructed unfairly or for any 'hidden' reasons. Friends may end up working together, but they may not.

We do think that students are less uncomfortable if the peer scoring is based on quantifiable data such as attendance records and meeting notes. As well as enabling the process of peer assessment to be carried out more objectively, such record keeping is transferable to the business environment, especially in PR consultancy, so students can see the wider benefits.

Although this model of peer assessment is now well established and an integral part of the PRPM module, we know the process does require careful preparation and continuous reinforcement by the teaching team. As Brown and Knight (1994) point out, the energy and effort involved in peer and self-assessment tend to be 'front-loaded'. Students who feel least committed to working groups pick up quickly any inconsistencies in approach or doubt in the minds of tutors about their confidence in the assessment. We conclude, therefore, that, while the benefits of peer assessment to both tutors and students outweigh the drawbacks, peer assessment should ideally form part of the assessment strategy for all modules (certainly at Levels 2 and 3) where group work is undertaken. We know that such a 'whole course' approach has implications for staff development and course design, but we envisage that such a 'peer assessment culture' could in the long term help to spread the set-up costs (such as briefing and ongoing support for both tutors and students), and ensure that by Level 3 students feel confident enough to negotiate assessment criteria, thus achieving greater independence as learners. Our model of peer assessment has changed, but the changes have been organizational rather than fundamental.

References

Boud, D (1995) *Enhancing Learning through Self Assessment*, Kogan Page, London

Brindley, C and Scoffield, S (1998) Peer assessment in undergraduate programmes, *Teaching in Higher Education*, **3** (1), pp 79–90

Brown, S and Knight, P (1994) *Assessing Learners in Higher Education*, Kogan Page, London

Burden, T (1989) *Developing Independent Learning*, Leeds Polytechnic, Leeds

Greenan, K, Humphreys, P and McIlveen, H (1997) Developing transferable personal skills: part of the graduate toolkit, *Education and Training*, **39** (2), pp 71–78

Lejk, M and Wyvill, M (2001) Peer assessment of contributions to a group project: a comparison of holistic and category-based approaches, *Assessment and Evaluation in Higher Education*, **26** (1), pp 61–73

Useful URL

Quality Assurance Agency: http://www.qaa.ac.uk/public/COP/COPaosfinal/intro.htm

Contacts

Anne Gregory and Liz Yeomans
Leeds Business School
Leeds Metropolitan University
Beckett Park
Leeds LS6 3QS
e-mail: a.gregory@lmu.ac.uk and l.yeomans@lmu.ac.uk

Chapter 9

Group work and the Web: FINESSE and TAGS

Rosa Michaelson, Christine Helliar, David Power, Donald Sinclair and Colin Allison

FINESSE (Finance Education in a Scalable Software Environment) and TAGS (Tutor and Group Support) are examples of Web-based learning environments. However, they provide a different kind of Web interface for group-based work from those virtual learning environments (VLEs) currently used in higher and further education.

FINESSE is a Web-based portfolio management game for student groups, used in a final year honours course in an accountancy and business finance department. The game sits within the TAGS system. The software for TAGS provides easy-to-use administrative tools for lecturers administering group work: it allows for real-time data to be integrated with the totality of the Web interface and goes beyond the typical multiple choice assessments currently available on the standard VLE. TAGS was originally developed as the system framework for the FINESSE portfolio management facility, but now provides resources for a range of subjects and administrative tasks. Currently part of a JISC-funded project, the TAGS group is exploring managed learning environment requirements from a student-centred viewpoint (INSIDE, 2001). The project consortium for FINESSE consisted of finance lecturers and computing specialists, who worked together during 1996–98. TAGS (1999–2001) has expanded the subject base and extended the consortium to include academics from, among others, physics, language, education and medicine.

This chapter focuses on the story of FINESSE. It outlines how we developed the software and describes how it is used. First, we highlight the rationale for and the objectives of the FINESSE project; then we describe the educational context and how the students use the software. Next we give a history of the development of the software, and then we discuss the resources that constitute the portfolio management game. We summarize the evaluation methods used for the FINESSE project and offer an overview of TAGS. Our final section explores some lessons learnt by the team and implications for collaborative software development in business education.

Rationale

Why did we start on these projects? The simple answer is that there was funding available from the Scottish Funding Council's investment in wide-area networks (UMI, 2001). FINESSE was funded under the SHEFC Use-of-the-MAN Initiative II; TAGS is funded by SHEFC SCOTCIT. We already had experience of a joint project between the educational experts at Dundee and the software team at St Andrews, which explored a business game on a multi-user spreadsheet. It was easy to identify a specific educational need (that of improving the group game already in use in a different subject area) that could be transferred to newer technologies. In addition, we understood the technological requirements of the proposed task, and we knew that we could work effectively as a group despite the different subject areas and institutional settings involved.

We continued with the project because FINESSE was very successful in meeting our educational objectives. Working on FINESSE also matched the different academic interests of the various group members. Some wanted to explore system administration issues for computer-assisted learning (CAL). Others were interested in group work and group assessment issues, and others in the practical need for integration of real-world data in learning environments – a topic not addressed by software such as WebCT. Some wanted to show that it was possible to go beyond using the chat room as a group communication method (which is the main group support resource offered by most VLEs). FINESSE and TAGS minimize administration of student groups and avoid the overheads that are often incurred in managing the educational process when using chat rooms for group work. We shall describe both learning environments, but first FINESSE.

Objectives

FINESSE's specific objectives were to:

- provide a realistic setting where students could manage a portfolio of investments;

- let students explore theoretical issues associated with portfolio management;
- allow flexible access – enabling self-study;
- help students develop group skills;
- allow lecturers to assess this group activity in a meaningful way;
- minimize staff time in administering the facility;
- support the needs of group work;
- support the project consortium.

These objectives were identified at the start of the process and used as benchmarks for project management.

Context

Accountancy staff at the University of Dundee offer a final year honours module called Security Analysis and Portfolio Management (4PM) for which we developed FINESSE as a Web-based game that requires groups of students to manage a portfolio of equities with a notional value of £100 million. This computerized portfolio management system is based on an earlier manual game that used Lotus spreadsheets. The manual version had serious problems: the portfolio could only change once a month, no dividend income was recognized and securities could only be selected from a small range of stocks. It did not appear to promote group work since one individual usually took all portfolio investment decisions. Also, because share prices had to be manually updated each month there was a high cost in staff time.

With FINESSE, each student group can spend the £100 million on a wide range of equities traded on the London stock market and the Alternative Investment Market (AIM). In addition, shares of other investment securities, such as trusts that can hold foreign equities, can be bought and sold, thereby facilitating a portfolio strategy that can incorporate non-UK securities. The game introduces a level of realism into the analysis by incorporating dividend income and capital gains, by including transaction costs and by using real-time share price data updated on a continuous basis, although subject to a 20-minute time lag. The real-time financial data are provided by two sources: Datastream and UpData. Datastream supplies daily batched data whereas UpData provides 20-minute price changes (and can also offer five-minute changes if required). The game is an integral part of the course – the students' assessment is based on their group use of FINESSE, the portfolio strategies adopted, an individual report about the project, and a joint presentation of the investment strategies that each group has employed during the academic year. The FINESSE component contributed 10 per cent of the final mark for the course for each student in 1999/2000 and 15 per cent in 2000/01.

How students use FINESSE

An initial lecture explains the game, assigns the students to the appropriate groups and briefly covers FINESSE facilities. The method of assessment of the group work is also discussed at this initial lecture. Students are told that their group Notebook resource (described below) will act as a logbook of their strategies and choices; as such it is used as qualitative evidence for the group task. The students are also given an introductory lab session in using FINESSE at which each student is given a user ID and password. After students log in to FINESSE, they can access their group portfolio – each student can buy or sell shares for that group portfolio – and their group Notebook. The students are then free to explore FINESSE individually, or as a group, in order to develop their group portfolio, and to organize their style of working together over the next six months. As the lecturer is also a member of each group we can observe portfolios and Notebooks for evidence of the internal group processes. We know that many groups choose regular times for face-to-face meetings as well as using their Notebook and e-mail for communication (this issue was explored in the post-questionnaire described in 'Evaluating FINESSE' below). We have also established that there is much more group activity amongst the students than before the introduction of FINESSE. We noted the increased level of student use of the computing labs, where the groups often met. We also observed the number of transactions for each portfolio, and the messages concerning those transactions sent via the Notebooks.

Development

The FINESSE software was originally developed collaboratively by computing staff at the University of St Andrews and finance staff at the University of Dundee; afterwards there was further development in conjunction with finance academics in two other universities. Development called for a variety of management methods since the staff members were drawn from several disciplines and four different sites. The team used videoconferencing for regular meetings, while agendas and minutes of the meetings were posted to a developers' Web site. A useful resource called a Notebook was produced for the team in which all members could write messages as they used the Web site. Messages placed on the Notebook could be e-mailed to the group. These messages gave a historical record of questions and answers, accessible by all team members, of the development process. The Notebook was linked to each page of the Web site. It allowed for informal project control by all participants, and for direct responses to problems encountered by the finance lecturers as the prototype evolved. E-mails and phone calls between the finance lecturers and the programming team helped too. Desktop video communications between the two main sites enabled developers to see the same Web pages, with error messages in one window. They could talk to and see each other on video, thereby debugging the underlying code in an efficient and effective way.

Another factor in the development of FINESSE was our interest in group-based learning. The department had identified a need for students to experience working in groups within the degree. As a result we investigated the educational basis for group work. Group learning has been promoted in higher education for a variety of reasons over many years (see, for example, Tribe, 1994; Thorley and Gregory, 1994). In particular, group learning is regarded as important when preparing students for the world of work by introducing teamwork skills (Johnson and Johnson, 1996; Jaques, 1985). The skills fostered by teamwork are often ignored in higher education; subsequently employers complain of the lack of critical thinking or negotiating skills evident in recent graduates. Further, there is the hope that group learning will foster 'deep' learning strategies as opposed to 'shallow' ones and 'active' versus 'passive' learning (Gibbs, 1992; Tribe, 1994). Research in accounting education, however, contains few examples of group learning (Rebele, 1998). Two contrasting examples (Lane and Gibbs, 1992; Hassall and Lewis, 1994) give an idea of the work involved in constructing a course around group-based learning. The problems encountered included resistance from staff and students; increased staff input in supporting group work; and difficulties in assessment and motivation. Practitioners often emphasize the need for an appropriate educational culture to support the introduction of group-based learning. Many discuss the change in the lecturer–student relationship that occurs as a result.

Successful group learning seems to be an *active* process in which the group tackle a realistic problem. It is: a process in which the learners construct meaning and systems of meaning; a reflective activity in which 'hands-on' processes inform 'mental' ones; a social activity during which learning happens through discussion and interaction with others. Group learning is context-dependent, requires a long period for assimilation and is heavily dependent on motivation (Michaelson, 1999). It is possible to evaluate the educational context of FINESSE with reference to these group-based learning criteria (see Appendix 9.1).

In FINESSE, to help members of each group to reflect on the work process and to provide evidence of strategic choices, they keep a diary or logbook throughout the period of the task, using the Notebook resource (see below). A difficulty with group learning in higher education is that motivation is closely linked to assessment, and particularly in a degree programme students need to be reassured about how individual marks are awarded for group work. Such pedagogic issues informed the design of FINESSE and influenced how it is used within the course.

FINESSE in 2001

Three kinds of people use FINESSE: tutors, students and the system developers. Each has a user ID and password. A tutor can allocate resources such as a Notebook or a portfolio to a user or a group, and can allocate users to groups. The game is accessed through a Web browser and, on submitting a user name and password, the students can choose between communicating with the group or their tutor via the group Notebook or by using the group portfolio.

The Notebook is now an important resource for the game. Although originally an administration tool for the development of FINESSE. It proved so useful that it became a feature of the game as the 'logbook' for group work, and also provides qualitative data for the assessment process. The original Notebook had some similarities to e-mail and other Web-based computer-supported cooperative work tools such as Hypermail and Lotus Notes (Hughes, 1994; Lloyd and Whitehead, 1996), but was designed to be as simple as possible. The underlying application is a common gateway interface program that manages several notebooks. The Notebook was designed so that a user first sees a blank comment window where any new comments can be added; a list of the most recent messages together with the date and author of each comment is also shown. Older messages can be viewed by clicking on a button.

During the development phase there were requests for added features, such as the option to e-mail a comment to the members of the group when adding it to the Notebook, and the ability to send messages to the Notebook from a user's e-mail application. Thus, a group Notebook provides a written history of past discussions, with a 'push and pull' e-mail facility whereby each message posted to the Notebook can be sent to the group, and any member of the group can e-mail a message to the Notebook. Each message has a time stamp and the name of the person who added the message. A message can be deleted by its writer or a systems user. In FINESSE, every page in the site has a link to the Notebook, so that a group member can make a comment to the rest of the group about the portfolio's performance or market anomalies as they are spotted. The Notebook is designed to make communication easy and intuitive. The portfolio resource offers the options shown in Figure 9.1.

By choosing 'Current share prices', students can view 1) all securities, 2) all the securities within a certain sector or 3) those securities beginning with a particular letter of the alphabet. They can select all stocks, just AIM stocks or just investment trust stocks. If students want to view historic prices they can type in a date from the last 10 years and the closing price for that date will be displayed. This retrospective information is useful when undertaking any fundamental analysis of a particular stock.

By choosing 'Sector History' (Figure 9.2) students can see detailed historic information for an industry, including price data. The price information goes back for five years and the profit earnings per share and price/earning (P/E) ratios are also shown. Graphs are available for each item in every sector. These facilities are provided to help students to determine how a sector has performed in relation to other sectors, and how well a particular stock within a sector has performed relative to the sector average.

On the 'Transaction' screen (Figure 9.3) all the current outstanding positions for the portfolio are shown so that students just need to click on a security if they wish to sell all of their holding or part of a holding, or wish to buy more of that stock. If they wish to buy or sell another security, they can highlight the letter of the alphabet that the security's name begins with. This brings up a list of all

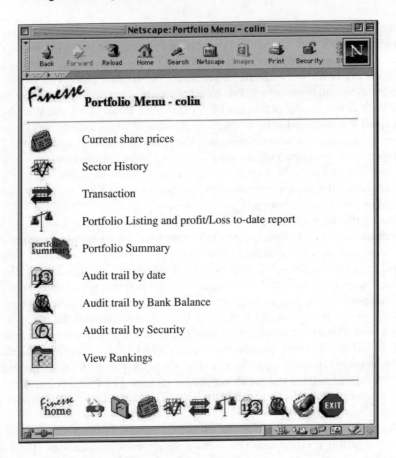

Figure 9.1 *Example of a FINESSE Portfolio Menu*

securities beginning with that letter from which the required security can then be quickly chosen. Students then select the buy or sell option and enter the quantity to be transacted. The system calculates the settlement amount including transaction costs and displays the data on the screen; students then choose whether to accept or cancel the transaction.

The 'Portfolio Listing and Profit/Loss to date report' and 'Portfolio Summary' options (see Figure 9.1 again) supply a calculation of the profit or loss to date and summarize the portfolio's performance. These screens enable students to see how much realized profit or loss has been made on closed positions for each security, and how much unrealized profit or loss exists on each open position by security. A profit or a loss is realized when a security is sold by subtracting the sales price from the purchase cost. A profit or loss is unrealized when the security is not yet sold; therefore the profit is a notional amount calculated by subtracting the share cost from its current price. Students can investigate the average purchase cost and

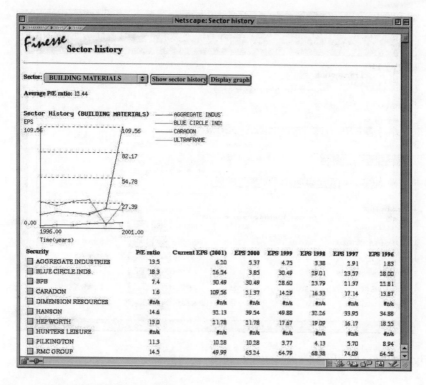

Figure 9.2   *FINESSE's Sector History option*

the current value of each share, the dividend income received and interest income they have earned, as well as the size of transactions costs incurred. All of these features are commonly calculated by practising fund managers.

The 'Audit trail by date' enables students to view audit trails by security and by date, to check their purchases and sales and also to examine which members of the group have conducted each trade. The 'Audit trail by Bank Balance' tells students how much money they have left to invest. These trails provide useful information to students and to staff who supervise the game and monitor student activity.

Finally, 'View Rankings' enables groups to see the performance of other groups in the class. This brings a competitive element into FINESSE and has students pitting their performance against that of other groups.

Evaluating FINESSE

Our evaluations of FINESSE have taken into account:

- the objectives of those who required the evaluation;
- the goals of those who carried out such an evaluation;

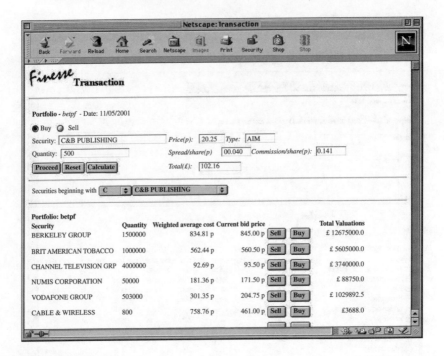

Figure 9.3   *FINESSE's Transaction option*

- the appropriateness of the software design and the success of its implementation;
- how FINESSE met the educational goals of the accountancy and finance lecturers;
- the extent to which the portfolio management game was successfully integrated into the educational process (Helliar *et al*, 2000);
- the extent to which educational outcomes were achieved (Helliar *et al*, 2000).

In FINESSE's second year of operation, we used various types of formative and summative evaluation of student learning (Michaelson *et al*, 2001). Our evaluations covered the software, the educational content and the integration and use of the software into the teaching of the course. We chose these three areas because 1) they were the main focus of interest for those involved in the project including the grant body, the finance lecturers, the software experts and the students; and 2) no one evaluation method would be sufficient for a project with such a mixture of different stakeholder groups. Each of these groups had their own objectives for the project: to evaluate FINESSE against these different objectives using a single approach would have been difficult, if not impossible. We chose both qualitative and quantitative methods (Mulholland, 1998; Jones *et al*, 1996).

The software was evaluated against other existing VLEs. These comparisons showed that at that time no existing software would allow the integration of a Web-based teaching environment with the database of information obtained from a real-life stock market source (Michaelson, 1999). We also needed an assessment mechanism for group work. Existing systems simply could not supply the rich qualitative data that FINESSE provided via the Notebook (as discussed above), or the filters that could be set by the tutor to signal important events in student activity.

The software development for FINESSE was evaluated by the finance staff at the different universities and by two experts engaged for the purpose. Staff involvement began at the start when they outlined the requirements for the system and provided a specification of what was wanted from the game. In addition, development versions of the game were scrutinized by staff and feedback provided to the programmers. This developmental phase was an iterative process that lasted for over a year before students were introduced to FINESSE as part of a course. The experts were invited to examine the game: one had many years of experience in the development of computer-assisted learning while the other had managed portfolios of over £1 billion for nearly two decades in the investment-management industry. Both experts interacted with FINESSE over many months, suggesting improvements and indicating how further realism might be injected into it.

We made presentations of the FINESSE software to an advisory body that had been established by the grant holders and we wrote reports for the grant coordinators. We read papers at conferences, wrote articles for the academic press and demonstrated FINESSE at a number of presentations. We collected feedback from interested experts, discussants and referees, which led to further evaluations and improvements in the game.

We also gained insights from students into how the game could be improved: they completed course evaluation forms and supplied feedback in staff–student committees. The first students to use the manual version of the game were introduced to FINESSE in a one-off lab at the end of the 4PM course. We asked them how the manual version compared with its Web-based counterpart, and their responses were strongly in favour of the new FINESSE (Helliar and Michaelson, 1998). We used pre- and post-questionnaires with two subsequent cohorts of students (Michaelson *et al*, 2001). Informal comments to staff about issues raised in the Notebook also contributed to FINESSE's development.

There has been a noted increase in group activity as a result of using FINESSE. As stated above, the students are observed working together in the computing labs; their use of the Notebook provides evidence of group communication; and they provided details of the frequency of meetings and comments about working together in the post-questionnaire.

Since FINESSE has been used at Dundee for two academic sessions, and is now in use at two other sites, one of the main criteria for success has already been achieved: that of integrating the software with the teaching process. This result is also consistent with Gunn (1996), who discusses evaluation based on 'integration' of CAL when software is designed and written for educators with clear objectives.

TAGS

As we said earlier, FINESSE runs within TAGS, which is a framework for the development, deployment and maintenance of Web-based collaborative learning environments. We believe that from the perspective of good educational practice such an environment should:

- support learners' group work;
- be interactive, engaging and responsive;
- provide for real-world inputs;
- be student-centred;
- be available any time and anywhere.

These pedagogical goals imply certain technical requirements (Allison *et al*, 2001) and, to date, the project has addressed issues of usability, security, responsiveness, concurrency control, availability and infrastructure quality of service that would have been unlikely to arise in a pure research environment.

Much of the utility of TAGS comes from its strong support for group-based learning, which has in turn resulted in the group ethos permeating the system. TAGS can support many functions, such as:

- privileges and access control;
- information dissemination and event awareness;
- group work involving shared, multi-user educational resources;
- the management of online collaborative learning;
- user-centric portal generation;
- collaborative development.

In practical terms, tutors construct a collaborative learning environment by using the Users, Groups and Resources management tool. This tool sets up arbitrary relationships between users and resources, using groups as the basis for the mapping. Users and groups are unique by name; resources are unique by name and type. Access rights can be specified when a resource is allocated to a group. The concept of a learning resource in TAGS is deliberately loose. It can be a simple timetable, an automated assessment exercise or an interactive multi-user simulation. Resources may be broadly classified, however, as generic or subject-specific. For example, a customizable timetable or mark sheet could be termed generic whereas a continuously updated French current affairs digest is subject-specific to language teaching. Instances of resources can be created by tutors and assigned to groups. Some resource types offer the option to 'subscribe' to them.

This means that e-mail messages can be sent to the appropriate user(s) whenever something of interest occurs, such as a new message being added to a shared Notebook or student work missing a deadline (Allison *et al*, 2000, 2001).

Lessons learnt from FINESSE and TAGS

One important lesson we learnt from developing and using FINESSE is that Web-based software that uses real-time data requires software maintenance. We encountered problems with Internet connectivity, such as the use of intranet fire-walls by one IT service, which inhibited student access. There were different computing facilities and levels of IT support across the collaborating institutions, which required both administrative and technological support.

Second, we also learnt that students can find unexpected ways of using such a tool. Some students tried out day-trading strategies, which were countered by the deployment of a five-minute data source. We did not expect that FINESSE would be used in lab-based sessions, as the ethos was one of long-term group work. However, lab-based trials of the software were very useful in the production of a robust system and in understanding the need for responsiveness from Web-based learning environments (Allison *et al*, 1999).

Third, we found that, as the number using TAGS and FINESSE increases, help is needed to update the system to meet a range of educational requirements. For example, lecturers in finance required additional features for FINESSE to improve the realism of the game such as screen-based trading and better research facilities. Staff also sought better feedback from the system to help in their monitoring of student progress and in the assessment of student performance. Details about each individual's contribution to the success of a group's portfolio performance within FINESSE required modification to the system to gather and document this information.

The overall lesson to emerge from the development of FINESSE and TAGS is that the systems are constantly evolving to meet the needs of different user groups. In addition, feedback from our evaluations has added to the requirements for improvement. As teaching is a self-reflective process and since teaching approaches change over time, educational software tools such as FINESSE may need further development as lecturers explore and invent new facilities. Extra work is required to administer and support new cross-institution and cross-department projects. As with earlier computer-based educational initiatives, funding continuation for the above work is difficult to secure once novel products are in place.

The implications of our experiences for software development for business education are that collaborative methods that allow educationalists and software developers to work together are crucial. The 1990s UK Teaching and Learning Technologies Project highlighted the problems associated with assuming that academics will have the required project management skills to produce software

(Michaelson, 2001). It is difficult to be truly interdisciplinary in higher education. There are few individuals who have the depth of experience required to mediate between disciplines for successful computer-based educational projects. Any group embarking on tasks like those discussed here needs to understand the time required for communication and administration of such collaborative work where staff have a wide spread of abilities.

We have evidence that our Web-based learning environment successfully supports and promotes group work in a campus setting. It highlights the difference between simple uses of a generic VLE within existing educational practice and our exploration of computer-based educational support in specific contexts. We do not expect the Web to fulfil all aspects of student learning. However, given real-time data online, an understanding of educational factors associated with group-based learning, and thorough project management, computing technology can provide new and valuable teaching tools like FINESSE and TAGS.

References

Allison, C *et al* (1999) An integrated framework for distributed learning environments, *Advances in Concurrent Engineering: CE99*, ed P Chawdhry, P Ghodous and D Vandorpe, International Society for Productivity Enhancement, London

Allison, C *et al* (2000) Using TAGS for distributed IT project management, *Proceedings of the LTSN-ICS 1st Annual Conference*, August, Heriot-Watt University, Edinburgh

Allison, C *et al* (2001) A group based system for group based learning, in *European Perspectives on Computer-Supported Collaborative Learning: The proceedings of Euro CSCL 2001*, ed P Dillenbourg, A Eurelings and K Hakkarainen, pp 43–50, March, Maastricht McLuhan Institute, Maastricht

Ewing, J M, Dowling, J D and Coutts, N (1998) Learning using the World Wide Web: a collaborative learning event, *Journal of Educational Multimedia and Hypermedia*, **8** (1), pp 3–22

Gibbs, G (1992) Introduction, in *Improving the Quality of Student Learning*, ed G Gibbs, Technical and Educational Services, Oxford

Gunn, C (1996) CAL evaluation: what questions are being answered? A response to the article Integrative Evaluation by Draper *et al*, *Computers and Education*, **27** (3/4), pp 157–60

Hassall, T and Lewis, S (1994) The development and implementation of group-based learning on an accounting degree, in *Using Group-Based Learning in Higher Education*, ed L Thorley and R Gregory, Kogan Page, London

Hein, G E (1992) The significance of constructivism for museum education, in *Museums and the Needs of the People: Proceedings of the 1991 CECA (International Committee of Museum Educators) Conference*, October, Jerusalem, Israel National ICOM Committee, Haifa [Online] http://www.exploratorium.edu/IFI/resources/constructivistlearning.html

Helliar, C V and Michaelson, R (1998) Evaluating FINESSE: experiences from the first year, British Association of Accounting Scottish Conference, September, Stirling University, Stirling

Helliar, C V *et al* (2000) Using a portfolio management game (FINESSE) to teach finance, *Accounting Education*, **9** (1), pp 37–51

Hughes, K (1994) Hypermail software [Online] http://vancouver-webpages.com/vanlug/hypermail.html

INSIDE (2001) Institutionally Secure Integrated Data Environment [Online] http://www.dcs.st-and.ac.uk/inside/

Jaques, D (1985) *Learning in Groups*, Croom Helm, London

Johnson, D W and Johnson, F P (1996) *Joining Together: Group theory and group skills*, 5th edn, Allyn and Bacon, Boston

Jones, A *et al* (1996) Evaluating CAL at the Open University: 15 years on, *Computers and Education*, **26** (1–3), pp 5–15

Lane, D and Gibbs, G (1992) Active and passive learning in management accounting, in *Improving the Quality of Student Learning*, ed G Gibbs, Technical and Educational Services, Oxford

Lloyd, P and Whitehead, R (eds) (1996) *Transforming Organisations through Groupware: Lotus Notes in action (computer supported co-operative work)*, Springer Verlag, Berlin

Michaelson, R (1999) Web-based group work, *Proceedings of the10th Annual CTI-AFM Conference*, pp 58–64, August, CTI-AFM Publications, University of East Anglia, Norwich

Michaelson, R (2001) Learning from our mistakes: 10 years of UK-wide C&IT initiatives, BAA Accounting Education SIG Annual Conference, July, Glamorgan

Michaelson, R *et al* (2001) Evaluating FINESSE: a case-study in group-based CAL, *Computers and Education*, **37** (1), pp 67–80

Mulholland, C, Au, W and White, B (1998) Courseware evaluation methodologies: strengths, weaknesses and future directions, ACEC98 Conference Proceedings, University of South Australia, Adelaide

Rebele, J (1998) Accounting education literature review (1991–1997), Part II: Students, educational technology, assessment and faculty issues, *Journal of Accounting Education*, **16** (2), pp 179–245

Thorley, L and Gregory, R (eds) (1994) *Using Group-Based Learning in Higher Education*, Kogan Page, London

Tribe, D M (1994) An overview from higher education, in *Using Group-Based Learning in Higher Education*, ed L Thorley and R Gregory, Kogan Page, London

UMI (2001) [Online] http://www.use-of-mans.ac.uk/

Further reading

Allison, C *et al* (2000) The TAGS framework for Web-based learning environments, *Web-Based Learning Environments 2000*, 5–6 June, Portugal, FEUP Editions, University of Portugal, Lisbon

Allison, C *et al* (2001) The architecture of a framework for building distributed learning environments, in *Advanced Learning Technologies*, pp 29–35, IEEE Press, Wisconsin

Michaelson, R (2002) Re-thinking Laurillard: universities, learning and technology, *International Journal of Management Education*, **2** (2), pp 15–29

Power, D M, Michaelson, R and Allison, C (1998) The FINESSE portfolio management facility, *Proceedings of the 9th Annual CTI-AFM Conference*, pp 119–25, CTI-AFM Publications, University of East Anglia, Norwich

Useful URLs

FINESSE: http://www.FINESSE.ac.uk
INSIDE (Institutionally Secure Integrated Data Environment): http://www.dcs.st-and.ac.uk/inside/
Scottish Higher Education Funding Council (SHEFC) SCOTCIT: http://www.scotcit.ac.uk/
TAGS: www.tags.ac.uk
UMI: http://www.use-of-mans.ac.uk/

Contacts

Rosa Michaelson
Administrator
Accountancy and Business Finance
University of Dundee
1 Perth Road
Dundee DD1 4HN
e-mail: r.michaelson@dundee.ac.uk

Colin Allison
Project Leader
School of Computer Science
University of St Andrews
Fife KY16 9SS
e-mail: ca@dcs.st-and.ac.uk

Christine Helliar
Accountancy and Business Finance
University of Dundee
1 Perth Road
Dundee DD1 4HN
e-mail: c.v.helliar@dundee.ac.uk

David Power
Same address
e-mail: d.m.power@dundee.ac.uk

Donald Sinclair
Same address
e-mail: c.d.sinclair@dundee.ac.uk

Appendix 9.1

We applied Hein's (1992) and Ewing, Dowling and Coutts's (1998) criteria for a constructivist framework for successful group-based learning to analyse the use of FINESSE, as follows:

- The students are involved in an active process, that of constructing and maintaining a portfolio of shares. They also produce a joint presentation reporting on the strategic choices.
- The game allows the student to construct meaning and systems of meaning.
- Reflective activity: in which 'hands-on' processes inform 'mental' ones. (What happens if you sell these shares today? What happened to the shares bought last week? What strategy does the transaction support?)
- Social activity: learning takes place through discussion and interaction with others. Members of a group meet together during the course and use the Notebook tool to justify their purchases and sales. They also write a report together concerning different strategies and give a joint presentation to the class and lecturers.
- Context-dependent: without real stock market data and the group-owned portfolio it has been difficult for finance educators to present more than theoretic views of portfolio management strategy in their teaching.
- Time-dependent: such learning requires a long period for assimilation – the game starts at the beginning of the course (typically October) and is played over several months (until May).
- Motivation: as such learning seems heavily dependent on motivation the game is assessed for a final course mark and the students play competitively. Early feedback from students asked for the capability to see summaries of other group portfolios.

Chapter 10

Using learning technology resources in teaching management accounting

Greg Stoner

At the University of Glasgow, we have succeeded in integrating learning technology resources into our teaching of a first-level management accounting undergraduate course. In this chapter I review how this development evolved over seven years and the benefits it brought. I also report on the evaluation and subsequent adaptation needed to enhance the students' learning experience. Finally, I attempt to draw lessons from our experience as staff, particularly about how different kinds of learning resources can be integrated into course design and later evaluated.

Objectives

Our initial objective in this project was to respond to evolving changes in the university teaching and learning environment by integrating learning technology resources into our teaching of a first-level undergraduate course in management accounting. We were concerned to maintain high educational standards and to enhance the students' learning experience despite worsening staff: student ratios and, through evaluation, we sought to draw lessons of possible benefit to staff in other educational environments. Throughout the seven-year period of this review changes have been made to improve the implementation of learning technologies and to respond to the ever-changing educational environment.

Context

The course

The University of Glasgow's Department of Accounting and Finance has offered for many years a specialist accounting degree. Now modular, it consists of core courses in financial and management accounting, finance, information systems, quantitative methods, economics, law and taxation (mostly taken in Years 1 and 2), together with ordinary and/or honours degree courses (in Year(s) 3 or 3 and 4). To graduate, students have to pass all courses individually; there is no cross-compensation of marks between courses.

Management accounting was taught at our university until 1997/98 as the second half of a Level 1 course called Accounting 1. Since that year, we have offered Management Accounting 1 (MA1), as a compulsory 10-week element of the Bachelor of Accountancy (BAcc) and Bachelor of Financial and Legal Studies (BFLS) degrees and as an option for students on other degree courses in the university.

MA1 aims to teach students how to create management accounting numbers, and encourages them to learn about the interpretation of those numbers in businesses and organizations. It covers the recording and control functions of management accounting (see Appendix 10.1), leading to our Level 2 course on management accounting information for decision making.

The students

Most students taking MA1 are specialist accounting and finance students. Annual intake to the BAcc and BFLS degrees 1994–2001 has been approximately 100 to 120 students, mostly on the BAcc degree, though the number of students entering the BFLS degree, introduced in 1997, has increased. Admissions policy has remained stable and so have the composition and grade scores of students entering the degrees. The BFLS degree has slightly lower entrance requirements than the BAcc.

On entry to MA1 most students are considered to be reasonably numerate and most seem to have chosen accounting/financial studies degrees expecting the subject to require good numeracy skills. We know from recent surveys (Stoner, 1998) that on entry students' IT skills are fairly good. Most are fairly confident in their basic IT skills and some have access to a computer at home. All first year students have to take a short basic information technology skills (BITS) course to ensure that their IT skills are adequate for their studies. IT skills acquisition is also engendered through non-assessed instruction in the use of spreadsheets, through assessed IT skills training in a few of the core courses and through IT elements integrated into most courses.

Since MA1 started in 1997/98 we have seen a significant increase in the number of non-specialist accounting and finance students taking it, rising to nearly a third of the total in 2000/01. These students are attracted from other faculties and degree programmes, mostly from science and social science, and are typically less well academically qualified, based on pre-university exam grades, than the specialist students.

Rationale and design strategy

The most visible recent change within the core accounting courses has been the reduction in formal class contact time. In part, this change was made for positive reasons: in particular the number of lectures per course has been reduced to provide less directive teaching and more time and responsibility for student learning activities. However, a potentially negative effect of time pressure has been to reduce the extent of small class teaching. Tutorial group sizes were marginally increased and the number of contact hours per student was reduced. Practical classes were stopped in the early 1990s, leaving only the weekly tutorial classes. The small group practical classes were recently 'replaced' in some courses by workshop classes, which are multi-staffed large class sessions. Some of these changes were facilitated by the gradual introduction of learning technology (LT) resources, particularly for the financial accounting parts of the curriculum.

Why did we change how MA1 (and its predecessor within Accounting 1) was structured, delivered and developed? Our rationale for change was directly linked to our desire to follow a particular course design strategy. Our reasons ranged from the principled to the pragmatic.

Among the principles were our desire to improve, or at least maintain, the quality of student provision, student learning outcomes and student motivation. We wanted to do so despite the economic pressures on teaching within the HE sector. Personally, I also wanted to put into practice lessons I had learnt whilst on secondment to the Learning Technology Dissemination Initiative (LTDI) during 1995/96. On returning to my permanent post I became course co-ordinator for MA1, a course with which I had not been associated for several years.

Pragmatically, we had to change the course. The teaching of accounting has changed during the last decade in response to changing perceptions of the nature of teaching and learning and changes in resourcing levels with resulting pressures on staff time. There has also been a move towards graduates leaving with a broader base of generic transferable skills.

Design strategy: integration of learning technology

MA1, and the inclusion of learning technology within it, have evolved gradually rather than being a result of a radical change. We believe a holistic approach helps in the development of courses, and that students' learning depends on the overall integration of the individual elements into the course. We also believe that a major factor in determining whether LT resources are successful in aiding students to attain specific learning objectives is how the resources are integrated into the curriculum (Stoner, 1996b, 1997; Draper, 1996).

How well have the two kinds of LT resources (see below) been integrated into the teaching of MA1? This question can be best answered by looking at students' use of, and attitudes towards, these LT resources. To provide a broader picture, I also discuss here students' perceptions of the extent to which the traditional and LT-based elements of the course were interrelated and supported each other.

Description

The initial LT resources integration strategy

Following changes in staff during 1996/97 we decided to investigate ways of embedding LT resources into the management accounting part of the Accounting 1 course. Our integration strategy involved being explicit about the role of the course's different elements, including the role of the LT resources. The lecture load was reduced. LT resources and workshop classes were introduced. The latter are large class sessions in which several staff helped students with problems they had met in answering pre-set questions, primarily calculative, and then discussed with students the generalization, adaptation and application of the calculative techniques they had used.

When the two elements of the accounting course were split the next year (1997/98) the changes made in 1996/97 were maintained, with some adaptation and improved integration, to form the basis of Management Accounting 1 (MA1). For 1997/98, the course was provided through an integrated combination of the elements listed in Table 10.1 (based on a handout for students), plus students' private study. We were explicit about the nature and purpose of the different course elements.

The handout also gave a detailed breakdown of the reading and computer-based learning (CBL) work required for each topic (with a suggested timetable), plus details of the course aims and learning objectives (see Appendix 10.1). In an attempt to ensure that students didn't treat the material taught outside lectures as unimportant, we told them: 'The material covered in the CBL is examinable regardless of whether or not the same material is covered in the lectures and other formal classes of the course.'

We expected that this strategy would make it easier to reduce the amount of didactic lecturing, thereby freeing time in lectures and tutorials for discussion of

Table 10.1 *Teaching and learning elements for Management Accounting 1*

Element	Number	Stated Purpose
Lectures	*c.* 23 of 1 hour	Lectures introduce the main topics of the course and direct students' attention to the main areas of interest within these topics.
Workshops (led by lecturers and tutors)	*c.* 7 of 1 hour	Workshops help students with calculative aspects of the term's work.
Tutorials (some led by external tutors or doctoral students)	*c.* 8 of 1 hour	Tutorial classes concentrate on discussion of issues raised by management accounting calculations, rather than on calculation procedures. Calculative issues are covered in workshops and by the use of learning technology resources. Even where tutorial assignments do include calculative examples students should prepare to discuss the issues raised by the relevant accounting techniques.
Learning technology resources (self-learning, no tutor)	2 software packages	These resources are an integral part of the course, covering (in combination with the workshop classes) most calculative issues of the course, some of which are not dealt with in detail in lectures and tutorials. Students are expected to study these resources in their own time in the department's computer labs.

accounting and interpretation issues. We also hoped that the improved use of LT resources would give students more formative feedback, particularly on calculative problems.

We also changed assessment procedures. In 1996/97 an assessed essay, weighted at 30 per cent of the course mark, was introduced to replace the end-of-term examination. In 1997/98, in addition to MA1 being assessed as a separate course, students had to complete computer-based tests weighted at 10 per cent of the course mark.

The learning technology resources: Understand Management Accounting and Byzantium

Understand Management Accounting is a fairly traditional computer-based learning software package distributed by EQL International. It presents core material as text and graphics, and then offers examples, most of which require student input. The lessons are interspersed with questions and tasks requiring student interaction. The formative feedback is basic but broadly encouraging and helpful, normally avoiding the unhelpful 'wrong – try again' type of response.

The package covers major parts of six of the 12 core MA1 topics as well as other topics not covered in MA1. We tell our students which lessons to complete and suggest how long it may take. We expect them to study the lessons in their own time, over the period when each topic is being covered in the lecture/workshop/tutorial schedule. Though monitoring of student use is possible, we did not formally monitor their progress.

The Byzantium human tutor emulation software (see Chapter 6) was developed during the UK HE funding bodies' Teaching and Learning Technology Programme, and is now distributed by Blackwells. Of the five calculation-intensive topics available, three are used by students taking MA1. We chose this package because we thought it would help our students to acquire and understand the basic calculative techniques covered.

Byzantium provides practice in numerical management accounting by generating random variations on standard example questions and by providing the tools to complete them. Questions are presented in a spreadsheet-like format, as structured spreadsheet templates but with the underlying structure, cell formulas and spreadsheet functions hidden. The software randomly selects which cells contain data as well as the actual data content for each question. Students may therefore have to work out answers from base data towards solution values, vice versa, or in both directions. The software emulates the range of question types, including incomplete records, typically used to enhance and test students' understanding of accounting techniques.

Byzantium gives structured and helpful feedback to students who make errors in completing the problems. The feedback is graded, typically providing automatically two or three levels of help before resorting to providing an explanation of the correct answer.

Each Byzantium module includes on-line text accessed via the help keys. This text is not hypertext or enhanced with graphics, but is also in the textbooks that students are officially encouraged to purchase. We told students to refer to the books while studying the software only if they thought they needed to do so.

We have used Byzantium since 1997/98 in test mode as well as in the learning 'interactive' mode. In test mode, feedback is suppressed and students' submitted work is batch-marked automatically, but only when staff give the command. After marking, the work is available for students to review. The assessed questions have contributed 10–15 per cent (depending on the year) towards the overall course mark, and minimum performance levels (allowing re-submission) have been required as a compulsory element of MA1.

Students were provided with minimal printed instructions on how to use both software packages. More help was available if they asked, mainly from the departmental computer laboratory manager.

Evaluation and adaptation

Initial formal evaluation

Each year we have adapted MA1, based on feedback from our evaluation and changing administrative factors. The initial intervention and integration strategy of 1997/98 was formally evaluated in 1998 (see Stoner and Harvey, 1999). We used a case-specific questionnaire completed by students and student focus groups, in addition to the normal professional and departmental evaluation procedures.

Statistically, we compared examination performance in management accounting questions before and after the intervention. Our tests indicated significantly improved performance in 1997/98 compared with 1995/96 and 1996/97, particularly in answering the numeric questions. For essay-style questions, differences were only significant between 1995/96 and 1997/98. These statistics provide some comfort that students were probably learning at least as well after the intervention as they were before, though this was not a controlled experiment.

Our 1997/98 students told us that they preferred Byzantium to Understand Management Accounting, but their detailed comments suggest that they liked both, for different reasons. They liked Byzantium for being more interactive and providing instant feedback on calculation problems, with lots of examples. The practice provided by Byzantium and the interactive nature of the feedback seem to outweigh possible concerns over the package's dated appearance, a criticism of the package raised by some academics. Some students found the EQL package tedious to read on-screen, though others said it was useful because of its clear explanations and because it reinforced the text book and class material.

The vast majority of students thought the LT resources were of good quality and, importantly, that they fitted well within the course. Students reported some problems of access to the resources. Some had difficulties with terms used differently, and with different solution formats, in the LT resources, their textbook and the formal classes. Students were positive about the freedom to work at their own pace and being able to make mistakes in private. They said the LT resources had helped them to understand the calculative techniques covered in the course. They were happy about the Byzantium test being included within the summative assessment. Some wanted more such resources, on other topics.

The formal evaluation also looked at the usefulness of different learning modes within the course. We asked students' about their preferences regarding different aspects of the course and the extent to which the course components were supportive of or possible alternatives for each other.

We found there was little consensus among students on their least liked and most preferred learning modes for different aspects of the course. This diversity is unsurprising, given the potential effects of students' learning styles on learning preferences (Honey and Mumford, 1992; see Wilson and Hill, 1994, for a review of this area related to students of accounting). Students strongly preferred Byzantium and the workshops for achieving calculative objectives, while they saw lectures and tutorials as relatively weak for this purpose. They saw lectures as particularly useful for non-calculative learning. However, given that our course documentation was explicit about our strategy, possibly students were reflecting our position, rather than expressing their own independent opinions. If they were doing so, this would be consistent with students exhibiting traits of the lower dualistic or multiplistic stages of intellectual development (Perry, 1970; Harvey, 1994).

We also tried to evaluate the extent to which different learning methods and resources were seen as supportive of or possible alternatives for each other, but this proved to be problematic and less conclusive. We tentatively concluded that students are more likely to see the different learning modes as supportive of each other rather than as alternatives. Students saw books and lectures as the least replaceable and most supportive learning modes. They said that Understand Management Accounting and the workshops were the most replaceable, though even these are seen as supportive by many more students than those who saw them as replaceable. Our students saw relatively little opportunity for using any learning modes to replace other modes, but they saw the LT resources as an integral part of the learning required. Students generally did not seem to view the LT resources as optional extras 'bolted-on' to the course, and were motivated to use them (Goldfinch and Davidson, 1998; Thornbury, 1998).

Our results supported the view that different modes of learning or methods of teaching are preferred for different learning aims by different students. There is an eclectic mix of students' learning styles and learning preferences. Perhaps the main benefit of LT resources is as alternatives. The LT resources did help students to fill perceived gaps in the building of calculative accounting skills. Our students commented on feeling secure knowing that there were resources 'to fall back on' if they hadn't 'quite picked up a concept in formal classes'. By the end of our initial evaluation, however, we felt it was still an open question (and it still is) whether the strategy could be deemed a success on wider grounds of efficiency and effectiveness.

Ongoing evaluation

Formal evaluation of courses within the department is centred on annual course monitoring reports (ACMRs). These are formal reports drafted for discussion within the department and with students at the end of each course. ACMRs are finalized after incorporating any additional feedback and when final and resit course results are available.

Since 1997/98, ACMRs have been the main vehicle by which changes in courses are planned, agreed and reported. Before that, evaluation was based on most of the same methods, though course review was less formally structured and documented. ACMRs cover the changes actually made as compared with those planned the previous year. They include feedback from students, staff and external examiners. They call for critical appraisal of operation of the course including appropriateness of learning aims and objectives; adequacy of resources; appropriateness of teaching, learning and assessment methods; quality control procedures; and student outcomes. The final section of the ACMR contains proposed changes based on the appraisal.

To collect student feedback for MA1 we used (and still use) a simple questionnaire, designed within a fairly flexible departmental standard. It asks students about 5–10 factors, for which they provide scores as well as providing comments and constructive criticism. The questionnaire for MA1 has included the two LT resources and workshops as well as lectures and tutorials.

We should probably add that further formal evaluation went on in normal departmental and programme academic committees, staff–student meetings, consultations with external examiners, and periodic management accounting subject stream progression review groups (in 1997 and 2001). Also MA1 issues were considered with other major programme issues at our department's teaching away-days in 1999 and 2001.

Besides these formal evaluation methods, we relied on informal and non-formal evaluation that facilitates continuous (within session) adaptation and throws light on the formal feedback. For MA1 we collected information from team meetings and reviews; discussions with student class representatives; in class, frequent direct questions to students about the course; and informal contacts with students. We drew further inferences from students' communications with staff (and sometimes with other students), via e-mail and assessed coursework.

Changes based on evaluation

We introduced changes based on the 1998 formal evaluation and the ongoing evaluation, and have made other changes dictated by external events (see Appendix 10.2). The LT resources have stayed in the course, both because of the balance they bring to the module and because the ongoing evaluation supports their use. Students still see them as providing essential support to the calculative aspects of the course. Students consistently rate Byzantium very highly and Understand Management Accounting moderately well. Both fare much better with students than the textbooks. The main change has been in the need to reinforce the messages conveyed to students about the relative responsibilities of themselves, to learn, and the department and staff, to provide the appropriate learning resources and activities.

Staffing of tutorial classes changed marginally in 1998/99, by when it became too difficult to get local accounting firms to commit staff to teach for the department during their busy January–March period when this course is taught. We used instead more internal staff and doctoral students. Our students' questionnaire scores improved and we decided to stop using external tutors, though they still teach on our financial accounting courses.

We introduced an e-mail discussion list in 1996/97. Use of it has remained essentially the same, although students' early enthusiasm to communicate with each other, as well as with course staff, has vanished. Students now rarely if ever post messages to the list, though staff still use it for responses to student queries and for issuing notices and additional advice. Possibly this change is due to e-mail being less novel now and students having access to other messaging services.

One concern of ours throughout has been the perceived level of students' calculative management accounting skills. Initially the LT resources were integrated to aid the improvement of these skills, and to some extent they have done so. However by 1998 the apparent improved ability of students to enumerate techniques had not been matched by improved student ability to apply these management accounting techniques in practice. For this reason, from 1998/99 we provided increased practice in applying techniques by marginal changes to course delivery and the introduction of summatively assessed case-based group work, to replace the more traditional assessed essay. This change was designed to improve the learning structure and to motivate students to alter their learning strategies. We appealed to students' inherent instrumental motivation by increasing and making explicit the summative assessment of technique application. We reinforced this by reducing the summative weighting of the Byzantium tests, which called for enumeration rather than application.

We are not entirely sure how successful these changes have been. We made further adaptations for 2001/02, including the explicit integration of a revised formative and summative case exercise, as problem-based learning. We think that the introduction in 2001/02 of a separate non-specialist managerial accounting course for all non-accounting students will reduce the range of student abilities, backgrounds and motivations in MA1. This may facilitate student learning.

The multi-staffed workshops have changed substantially, too. One lecturer decided to phase them out because he thought the advantages of multi-staffing were outweighed by the improved flow of delivery available by incorporating workshop-type exercises within some lectures. However, many students seem to prefer workshops to lectures for dealing with calculative techniques. This is one reason why workshops are being used as part of the problem-based learning case study exercise in 2001/02.

Topic coverage has changed only slightly over the six years since the initial intervention, but for 2001/02 it was marginally reduced to provide more time for students to develop their depth of understanding of the application of calculative techniques and for the partial application of a problem-based learning approach.

Discussion

Our formal evaluation (Stoner and Harvey, 1999) came to the tentative conclusion that the integration strategy for the LT resources was successful, within the changing context provided by MA1. Students preferred Byzantium and workshops for learning calculative techniques, but tutorials, lectures and textbooks were preferred for developing understandings of concepts and their application. Byzantium was more popular than Understand Management Accounting, but students perceived both as valuable for the course. These conclusions suggest that, even on a course with a fairly homogeneous student entry, there is student demand for and pedagogic benefit from providing a rich and varied learning environment.

My review of MA1 highlights how continued evaluation, coupled with thoughtful adaptation, can take into account course and subject-specific factors, changes in the background and education of the student body, and in the development and learning of individual teachers.

We also looked at more general factors, such as student motivation and the development of students' maturity of learning in terms of, say, Bloom's taxonomy or Perry's scheme of intellectual and ethical development. For example, did the introduction of LT resources (particularly Byzantium) increase students' instrumental motivation to concentrate on surface learning? Our change towards using case studies of applications as part of summative assessment has helped students to focus on learning to apply techniques, and we are moving them now towards problem-based learning.

Overall, I regard our attempts to use learning technology resources in management accounting as broadly successful, not least in how we have integrated them into the MA1 course. That said, we are keenly aware of constant change in business education and we shall continue to adapt our teaching in order that our students may learn and understand.

Acknowledgement

I carried out the initial formal evaluation of this project with the considerable help of Jen Harvey, my previous colleague in the Learning Technology Dissemination Initiative at Heriot-Watt University, who is now the Distance Education Officer in the Learning and Teaching Centre at The Dublin Institute of Technology.

References

Draper, S W (1996) Observing, measuring or evaluating courseware: a conceptual introduction, in *Implementing Learning Technology*, ed G Stoner, pp 58–65, Edinburgh, Heriot-Watt University Learning Technology Dissemination Initiative, Edinburgh

Goldfinch, J and Davidson, K (1998) How to add value, in *Evaluation Case Studies*, ed N Mogey, Heriot-Watt University Learning Technology Dissemination Initiative, Edinburgh

Harvey, J (1994) An investigation into ways of encouraging the development of higher level cognitive skills in undergraduate biology students with reference to the Perry scheme of intellectual development, PhD thesis, Napier University, Edinburgh

Honey, P and Mumford, A (1992) *The Manual of Learning Styles*, Peter Honey, Maidenhead, Berkshire

Perry, W G (1970) *Forms of Intellectual and Ethical Development in the College Years*, Holt, Rinehart and Winston, New York

Stoner, G (1996) A conceptual framework for the integration of learning technology, in *Implementing Learning Technology*, ed G Stoner, pp 6–13, Heriot-Watt University Learning Technology Dissemination Initiative, Edinburgh

Stoner, G (1997) Implementation issues: leaning towards learning, *Account*, Computers in Teaching Initiative Centre for Accounting, Finance and Management (CTI-AFM), Summer, pp 13–23, also in *Selected Proceedings: 8th Annual CTI-AFM Conference*, ed K Fletcher and A H S Nicholson, pp 40–50, April 1997, Newport, Gwent, CTI-AFM, University of East Anglia, Norwich

Stoner, G (1998) IT is part of youth culture, but are accounting graduates confident in IT?, in *Selected Proceedings: 9th Annual CTI-AFM Conference*, ed K Fletcher and A H S Nicholson, pp 13–30, April 1998, York, CTI-AFM, University of East Anglia, Norwich

Stoner, G and Harvey, J (1999) Integrating learning technology in a foundation level management accounting course: an e(in)volving evaluation, in *Selected Proceedings: 8th Annual CTI-AFM Conference*, ed K Fletcher and A H S Nicholson, pp 146–60, April 1997, Newport, Gwent, CTI-AFM, University of East Anglia, Norwich, pp

Thornbury, H (1998) Using confidence logs and questionnaires as part of the Mentor project, in *LTDI Evaluation Cookbook*, ed J Harvey, Edinburgh, Heriot-Watt University Learning Technology Dissemination Initiative., Edinburgh [Online] http://www.icbl.hw.ac.uk/ltdi/cookbook/contents.html

Wilson, R M S and Hill, A P (1994) Learning styles: a literature guide, *Accounting Education*, 3 (4), pp 349–58

Courseware sources

Byzantium is published in institutional and student versions by Blackwell Publishers, London, and was produced by the Byzantium TLTP project led by G Wilkinson-Riddle, De Montfort University, Leicester [Online] http://www.blackwellpublishers.co.uk/static/electron.htm and http://www.blackwellpublishers.co.uk/asp/book.asp?ref=0631207503.

Understand Management Accounting is distributed by EQL International Ltd, Livingston Software Innovation Centre, 1 Michaelson Square, Kirkton Campus, Livingston, EH54 7DP, [Online] http://www.eql.co.uk/.

Contact

Greg Stoner
Department of Accounting and Finance
University of Glasgow
65–73 Southpark Avenue
Glasgow
G12 8LE
e-mail: g.stoner@accfin.gla.ac.uk

Appendix 10.1 Topics and learning objectives for MA1 (a student handout)

Topic	Learning objectives By the end of the course, you should be able to:
1 Introduction and historical development	Describe historical developments in management accounting. Appreciate why management accounting practice is what it is. Appreciate the nature of the development of management accounting theory.
2 Functions of management accounting	Describe and explain some of the differences between the theory and practice of management accounting. Differentiate between cost accounting, management accounting and financial accounting. Describe and explain the major functions of management accounting. Differentiate between score-card keeping, attention directing and problem solving.
3 Management accounting in changing business environments	Explain the major criticisms of contemporary management accounting practice. Be aware of the changing nature of the contemporary business environment and be able to appreciate the potential effects on management accounting – theory and practice.
4 Cost concepts and cost behaviour	Explain the various definitions of cost and cost classification systems. Relate the cost classification to cost objective. Identify cost objectives, such as costs for stock valuation, costs for decision making and costs for control.
5 Job costs and overhead allocation	Distinguish between job costing and process costing. Review the different traditional methods of allocating overhead costs. Understand the different methods used to apportion overheads to production and be able to calculate overhead recovery rates and production costs under the traditional methods. Explain why departmental overhead rates may be implemented in preference to an overall factory rate. Differentiate between the different capacity measures that might be used as the denominator in calculating overhead rates. Justify the use of predetermined overhead rates in preference to actual overhead rates.
6 Absorption and variable costing	Explain the difference between an absorption and variable costing system. Understand the distinction between profit and contribution. Prepare profit and loss accounts based on absorption and variable costing. Explain the advantages and disadvantages of employing different costs for the costing of stocks; absorption and variable costs; FIFO, LIFO, average cost, replacement cost and standard cost methods of stores valuation.

Topic	Learning objectives By the end of the course, you should be able to:
	Be aware of, and able to evaluate, the appropriateness of absorption and variable costs for a variety of purposes.
7 Activity-based costing	Describe activity-based cost accounting and be able to draw comparisons with other forms of costing, including traditional methods and the German/Dutch cost pool system.
8 Process costing	In process costing, distinguish between normal and abnormal losses and describe appropriate accounting treatments. Prepare process cost accounts using the weighted average method of valuing work in process.
9 Standard costing and variance analysis	Prepare flexible budgets and analyse variances according to price and quantity. Explain how standard costs are set. Identify the causes of and calculate labour, material, variable and fixed overhead variances. Construct a departmental performance report.
10 Budgeting and performance measurement	Describe responsibility accounting systems. Differentiate between the planning and motivational aspects of budgeting. Distinguish between different styles of evaluating performance.
11 Behavioural aspects of accounting control systems	Explain the impact of human behaviour on a variety of budgeting issues, including budget bias, organizational slack management and the relationship between the planning and motivational aspects of budgeting.
12 Management accounting in organizational context	Describe and evaluate the effects of organizational context on the selection, operation and outcomes of management accounting control systems. Explain the major variables in the contingency theory of management accounting. Relate the importance of technology, organization structure and environment to the design of accounting information systems.
13 Developments in management accounting	Describe some of the newer developments in management accounting and be able to relate them to criticisms of conventional management accounting, including new manufacturing technology, just-in-time manufacturing, increasing emphasis on quality measurement, life cycle costing and strategic management accounting.
and Additional general and overall learning objectives	Demonstrate an ability to gather, organize and interpret information. Communicate effectively both orally and in writing. Work with others in tutorials and workshops. Use information technology. Learn and study effectively and demonstrate a degree of self-management and organization.

Appendix 10.2 Significant structural changes in module/module delivery

Year[§]	Separate module	Lectures[§]	Use of workshops	Use of external tutors[ç]	Use of EQL (MA) [#]	Use of Byzantium [#]	Other summative assessment[Þ]	Exam summative assessment	Topic changes[±]	Use of e-mail discussion[ø]
1995/96	No	L1 + L2	No	Yes	(FA)	No	Individual essay 25%	75%	n/a	No
1996/97	No	GS + L3	All	Yes	FA	FA	Individual essay 25%	75%	Yes + Order	N, Q + R
1997/98	Yes	GS + L1	All★	Yes	FA	FA + SA 15%	Individual essay 25%	60%	Order	N, Q + R
1998/99	Yes	GS + L1	½ + ^	Yes, some	FA	FA + SA 10%	Group Case 1 30%	60%	No	N + R
1999/00	Yes	GS + L1	½ + ^	No	FA	FA + SA 10%	Group Case 1 30%	60%	No	N + R
2000/01	Yes	GS + L4	½ + ^	No	FA	FA + SA 10%	Group Case 2 30%	60%	Yes + Order	N + R
2001/02	Yes	GS (all)	All	No	FA	FA + SA 30%	Group Case 2 30%	60%	Yes + Order	—

§ 1995/96 shown as base year, before interventions described in this paper. Information for 2001/02 is as planned, not implemented at the time of writing.

§ GS – the author; L1, L2, L3 and L4 are other academic staff from the department (bold = module director/coordinator).

ç Professional/trainee accountants from local professional accounting firms used as external tutors for the majority of tutorials pre-1998/99; post-1998/99 the majority of tutorials were staffed by the module coordinator/director with others staffed by doctoral students.

CAL material used as learning resources and as assessment: FA = formative assessment; (FA) = package available for formative evaluation but not specifically integrated into the module delivery/documentation; SA = summative assessment, with indication of % contribution to final marks.

Þ Indication of nature of assessment, its contribution to the final marks and whether it was based on individual or group-based work. Group work is typically in groups of three or four students.

★ Used less formally for the second half of the course.

^ Some lecture slots in the second half of the course used for numerical exercises but not as multi-staffed workshops.

± Though there was no overall change in the learning aim of the course, there were changes to some detailed learning objectives and the way in which the learning objectives were presented as differentiated topics. Only significant topic changes are indicated: minor changes/updates were made each year. 'Yes' indicates substantive revision/swapping of topics (2000/01: final topics only). 'Order' indicates substantive changes in order of topic coverage.

ø E-mail discussion list set up and operated in all years, but student use of the list differed between years, resulting in different affective modes of use: N indicates list used for course staff to issue notices; Q indicates students asking questions on the list (with occasional student answers); R indicates staff replying to student questions/queries to the list.

fi In 2001/02 the summative case assignment is to be significantly revised and integrated into the timetabled learning activities of the course, as a problem-based learning exercise.

Chapter 11

Creating a Web site for studying strategic management

Colin Clarke-Hill and Ismo Kuhanen

This is the story of how we created, through a do-it-yourself approach, a Web site for students studying strategic management, research methods and management ethics at our universities, Gloucestershire and Plymouth. We had clear objectives and a rationale for what we were attempting to do. We were fortunate in possessing some of the IT skills required but had to learn the rest.

We based the design of our site on the A T Kearney 3-C model, which we adapted to meet the students' needs. Here we describe the site and its design and explain how it expanded through links to other sites. We also provide details of our students' evaluation of it.

We discuss the use of Internet technology as a means of reducing costs and facilitating radical transformation of business and university systems. We argue against centralized Web portals for delivering an e-learning strategy, and in favour of a distributed one controlled by individuals and /or small academic groups. We discuss the creation and use of business Webs and application of the extended enterprise model to the university. Finally we argue for wider use of personal controlled learning Webs that are free to access and use, to further students' understanding of the subject area.

Objectives

Together, we started in 1999 to develop a Web site (http://www.strategios.co.uk) devoted to the study of strategic management, research methods and management ethics. We have operated and maintained it ever since: jointly, we pay for, run and control it, although one of us (Ismo Kuhanen) is now a consultant and no longer teaching in a university.

We deliberately chose to be independent from the bureaucracies of our universities. This enabled us to develop the site in any way we saw fit. In 1999 we wanted to create a site and deploy e-learning methodologies that were in advance of what our universities could offer. We wanted flexibility to change material, add new links and respond to our students' needs quickly. Our universities at that time could not deliver the flexibility that we required, so we embarked on a DIY approach.

We knew that our objectives were to:

1. create a Web site for our subject with a consistent theme through the many pages;
2. have a showcase for our teaching material;
3. build an interface with the wider scholarly community;
4. provide access to and use of the site free of charge;
5. control our teaching content, bearing in mind the course requirements of our universities;
6. enable our students to broaden their horizons through interactive links, germane to the subject of strategic management;
7. share our enthusiasm for our subject with others.

Rationale

Teaching and learning are changing. Content is changing and so are teaching styles. But the most rapid changes have been in the technology available for learning (for example, see De Montfort University's excellent Web site at http://www.dmu.ac.uk/ jamesa/learning/contents.htm).

The 1990s heralded the dot.com era: there was an exciting technological crossover between developments in e-commerce and what could be achieved in teaching and learning in universities and colleges. The commercial e-hubs (Kaplan and Sawhney, 2000) that were being created for procurement and value chain management (Rayport and Sviokla, 1996) might with modifications be applied to universities and colleges. The rationale for Web-based systems had arrived and they were seen to work for e-commerce. Adapting e-hub and portal models to a university environment would look something like Figure 11.1, a diagrammatic overview of an e-learning portal.

In Figure 11.1 the e-learning portal is controlled from a Web site and is designed around a set of appropriate learning models. The Web site and its pages are linked to a block of appropriate resources in the form of content available to

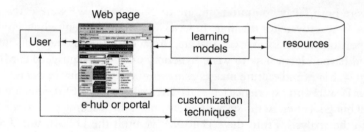

Figure 11.1   *Diagrammatic view of a learning portal*

the students through two main filters. These are the learning models being used and customization techniques designed to meet broad users' characteristics and learning needs. Customization borrows from the fields of customer relationship management and mass customization models used by financial services and e-retailing companies. The e-learning portal is controlled and operated by the provider, and users must interact with the provider's agenda. Password protection locks out users who are not part of the system and all interaction with external links is strictly controlled. The intention is to create something of a 'walled garden' within which learning will occur.

Implementation of e-commerce has proved very costly and many systems have failed. The crossover between e-commerce models and e-learning systems certainly could not be achieved at zero or minimal net cost. Despite government funding for much of the technological infrastructure, the biggest cost to the universities and colleges is in transforming academic processes, such as conceiving, writing, commissioning and paying for content. E-learning portals are expensive to set up and maintain.

An alternative to the central hub may lie in small-scale Web sites controlled by individual or small groups of academics. This approach had its attractions for us. For many like us, it became a personal challenge. If universities and colleges were 'slow on the curve' for all sorts of reasons, interested individuals could blaze the trail alone or with a few others, we argued. Doing so turned out to be easier and more fun than we thought it would be.

Besides the technology push, we potentially had the pull of student demand. By the time we started, many of our students were technologically literate, had a job to pay their way through university and were demanding out-of-hours access. Their 24/7 lifestyle demanded a response. We had a vision and we prepared to meet the challenge.

Context

We selected and marshalled academic content that would be useful to our students, of course. We had to teach ourselves some new skills, too. Fortunately, we were both fairly computer-literate to begin with. We were early users of PowerPoint software for teaching. Indeed, we used to give our whole PowerPoint slide portfolio to our students on diskettes to save printing and reproduction costs. We did have to learn how to write hypertext mark-up language (HTML) code, design Web sites and capture images using scanners and digital cameras.

Our PowerPoint experience led to us developing a CD ROM, which was crude at first but got better. At the start it merely linked the teaching plan to the lectures and to the analysis. From the CD ROM we built the HTML full Web-based service that we have now. Along the way, we learnt to program using Asymetrix's Multimedia Toolbook program suite for the CD ROMs and, later, the HTML editors for the Web pages.

What we did, in effect, was learn how to develop and write a set of electronic teaching and learning materials, available online: you could call it an e-book resource. And it is available to all, on the Web, free of charge.

Description

When we began to develop our site, we did not have to start from zero. There were several well-known and easily accessible models for building Web pages. The question for us was how to mimic the e-learning portal at the micro-level of the Web site and Web page, for our own subject of strategic management.

The model for our Web site was adapted from A T Kearney's 3-C model described in the company's white paper, 'Building the b2b foundation' (Kearney, 1999), originally designed for Internet market makers interested in business-to-business commerce. We adapted the original 3-C model of Commerce, Content and Connection, which became Connection, Content and Community. In a later paper, A T Kearney proposed a 7-C model, and incorporated this in another white paper called 'Creating a high-impact customer experience' (Kearney, 2000). These two linked models were developed by the firm to enable e-commerce companies to design their pages and portals. For our purposes, the adapted 3-C model (Figure 11.2) explains our underlying design philosophy adequately.

We drew a map of the Web site consisting of many Web pages and sub-directories. This gave us an integrated picture of the design. The front page would be the welcome on entry to the site. The whole conception of the site was to focus on issues that were linked to the teaching of strategic management, international business, management ethics and research methods. These subject fields were of direct importance to us: they were our subject areas of expertise; therefore we included all four in the model.

Connection to the Web site was through two Internet service providers; it was controlled by us via passwords and registered Web site names. The main name was Strategios, which became the registered home page for the site. Connection through these two servers was quick and straightforward. We were able to upload

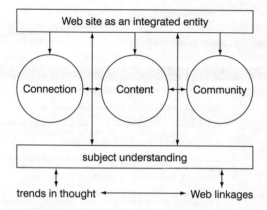

Figure 11.2   *The 3-C model of the Web site as an intetgrated entity*

teaching and other material by using the usual file transfer protocol (ftp) connections. The design values of the directories, sub-directories and individual files had to conform to the speed of upload and be visually simple. But we aimed to have rich content and simple design values.

One or our objectives was to create interactivity with the wider scholarly community. We wanted to create a virtual 'interactive classroom' for our users. We decided, very early on, that access to the Web site would be free to all and not password-protected. The foundation of the site was the subject material. We enabled our students and other users to explore trends in the four subject fields, both through content that we had generated and through links to other sites where the subject fields are being developed. For our own students the site supplemented the material they received in the classroom.

We wrote, and still maintain, the Web pages by using Microsoft's HTML editor, FrontPage. This allowed us to avoid buying the very expensive, but industry-standard, Web design tool, Dreamweaver. The FrontPage software has the advantage of being integrated into the Microsoft Office suite of programs and works seamlessly with Word and PowerPoint. FrontPage allows the user to define backgrounds, layouts and page structures. The program automatically converts the text and graphics into HTML code. The user does not need to know how to program in this code. Pages are stored on disk and we upload them to the site using standard ftp software that we found on a free disk on the cover of a computer magazine.

Our costs were thus minimized. We do the uploading from home using standard access facilities available through BT Openworld. Unmetered Internet access, in recent years, has helped to cap the cost of maintaining the site. Registration of the domain name, Strategios, costs us about £50 a year. By using two Web sites linked together, the site has a capacity of over 100 mb of space.

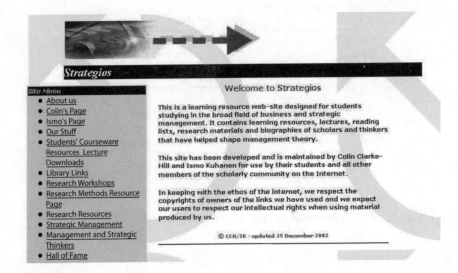

Figure 11.3 *The main Strategios site*

Examples

Here are four examples of what we have developed, from within our main Strategios site, shown in Figure 11.3. The key parts of the site are listed in the left-hand column.

Example 1

Students said the 'Library' (http://www.strategios.co.uk/library.htm) was particularly useful. This page offers links to relevant online journals, management consultant Web sites that publish their research and key reports, home pages of important academic journals and popular management magazines. Students also find on it other links that may be useful, such as online tutorials in using the SPSS package for statistical data analysis, designed and run by an individual at the University of Teesside. A link to the very informative and well designed site for business education, Bized (http://www.bized.ac.uk/fme/), takes users to a wealth of business-related material, lecture notes, case studies and other useful information.

Example 2

The 'Research Methods' page has a wealth of information for students doing their research projects and writing dissertations (http://www.strategios.co.uk/page%203.htm). It takes as its theme an online research methods module. Here the basic menu offers the user key research themes in the form of lectures and links. With links to online statistical pages, online textbooks and other sites of interest we attempted to create a holistic module. One very good example of a Web-enabled e-book for studying advanced statistical analysis for research purposes is at http://www.statsoft.com/textbook/ stathome.html. Another example of a Web site for studying research methods is Cornell University's Research Knowledge Database (http://trochim.human. cornell.edu/kb/). One of us (Colin Clarke-Hill) uses in his classes the lectures that this site makes available as downloads.

A link at the end of the 'Research Methods' page takes the user to more material on the research topic and, further, to more advanced sites that the user may find interesting. There is a link to a new module on research methods for the 2002/03 academic year.

Example 3

For the Web-enabled module Corporate Strategy, the welcome page (http://www.strategios.co.uk/mb428%20Webpage/gbs428.htm) shows simply the module title and semester dates. A click on 'Enter' takes the user to menus for the workbook and the main teaching items. The workbook menu has an introduction and five topics. The teaching material in the workbook is hot-linked to other Web sites of potential interest. The main menu includes an introduction to the module; reading resources; a teaching plan with topics linked to the workbook topics and to lecture notes in PowerPoint format; seminar topics with questions and reading lists that may be helpful; and contacts and other key information. A final item on assessment completes the main menu.

At the foot of the 'assessment' page are special links to help the user to gain further understanding. For financial valuation theory there is a link to a Web site (http://www.stern.nyu.edu/ adamodar/New_Home_Page/) designed by a leading US academic. This site is full of content: it develops theory and examples in a very thorough manner. For student use it also has numerous cases presented as spreadsheets. Allied to this personal Web site is another (http://www.cbi.cgey.com/ about/index.html) through which students can call up leading research studies on valuations and other papers from and about online company financial data, from sites such as Hemscott (http://www.hemscott.net/) and Thomson Financial (http://global.thomsonfn.co.uk/).

Example 4

Management Ethics is another Web-enabled module, based on much the same model as Corporate Strategy but with somewhat greater Web interactivity. In the academic year 2001/02 one of us (Colin Clarke-Hill) transferred the teaching material from the site (http://www.oldredlion.here2stay.org.uk/ethics/ mb430.htm) to a CD ROM and used it for a distance learning module, linking together the CD ROM and the site. The take-up of this optional module was too small for a scheduled face-to-face class, so remote delivery with two live seminars was chosen.

On the page 'Theoretical underpinnings', which is the opening section of the module's workbook, the reader is linked to an excellent publicly funded business site called BOLA – Business Online Archive (http://sol.brunel.ac.uk/jarvis/bola/index.html), run by Chris Jarvis at Brunel University. BOLA has a particularly well-developed set of resources on business topics, and, for students of management ethics, explanations of the key philosophers, case studies and other useful material. By clicking on BOLA's external links the user finds links to sites containing reports and white papers on ethical issues from campaigning and research groups in this field. The Christian Aid site is a particularly good example (http://www.christian-aid.org.uk/indepth/fulllist.htm), like that of the ethics research group at the University of British Columbia in Canada (http://www.ethics.ubc.ca/resources/business/).

Student courseware

Links (http://strategios.co.uk/Lectures/lectures.htm) enable students to download lectures for strategic management, management ethics and research methods, to support their learning.

Evaluation

If we give the impression that the Strategios site was created in a few days, we want to dispel that notion forthwith. The site as it stands has evolved over four years. It takes a considerable amount of time and effort to create, write and design the material ready for Web site formatting. The material has to be structured for remote access, links have to discovered and evaluated before they can be recommended for use and the new pages have to be uploaded on to the site. Regular maintenance is essential to keep the material up to date and all the links working.

Up to 2001, we used both a CD ROM and our Web site. The Web site was less well developed and we depended on the CD ROM. Our students told us what they thought of both, and we dropped the CD ROM as a result of rethinking our teaching strategy (Clarke-Hill and Kuhanen, 2000). We put much of the CD ROM material, reformatted in HTML, on to the site. We learnt from our students' experience, and our site as a whole benefited.

Today, students and academics heavily use our Web site. We know this through traffic data. Data for the site as a whole are difficult to obtain in usable form, but we know that traffic flow data for the key pages make interesting reading. For example, we extracted data for page traffic for the MB428 Management Ethics sub-directory, accessed from the menu page through the link 'Colin's Page' (http://www.strategios.co.uk/colinmenu.htm). Table 11.1 shows figures supplied by the Internet service provider for two seven-day periods in 2002.

Table 11.1 *Web log data for Management Ethics*

Descriptor	Seven Days to 1 March 2002	Seven Days to 10 May 2002
Successful requests	611	420
Average successful requests per day	87	61
Successful requests for pages	221	177
Average successful requests for pages per day	31	25
Distinct files requested	50	50
Distinct hosts served	137	136
Data transferred	25.41 mb	14.2 mb
Average data transferred per day	3.65 mb	2.01 mb

The Web logs track every key-stroke made by visitors to the site. They note each page request, where it came from and even what link was selected, by time, in the minutest detail. From such data, we know that in February–May 2002 the site was particularly popular with users from the UK, Australia, France, Canada, the United States, Greece, Malaysia and South Africa. Users from both commercial companies and academic institutions used the MB428 Management Ethics sub-directory in equal measure. In an average week it registered some 400 page requests, with a download of some 18 mb of data transferred. The highest number of requests for pages came in the week ending 1 March, when 611 successful requests were logged and 25.4 mb of data transferred. Two months later, in the week ending 10 May, there were 420 requests for data and 14.2 mb transferred. When we looked at the Web logs for the quarter as a whole, the popular times for users to be online were between 1300 hours and 2000 hours at the weekend from Sunday to Tuesday. For the two weeks shown in Table 11.1, visitors to the pages came from 135 different locations, with about 26 per cent of visitors from the UK.

The Web log data, as displayed in Table 11.1, certainly indicate that this directory is very popular, and we have grounds to believe the site as a whole is popular too. Our detailed discussions with students support this view. At both our universities, evaluation questionnaires at the end of modules contained specific questions about the Web site, and most students evaluated the site very positively. They rated highly factors like interactivity, Web links and informative content. The popular pages with many students were the 'Library Links' that took users to the key journals and other online sources. Students who were building up bibliographies for projects and essays found this facility particularly useful. On the other hand, students found the lack of online full-text material frustrating. This problem cannot be avoided due to copyright.

Final year undergraduates and MBA students were particularly complimentary about the 'Research Methods' page. We do expect to revise this page, however, because in many institutions the teaching of research methods is often poorly backed up with materials. We think an online source would be a possible solution.

Interestingly, our students now expect such a site as a given for their courses and do not find our approach idiosyncratic. The pressure placed by students on colleagues who do not follow such a path could be quite intense.

Discussion

We can build parallels between the experience of commerce and the university. If we return to our earlier point on the technology solution to reducing cost transactions and other associated costs of running a business, which the Internet technology is seen as providing, this I believe is a myth. The literature and commercial history on this point are instructive. Read the excellent article on e-marketing failures by Varianini and Vaturi (2000) and that of Brash, Crawford and Grosso (2000) on the problems that e-retailers had in using their business models centred on their value chain costs and revenues. In particular see the data the latter authors display in exhibit 1 (p 100) on how e-tailers destroyed value with their Internet business models.

On the role of the Internet in business and business processes there is an interesting debate surrounding the differing views of Tapscott (2001) (http://www.dontapscott.com/Strategy_Business.pdf) on the one hand and Porter (2001) on the other. Tapscott argues that the Internet can lead to serious and far-reaching transformations of how businesses (and, by association, universities and colleges) work. This technology allows for what can be termed radical business model innovation. Brash, Crawford and Grosso (2000) have shown us convincing evidence of the downside to such radical transformations and over-optimistic business assumptions. Universities and colleges would certainly like to see the attack on costs that could follow introduction of the technology, but are reluctant to embark upon the transformation in staff and business processes that would follow. They should indeed be cautious about overblown claims for this technology. Porter (2001) does not deny this, and strongly urges caution. He exhorts business leaders to 'return to fundamentals' and to abandon any thoughts of new business models or e-business strategies and encourages managers to see their Internet operations in isolation from the rest of the business. According to Porter (2001), 'we need to see the Internet for what it is: an enabling technology. It is a powerful set of tools that can be used wisely or unwisely, in almost any industry and part of almost any strategy.' Porter further calls for integrating this technology into the overall strategy of the business if it is to be leveraged for competitive advantage. Vice-chancellors please note.

Tapscott (2001) sees that, in the future, strategists will no longer look at the integrated corporation as the starting point for creating value, assigning functions and deciding where the firm's boundary lies. Rather, managers will start with the customer's value proposition and a blank slate for the production and delivery system to be built around the customer: in other words, this is a radical form of customization. A firm will be part of a business web (b-web) that allows a lead firm to choreograph the process, acting as a context provider, and different firms in the b-web will service the customer in different ways but in a coordinated and seamless manner. Businesses, Tapscott argues, will operate within extended boundaries and in multiple and overlapping b-webs, depending on their relative position in the value chain. Exponents of this view term this the extended enterprise and embedded enterprise.

Synthesizing these two opposing views and putting them in the context of this article is not difficult. Clearly, there is significant scope for the development of e-learning systems using portals, databases and associated tools. Starting with the student as user (customer?) and building customized delivery of appropriate teaching and learning materials is both possible and desirable. Whether this will produce any significant cost savings is debatable. No doubt, universities and colleges will have to transform their business models very radically, perhaps question their very existence as academies in the classical sense. They should heed Porter's (2001) view and see this technology as 'enabling'. Doing so would allow for a mixed strategy to be adopted: the traditional with the technology, hugely advantageous to the student who would get the best of both worlds.

If we take on the Tapscott (2001) view of extended enterprises based on intricate and overlapping b-webs, then we can see new horizons for the university and indeed for the student. Expertise can be located at different points in the b-web and differential advantages of individual universities and colleges can be leveraged for the system as a whole.

In both cases there are practical difficulties that will need to be overcome. Business model transformations are inevitable as digital convergence becomes an increasing reality. Vice-chancellors will have to fund the intellectual efforts that will be needed to create these b-webs and the content therein. Universities and colleges will have to become adept at managing the complexity created by overlapping b-webs.

These b-webs, or perhaps learning webs or l-webs, will also change the nature of the university's rationale and the university teacher's role from that of a lecturer to that of a content provider. Familiar learning and teaching models may need to be redesigned. The student as the central focus will have to take personal ownership of his/her own learning. The onus to plan and execute the student's learning, with Web-enabled tools as a guide, will shift from the university to the individual.

To conclude, then, at the present moment of development in our own universities, we do not advocate centrally controlled learning webs based on central portals and huge database provision linked to customization systems. They are technically possible and likely to happen, but very expensive to implement and in our view potentially alienating. We advocate instead a distributive model of subject-based l-webs controlled by individual academics or small groups creating their own communities of Web sites with colleagues in other universities and colleges. These sites should be, in our view, accessible free of charge and cooperative in nature within the wider scholarly community. We also advocate that, in the interim, academics develop these extended subject webs themselves. They will thus keep control of their intellectual property and be free from the dead hand of bureaucracies that universities and colleges can so brilliantly develop.

We have shown how we realized our vision for our site. We shall continue to develop it as a personal attempt to create a subject l-web to serve our students' needs and, we hope, provide useful links to the wider academic community on the Internet. We have also shown some examples of sites created by individuals or small academic groups that advance research, knowledge and dissemination of their subject fields to the wider academic community. We feel it is a privilege to be part of this movement.

References

Brash, J, Crawford, B and Grosso, C (2000) How e-tailing can rise from the ashes, *McKinsey Quarterly*, **3**, pp 98–109

Clarke-Hill, C M and Kuhanen, I M (2000) Computer aided learning: developing a CD-ROM resource and aspiring to a networked classroom, *Journal of Teaching and Learning*, **5** (2), pp 10–13

Kaplan, S and Sawhney, M (2000) E-hubs: the new b2b market places, *Harvard Business Review*, **78**, May–June, pp 97–103

Kearney, A T (1999) Building the b2b foundation: positioning net market makers for success [Online] http://www.atkearney.com/main.taf?site=1&a=5&b=3&c=1&d=4

Kearney, A T (2000) Creating a high-impact customer experience [Online] http://www.atkearney.com/main.taf?site=1&a=5&b=3&c=1&d=10

Porter, M E (2001) Strategy and the Internet, *Harvard Business Review*, March, pp 62–78

Rayport, J F and Sviokla J J (1996) Exploiting the virtual value chain, *McKinsey Quarterly*, **1**, pp 21–36

Tapscott, D (2001) Rethinking strategy in a networked world (or why Michael Porter is wrong about the Internet), *Strategy and Business*, **24**, pp 34–41 [Online] http://www.dontapscott.com/Strategy_Business.pdf

Varianini, V and Vaturi, D (2000) Marketing lessons from e-failures, *McKinsey Quarterly*, **4**, pp 86–97

Contact

Colin Clarke-Hill
Reader in Strategic Management
The Business School
University of Gloucestershire
Pallas House
Cheltenham GL50 2QF
e-mail: cclarkehill@glos.ac.uk

Chapter 12

The live consultancy case study

Suzanne O'Hara, Steve Reeve and Stephen Flowers

Eight years ago we designed a 'live' consultancy case study, for use on our part-time MBA residential programme in the business school at the University of Brighton. Our experience of running this activity on more than 30 different occasions leads us to believe that it provides a rich learning experience for all those who take part. The live case study brings together the essential elements of a Master's-level qualification: implementable solutions to 'real-world' problems, informed by academic concepts and analytical thinking. We believe therefore that the case study exercise offers a vehicle for learning on any Master's-level, post-experience practitioner course.

We explain here how and why the original process was conceived and go on to outline its subsequent development. In so doing we hope that readers will be able to determine whether the live consultancy case study can be a useful learning vehicle on their own programmes.

Our rationale

In 1993 we launched our new MBA programme. In the participants' handbook, we stated that 'The ethos of the programme is that of mature people participating in an adult learning experience.' Key characteristics of the programme included adult-to-adult relationships with tutors and the management experience that participants brought to the programme.

Part of the new MBA was a two-day residential element. We believed it was important that its design should fit the ethos of the MBA as a whole and not be viewed simply as a bolt-on activity. In considering what form the residential session should take, we examined models that had been used within the university and elsewhere. Neither the classic 'outward bound' nor the simulation games model seemed appropriate. The deeper, person-focused model from management development practice seemed similarly inappropriate. The standard written case study approach, although popular on MBA residential sessions, appeared to us to have two major shortcomings: low fidelity and lack of immediacy.

Shortcomings of the written case study model

Written case studies, which are often out of date, offer an imaginary situation or an edited description of the 'there and then' as a vehicle for learning. They must necessarily be taken at face value, because a written account is all there is to work on. It is impossible to interrogate the data or dig any deeper into the problem than the level of information given in the text. It is not possible to ask questions of the people involved. Important contextual background is often missing. Interpretations of what might be the case remain exactly that: merely interpretations or 'guesstimates'. They are of low fidelity. Written case studies mean little to participants on a personal level. They lack immediacy. Although there may be similarities and connections to the participants' own work and to their organizational contexts, it is easy for participants to distance themselves from the learning vehicle and the solutions they generate. The reality level is low and there is always the safety net of being a third party. This combination may lead to idealized textbook solutions that could never be implemented in the real situation because of the dynamics and personalities involved.

We thought mature students on an MBA programme needed something more challenging than written case studies against which to pitch their own organizational experience and academic learning. We believed that real problems in the 'here and now' offered them more scope for significant learning than did written case studies. We also believed that participants would learn most from experiences that exercised their emotions as well as their intellects.

The live consultancy case study

After much discussion, the team decided to attempt to create a situation in which we would all learn from each other. We therefore designed a live case study consultancy exercise in which programme participants would act as clients and offer their own real, current managerial problems as live case studies. Small 'management consultancy' groups of other participants would analyse these cases and make recommendations to the client, in an attempt to solve the problem and learn about management. The learning during the exercise would be emergent (Megginson, 1996) and harvested during debriefings and reflection.

This approach seemed to offer both high fidelity and high immediacy, because:

- the clients had real problems for which they wanted implementable solutions;
- the consultants could continue digging into the case by requesting more and more information, until the client cried 'enough!';
- in developing solutions, the consultancy group would feel a sense of responsibility to their peers and friends. The advice they gave would matter because they were addressing a real problem.

The live case study was a risky approach for us to take. It required from us, the staff team, new skills and methods of working. We had to give up 'control' on the micro-level and learn to live with the nature of emergent, unpredictable outcomes rather than pre-planned expectations. In addition, there was always the risk that, for various reasons, no suitable problems would be forthcoming and we would find ourselves at the residential session with a huge hole in our programme!

Experimenting with the first live case study

Several weeks before the residential session, we sent details to the participants. We asked them to volunteer as clients for the live case study exercise and to submit brief details of their problems. Only a few participants sent in problems for consideration, not enough for the number of groups we needed to run. With over 60 participants and with consultancy groups of seven members, we needed more problems to be offered if the new live case study model was to go ahead. Informal soundings indicated that participants were reticent about putting themselves forward as clients since they were unsure what this involved. Members of the staff team therefore talked informally to participants and answered any questions they had. Despite this we arrived at the residential session without the necessary number of clients.

At the start of Day 1, we explained we did not have enough problems. We described once again what was required of clients. We did our best to emphasize the benefits, especially the expectation that clients would return to work with solutions that could be implemented. We emphasized that confidentiality would be maintained and that clients would have a veto over which group they worked with. If, for example, other participants worked in the same organization or for a competitor, the client could ask for a transfer. We asked the participants to let us know by lunchtime if they wanted to offer a problem. It was an anxious morning.

By lunchtime however we had more problems than we needed. It seemed that, once participants had the chance to talk through what was involved with all the tutors at the residential session, many more than were needed were prepared to act as clients.

Over lunch, we considered the details of each case, looking for those which seemed to offer sufficient breadth and depth as learning vehicles. Here are some (unedited) examples of the kinds of problems we were offered:

- Decide what will happen to a satellite depot of a much larger company. The depot is losing money.
- Develop a set of procedures for dealing with stress in a high-stress occupation. In a time of cuts and uncertainty, people are feeling vulnerable if they admit to being stressed. The culture of the organization views stress as a weakness.
- Guidance on motivating a previously highly motivated work force that is now demotivated.
- How to reinvent a public sector service. How can a bureaucracy be innovative? What is the way forward?
- Following the move and merger of an NHS teaching centre, should the new centre be run like a business? What is the way forward personally for the manager?
- Following the rapid growth and development of a partnership, how can the owners be convinced that traditional management methods will constrain the business and limit further growth? A strategy for the future.
- Change management 12 months on: 12 months after a takeover and change management initiative, this part of the company is still underperforming. There is a feeling that the current underperformance will only be tolerated until the year end. The business seemed to incur the costs of the change but had not realized the benefits. There is no partnership between the old and the new. How to develop a partnership approach to management, hopefully resulting in improved performance.
- How to generate an increase in profit of 25 per cent for a business in the service industry by the end of the next financial year. Ideas to generate additional sales? Ways to maximize sales in existing outlets?
- Management following a major change involving the merger of 12 areas into four. How to get everyone working in the same way? For example, currently there are nine teams all with different points of contact. What is wanted is one point of contact. To achieve this we need to change their ideas about how to work, but this is seen against a cut in staffing levels of 12 to four in each team.

We looked for complex examples that posed problems, rather than puzzles (Revans, 1983). A little ambiguity, as in some of the examples, did not matter, because the problem could be explained further by the client. We knew we had to identify and exclude case studies that involved ethical or personal issues that might make them unsuitable: for example, we have been offered problems caused by extra-marital affairs between other managers in the organization.

Once the problems were selected, we allocated them to the groups we had drawn up before the residential session began. As far as possible these consultancy groups contained a balance of age, gender and organizational experience. Some groups needed minor changes when for example two people from the same group were to be clients. We then checked that clients were happy to work with the groups to which we had allocated their problems.

The live case study was planned to take up Day 2 of the two-day residential session. On the evening of Day 1 we met with everyone to explain the aim and structure of the activity. The consultancy groups met the same evening in their allocated rooms and clients visited them to explain very briefly the nature of their specific problem. Throughout Day 2 the consultancy groups worked on the clients' problems, with clients visiting at agreed times to answer questions and provide information. In the afternoon each consultancy group made a formal presentation to its own client who provided immediate feedback to the group on the usefulness and applicability of the recommendations.

After the residential session, feedback from participants about the live consultancy case study exercise was very positive. Here are three examples:

- 'The speed with which our group homed in on the key issues and reached practical solutions that could be proposed to our client proved to me that the module contents had been consolidated and that the effort I have put into the programme has been worth while.'
- 'It [the live case study] has enhanced my awareness of how valuable the programme has been to me as a management development vehicle to complement existing knowledge and skills that I have gained through practical, in-the-field experience.'
- 'The exercise made me really appreciate the worth and global validity of the material studied so far in the programme.'

Our first run-through had been successful, but we needed to make some improvements to the original model. How did we change it and why?

'Minders' to reduce clients' stress

We knew that the model was live, but were unprepared for the emotional stress experienced by participants who became clients. Clients found it very difficult to cope with the changed nature of their relationship with other members of the programme. During the exercise, clients almost immediately lost their group membership as participants on an MBA programme and became outsiders. The staff team was as shocked as the clients by the speed with which the group became 'consultants'. As the consultants cohered in their group the helpful, volunteering client seemed to become for them an external target, a manifestation of an organizational problem, no longer a course colleague. Our assumptions that the consultants might act as if they had been paid to undertake the consultancy and demonstrate politeness and customer service were somewhat confounded by the MBA cultural attitude of 'We'll sort this' that seemed to prevail.

The clients also experienced stress because of:

- loss of ownership of the problem, as the consultancy group took it over and excluded the client from the problem-solving process, other than as a supplier of information;
- frustration in seeing a group apparently go off target as they approached the problem in a way that the client could not understand;
- highs and lows of Day 2, in terms of whether or not the client would get a workable solution;
- the possibility of encountering a group whose members did not appear to address the problem well.

It was clear to us that clients were feeling isolated, interrogated and under great pressure. Many described themselves as 'reeling' out of consultancy sessions. One solution might have been to include the client in the consultancy group, but an important aspect of the exercise was to see what solutions could be generated by a group of managers who were external to the problem. We therefore decided that rather than include the client in the consultancy group we would build in formal support for clients to enable them to cope with this stressful role. All clients now have a member of staff, a 'minder', who stays with them throughout the day. The minder's role is to:

- protect the client from overzealous interrogation;
- hold debrief sessions with the client, outside the consultancy meetings;
- capture the learning, because the day is fast paced;
- observe the client–consultancy group interactions;
- help manage the client's expectations through the highs and lows of the day, reminding him or her that, whatever the outcome from the consultancy group, benefits and learning would flow from six hours of thinking about the problem and questioning the group's approach to it.

We now hold an initial meeting with clients on the afternoon of the first day of the residential session to talk to them about the above issues and to answer any questions. Throughout the second day, clients also attend frequent debriefing sessions with their minders, other clients and the rest of the staff team. At these meetings we all share reflections and observations and prepare for the next session. The clients also form themselves into a group for Day 2 to help counteract the potential loneliness of the client role. Feedback from clients since we made these changes suggests that they have gone a long way towards alleviating the potential stress of the client role.

Formal sessions to generate live cases to reduce staff stress

Staff stress mainly arose from now knowing until lunchtime on Day 1 whether there would be sufficient live cases to enable us to run the exercise. Our problem seemed not to be that managers had no problems that were suitable: far from it.

Most of them had a number of problems they were facing. Our problem was more that the managers were reluctant to volunteer for a variety of reasons. We therefore decided we would introduce a formal session to generate enough live cases to work on. At the start of a residential session, in the event of there being too fiew problems, we now ask participants to form groups of approximately five members. These groups work together for 20 minutes to generate two or more problems that might be used for consultancy case studies. It seems to us that, by working in small groups and discussing potential problems with their peers, participants are much more willing to come forward as clients. In our experience, each group always produces at least two problems. In some groups, all five members offer problems.

Adding a coordinator

We have found it useful to have one member of the staff team who, throughout the exercise, acts only as a coordinator or 'sweeper' and who does not work with a client. Since there can be as many as 9 or 10 consultancy groups operating at the same time, one person needs to have an overview of the whole activity. The coordinator ensures throughout the exercise that everyone keeps to time and answers any questions that individuals or groups may have.

The live consultancy case study model today

As a result of the changes that we made to the original model and our experience of running it on many different occasions, our current model runs as follows. Day 1 is spent on activities focused on reflective practice and deals with issues of managerial and personal relevance. In addition to these activities, if there are insufficient case studies to work on, a 20-minute session is used to generate them.

During the lunch break the staff team gets further details from the volunteers about the nature of their problems and what they hope the consultancy group will produce for them. This helps the team to determine which problems will offer the best learning opportunity for participants.

After the tea break, the consultancy groups are announced and form together to undertake a team-building exercise. During this time the staff team meets with the clients to help each one to clarify the nature of his or her problem and what he or she wants from the consultants.

After briefing everyone about the nature of the exercise, we distribute timetables and the consultants meet to consider group process issues. Meanwhile we brief clients about the implications of their role and answer their questions. We explain that their first visit to their consultancy group is to indicate briefly the nature of the problem the group will be addressing, so that the consultants can 'sleep on it'. Since the clients' minders have not yet joined the residential session, this first visit to the group is strictly limited to 10 minutes. Table 12.1 summarizes Day 1.

Table 12.1 *Summary of the live consultancy case study, Day 1*

Day 1	Groups	Staff
9.30 am	Welcome and introductions. Request for case studies (if necessary 20 minutes in small groups to generate more).	
1.00 pm	Lunch.	Meet case study volunteers: get further details of issue and desired outcomes. Select case studies to be used.
3.30 pm	Tea.	Meet with volunteers and inform them of selected cases, give rationale and thank those whose cases weren't selected.
3.50 pm	Team-building exercise in consultancy groups.	Meet with clients to discuss cases.
4.35 pm	Briefing for case study exercise: timetables distributed.	
4.45 pm	Consultancy groups convene to identify the qualities and strengths each person brings to group working.	Meet with clients to brief first visit to group.
8.30 pm	Meet in base rooms for first client visit (10 minutes) to introduce problem and outline desired outcomes.	

On Day 2, additional staff members join the core team as minders for the clients. These staff members need to be well briefed about the nature of the activity and in particular the role they play in it, especially since they have not been present on Day 1.

The role that minders play during the exercise is complex. It has elements of all of the following roles:

- facilitator to ensure the smooth running of the exercise and to enable the learning of the client and the consultant group;
- to push forward the boundaries of their own learning;
- supporter to the client when he or she feels alienated from the group;
- caretaker to protect the client from the facilitator, to ensure the smooth running of the exercise and to enable the learning of the client and the consultant group;
- mentor to establish rapport with the client and provide advice and feedback;

Table 12.2 *Summary of the live consultancy case study, Day 2*

Day 2	Consultancy Groups	Clients and Minders
9.15 am	Meet in base rooms to: define the problem; identify questions to ask client	Meet: for clients to be introduced to minders; to debrief after first visit; to clarify nature of relationship between client and group.
9.45 am	Second client visit (1 hour). Work with client to: obtain further information; agree terms of reference; agree outcomes.	Second client visit (with minders).
10.45 am	Work together.	Debrief second client visit with minders.
11.00 am	Coffee.	Coffee and debrief (continued).
11.15 am	Work together.	Meet together to: share observations; reflect on process; prepare approach to presentation.
12.00 noon	Can meet with client if required – groups need to pre-book sessions.	Can meet with group if pre-booked.
1.00 pm	Lunch.	Lunch.
2.00 pm	Presentations in base rooms: presentation (20 minutes); client feedback and discussion (10 minutes); observer feedback (10 minutes); general discussion (15 minutes).	Presentations. Minders brief group about next exercise.
3.00 pm	Evaluate learning from working as a consultancy group. Flip chart learning.	Evaluate learning from being a client (main hall). Flip chart.
3.30 pm	Plenary: each group outlines project and solutions (3 minutes). Poster learning from working as a group.	Clients give feedback to groups. Poster learning from acting as a clients.
4.00 pm	Close.	Close.

- coach when guiding and encouraging a client being hijacked by the group;
- process observer of client and consultancy group throughout the exercise.

It is important that minders hold back from providing solutions for the group. This can be particularly difficult for those staff used to a more interventionist role: many have commented on this aspect of the work. Allowing the groups to generate their own learning provides a different set of education rewards, which minders happily acknowledge even when they think the 'wrong' solution is being offered, or the 'wrong' questioning approach taken. Minders need to trust in the process, especially when it seems as if the group will not deliver a useful outcome. During the debriefing sessions, there is time for staff to offer their own ideas to the client about possible solutions if it seems that the group is unlikely to produce anything workable. Our own experience is that at the final presentation even what appeared to be the most unpromising of groups can produce good solutions for the client. The progress that groups make between the second client visit and the final presentation can be outstanding.

Throughout the day the consultancy groups work on the clients' problems. Clients, with their minders, visit the groups at agreed times to answer questions and provide information. The length of these visits is strictly limited to prevent groups spending too much time gathering information and too little generating solutions. Additionally, one of the aims of the consultancy exercise is to show how much can be achieved in such a short time. In the debriefing sessions that follow these visits, it can be useful if client and minder make independent notes about what they perceived to be the important points, before they begin their discussions. Following the presentations, both clients and consultants reflect in their respective groups on their learning from the activity. The consultancy groups, in particular, find it hard to let go of the problem they have been working on so intensely. Members of staff usually suggest that the groups take a few minutes' break and then re-form to reflect on their learning.

The residential session ends with a plenary during which the learning from the exercise is shared. Each group briefly outlines the problem its members worked on together with their recommendations. Clients are encouraged to voice their appreciation for the work of the group. Both consultants and clients describe the nature of their learning.

Learning outcomes promoted by the live consultancy case study

We argue that the live consultancy case study promotes five types of learning outcome better than any other method we know, although it would be impossible to devise controlled experiments to prove we are right. These five types of learning outcome are: integration of theory and practice; achieving holistic learning;

offering insights into other organizations; providing high-intensity group learning; and the subtle nature of clients' learning.

Integration of theory and practice

In developing solutions, the consultancy groups often use the models and frameworks that have been introduced during the MBA programme. This juxtaposition, of what are often generalized high-level models with the complex reality offered by the problems presented, creates an atmosphere in which the models are challenged and applied in order to provide useful outcomes. This analytical and critical process, combined with the practical experience of the members of the consultancy group, produces individual solutions that avoid the standard approaches commonly generated with written case material.

Achieving holistic learning

Participants perceive the live consultancy case study as being highly relevant to their experience and so it can lead to 'significant learning' (Rogers, 1969). In addition, it generates commitment and empathy among participants and so promotes whole-person learning (Rogers, 1969). It is difficult for participants to distance themselves from the learning vehicle. This is not a written case study of an organization that means very little to them. The 'case study' belongs initially to one of their colleagues with whom they have worked throughout the MBA programme. As their client, this colleague is being open about an area of work that is proving difficult and is asking for help. Participants can often closely identify with the situations in which the clients find themselves. As a result, the consultancy groups exhibit a high level of personal commitment to what they are doing. They feel a strong responsibility to the clients in terms of delivering a workable solution, which can then be taken back and implemented. After the residential session, some clients even update their consultancy group about senior management's response to the solution offered.

Offering insights into other organizations

The process of client–group consultation provides an opportunity for the group members to become immersed in the culture of an organization different from their own. This very rapid immersion creates a period of cognitive dissonance that is the basis for powerful client and consultant learning. Participants may for the first time be faced with trade union constraints, or the different ethos of working in the public/private sector, or ethical considerations. From this they can develop recognition of the limitations of certain approaches when applied to other sectors or disciplines and an appreciation of the relationship between academic models and experience, and their relative importance.

Providing high-intensity group learning

Because of the holistic nature of the learning process in which participants engage, the group learning is thrown into a much sharper focus than we have experienced with other group activities. The group has a clear aim: to present the client with a workable solution to the problem. There is a high level of personal commitment to this aim: because of the relationship the group has with the client, the group members really want to help. These factors, combined with the tight deadlines within which the aim must be achieved, serve to produce an intense group experience that provides valuable learning.

The subtle nature of clients' learning

We had assumed that the clients might obtain some extremely useful operational recommendations, but the bulk of the learning would be with the consultants. In fact it appears that the clients can gain some profound insights into themselves, their working lives, the behaviour of others and the nature of learning. The following are some typical responses from clients about this experience:

- 'We've worked through the problem time and time again, but it's a long time since we've asked ourselves some of these basic questions.'
- 'They asked some fundamental questions.'
- 'The group [members] are distant from the subject and so can provide a view that is uninfluenced by personal feelings.'
- 'Explaining something to someone else gave me insights I hadn't had before.'

At the final plenary sessions, the feedback given by clients is sometimes of a deep and emotional nature. It can be in the form of gratitude for a genuinely novel solution to a long-running problem. More often clients explain how they see themselves within their work context in a different light, with consequently profound effects. Very occasionally there has been an angry backlash resulting from clients' perceptions of their treatment during the process.

Variations on the model

For non-residential programmes

The live consultancy case study model is not restricted to residential programmes. We have used it to integrate theory and practice as a one-day activity during five-day intensive modules on change management and information systems management.

Taking forward the learning

An extra activity has also been added to the model to carry forward the learning from the case study. On the day following the exercise, participants were asked to review what they had written about their learning on Day 2 and add any new insights. The whole group's 'lessons' were later collected, typed up and sent out to participants.

The use of a reflective diary

Clients have also been encouraged to keep a reflective diary. The day is fast moving and this enables them to have a record of important insights and observations from the exercise.

Conclusions

As well as the learning outcomes detailed above, the live consultancy case study seems to have other benefits that extend beyond the actual activity itself:

- *A process for developing staff as facilitators of learning.* Taking part in a live consultancy case study moves staff away from centre stage in the learning experience. The structure of the exercise places them in the role of observers of the consultancy group process, not disseminators of knowledge. The structure prevents them from stepping in with help and guidance and in this way promotes learner autonomy.
- *The value of experience and academic knowledge.* The case study creates a symbiotic relationship in which both the participant and the academic benefit. It places value on both practitioner experience and academic knowledge and creates a two-way flow of knowledge and experience. This enables the live consultancy case study to be viewed as a microcosm of the interaction of higher education with its environment. The two engage, and new knowledge is created.
- *Students' as skilled practitioners.* The problems that are offered as live consultancy case studies provide staff with a valuable insight into the problems currently facing managers in organizations. In addition, throughout the exercise, staff members see participants not in their student roles but in their roles as skilled managers. This can lead to a shift in perceptions and it emphasizes that in the work context our 'students' are often highly skilled practitioners.
- *A process for reviewing course relevance.* Every time the live consultancy case study has been used it has brought to the surface a range of course and organizational issues that are at the heart of any programme of post-experience or postgraduate study. Besides discussions of case method process, we may have to review more fundamental issues regarding the relevance of individual module content and its sequencing, and even the structure of the MBA programme. This questioning approach to 'Why do we do what we do?' and 'How do we do it?' is perhaps the most important organizational outcome of the live consultancy case study method.

In designing the method, we believed that real problems in the 'here and now' offered more scope for significant learning than imaginary problems or edited descriptions of the 'there and then'. We also believed that participants learn more from learning experiences that exercise the emotions as well as the intellect. As a result of our experiences in using this activity, we believe it is not limited to use on MBA programmes, but can be used as a generic model on all postgraduate practitioner courses.

References

Megginson, D (1996) Planned and emergent learning: consequences for development, *Management Learning*, **27** (4), pp 411–28
Revans, R W (1983) *The ABC of Action Learning*, Chartwell-Bratt, Kent
Rogers, C (1969) *Freedom to Learn*, Merrill, Columbus, OH

Contact

Suzanne O'Hara
Brighton Business School
University of Brighton
Mithras House
Lewes Road
Brighton BN2 4AT
e-mail: S.Ohara@bton.ac.uk

Chapter 13

Building and maintaining distributed communities of practice: knowledge management in the OUBS MBA

Stephen Little, Wendy Fowle and Paul Quintas

Building and maintaining 'distributed communities of practice' is at the heart of B823 Managing Knowledge, a second-stage elective added to the Open University Business School (OUBS) MBA in October 1999. The course content reflects the expertise of its multidisciplinary development team headed by Paul Quintas, the first professor of knowledge management in the UK. In B823, technologies that support knowledge strategies are examined along with current best practice in knowledge management. A key feature of the course is the use of established and state-of-the-art knowledge technologies in creating the distance learning environment.

The original model for the Open University as a whole, founded in 1969, was one of mass delivery of a highly developed product. Radio and television broadcasts fronted purpose-designed print and audio media, and individual study was leavened with face-to-face activities in tutorial groups and at residential schools.

During the 30-odd years of the OU's existence, the generation and transmission of knowledge has been transformed by the same information and communication technologies that have also facilitated globalization of the world economy. It is now feasible to build and maintain distributed communities of practice among tutors and students, despite the distances between them.

The key to successful distance learning is that students engage with their materials at a time and place of their own choosing, rather than learning synchronously, face-to-face. However, electronic support of synchronous communication is also proving valuable at the OU. In B823, course objectives are served through asynchronous text conferencing using FirstClass™, plus synchronous voice-text-and-graphics conferencing using Lyceum, a new Open University software system implemented and evaluated for the first time in 1999–2000.

Objectives

The 'knowledge economy' is a term for an emerging global system driven by falling transaction costs delivered by information and communication technologies (ICTs). It requires working practices involving close collaboration across increasing distances, both physical and cultural. Different nations and regions are becoming increasingly linked, within networked and globalized organizations and alliances. As a consequence, management education is seeking a corresponding realignment. A concern with the accurate transmission of known information within a stable environment is being succeeded by a focus on critical exploration and the generation of new and relevant knowledge for the use of individuals, groups, businesses and not-for-profit organizations operating in a dynamic environment with uncertain boundaries. Just as business is discovering new forms of collaboration, exploring new communities, inventing new forms of enterprise, seeking resources, finding information and learning through interacting electronically on a huge scale, so business education must anticipate the consequent demands on graduates.

We were members of a team developing an elective in managing knowledge for the OUBS MBA to deal with a range of issues central to the effective management of knowledge and intellectual capital. B823 Managing Knowledge consists of 13 one-week study units. Students must complete three tutor-marked assignments, attend a short residential school and pass a written examination. Units deal with communication, the cost and value of knowledge, and the process of knowledge management within and between organizations. Intellectual capital and its measurement are dealt with in some detail, along with intellectual property rights, and the management of knowledge and innovation. The nature of and relationship between tacit and explicit knowledge is a central concern. The use of brands to encapsulate knowledge and values and the human resource dimensions of knowledge work are also dealt with.

Developments in business practice, in response to globalization (eg the 'network enterprise': Castells, 1996), suggest that such forms of collective practice will become increasingly significant during the career spans of current MBA students. B823 allows students and staff to create a collectivity through technologies that support new forms of community of practice, a key concept of knowledge management. The support of a vibrant community across distance is central to the course's success.

Context

The Open University

The UK's Open University (OU) was established in 1969, and more than 2 million people have studied with it since then (see http://www.open.ac.uk). The OU specializes in supported distance learning offered nationally and internationally. OU students study in their own homes or workplaces, in their own time, supported by locally based tutors. There is a network of 330 regional study centres in the UK and abroad and, for many courses, a residential school component. Media such as computer conferencing, CD ROMs and interactive Web sites provide students with support, in addition to the core resources of printed material, TV and radio broadcasts, audio- and videotapes, computer software and home experiment kits.

The Open University Business School

The Open University Business School (OUBS) was established in 1983 and now has some 30,000 students in 38 nations; 7,000 of these are participants in the MBA programme, launched in 1989, 2,500 of them outside the United Kingdom (see http://www3.open.ac.uk/oubs/). OUBS students are usually practising managers in public, private, not-for-profit and profit organizations. They draw on their diverse experience to contribute key resources to their learning environment. OUBS has about 250 permanent staff and 850 locally based part-time tutors, now known as associate lecturers, who provide face-to-face, telephone, online and correspondence tuition. Students often establish their own face-to-face and/or online self-help study groups.

Since 1991, OUBS has been developing computer-mediated communication (CMC) in MBA courses. At first conferences were provided, for students and tutors who wanted to use them, covering topics of the students' choosing. Typically 20–30 per cent of students (100–200 individuals per course) took up this opportunity. The academics' role developed from passive monitoring of these conferences to more interactive facilitation or e-moderating. Salmon's (2000a) action research identified distinctive e-moderating skills, and her five-step model is now widely used to train OUBS tutors in how to foster an effective online community among their students. The model is now a resource for developing skills appropriate to both synchronous and asynchronous CMC (see Salmon, 2000b).

Rationale

Six drivers of knowledge management

In the first unit of B823, students learn about six factors responsible for the high profile of knowledge management in the last decade of the 20th century:

1. *Wealth from knowledge.* Company value has come to be seen to be increasingly dependent on intangible assets, knowledge assets, intellectual capital and intellectual property.
2. *Human resources: people as the locus of knowledge.* Following the downsizing, early redundancies and outsourcing of the 1980s and early 1990s, organizations have rediscovered the importance of people. People are seen to possess knowledge, to create knowledge and value, and retain organizational memory. And they can leave, taking this knowledge with them.
3. *Knowledge interdependence.* Organizations in all sectors have become more mutually dependent. Even the largest companies must collaborate in order to deliver new products and services. Cross-boundary knowledge sharing creates new forms of knowledge interdependence between organizations.
4. *Organizational learning.* The global pace of change requires continuous regeneration of organizational knowledge bases: organizations and the people within them must be continually learning. The need to absorb knowledge across organizational boundaries is a key knowledge management issue.
5. *Technology: limits and potentials.* Information technology reached a threshold in the 1990s when the limits of traditional information systems were recognized. There has been a growing recognition that most of the information and knowledge that managers use in making decisions was not captured in computer-based information systems. At the same time, the communications paradigm has shown real potential: developments in communication technologies have led to the World Wide Web and other knowledge technologies.
6. *Innovation and knowledge creation.* Competitive advantage is more and more seen to be gained through innovation, which depends on knowledge creation, knowledge sharing and knowledge application.

Knowledge management as a new topic?

These six drivers of knowledge management underpin B823, but in many organizations there is a strong bias towards some at the expense of others. Onc focus eveident from any Web search on knowledge management topics is on explicit, codified, formal information capture. Another is on technology providing communication channels for knowledge sharing. Elsewhere the human resource and cultural issues surrounding networks, team working and knowledge sharing are emphasized.

The importance of knowledge is not a new idea. Drucker (1969), Penrose (1959) and even Alfred Marshall back in 1890 referred to the role that knowledge plays in the economy. Recently there has been new interest (Grant, 1996; Spender, 1996) in the notion of a knowledge-based theory of the firm, first explored by Penrose (1959) and others. Nonaka (1994) has developed a conceptual framework to account for how knowledge is shared between individuals and social groups, through the interplay of tacit and explicit knowledge. Cook and Seely Brown (1999) have built upon this type of approach, emphasizing first the importance of knowledge held by groups, and second the importance of knowing as action. In a contribution that owes much to Schön's (1983) notions of the reflective practitioner, they propose that knowledge is a tool of knowing: knowledge is drawn upon in the context of practice, that is, in the process of knowing as evidenced in action.

B823 also draws upon a different but related perspective articulated by Gibbons *et al* (1994), who proposed a radical rethink about how knowledge is produced or created. They challenged the view that knowledge is created in formal research environments, held in libraries and controlled by disciplines or communities of scientists, specialist professionals and scholars. This is Mode 1 knowledge. The new focus is on Mode 2 knowledge that is created in use, ie knowledge created by practitioners in their own contexts. Such knowledge may be transient, and a high percentage of it will be implicit (or tacit) rather than explicit. Mode 2 knowledge may be the key source of competitive advantage, but is largely ignored by economists, and is not easily captured by ICT systems. Mode 1 knowledge focuses on hierarchical, discipline-based homogeneous knowledge. Mode 2 is interdisciplinary, created by practitioners and embedded in reflective practice.

These conceptual themes point towards an emphasis in B823 on practice, knowing (as well as knowledge), learning and social contexts. They lead to the concept of communities of practice.

Communities of practice

A community of practice (CoP) is an informal social network in which the engagement of individuals in a joint enterprise is facilitated by a shared repertoire of concepts, actions, tools, story artefacts and discourse (Wenger, 1998). This self-perpetuating group differs from other teams and networks in that, although there is a diversity of experience and background, all members, through extensive communication and shared practice over a period, come to share similar goals and interests, beliefs and value systems without any formal organization. Wenger and Snyder (2000) differentiate between CoPs, formal workgroups, project teams and informal networks. In each of the latter cases the groups are brought together to work on specific projects or problems. CoPs stand out from the other groups in that they are informally bound.

CoPs enable expertise to be shared and best practice to emerge, freely and informally. The commitment to the CoP members overrides any reluctance to share knowledge, and the community, as it is cultivated, accepts the boundaries that their knowledge-sharing activities fall within. It is this trust among the CoP that demonstrates its uniqueness and ability to go beyond the team and networking practices.

CoPs enable learning through shared experience, creating knowledge that is socially held. In the case of a newly developing CoP (relevant to B823), all members of the community have different knowledge and expertise. Each member is differently knowledgeable about his or her own sphere of existing expertise and at the same time differently novice about others' areas, and about the context in which new practice-based expertise is emerging. Engagement in the new context of practice involves progressive negotiations between 'experts' and novices. Each member of the community assumes the role of novice in order to learn about aspects of others' expertise and, simultaneously, to learn through engagement in practice.

Learning in an established CoP may also be a guided process. Guided joint social activity mediates experience, decontextualizing it in order to enable the sharing of knowledge. Thus another vital role of the CoP is to provide a support structure between those who have greater knowledge and experience in a particular subject than others. Such practice draws on individuals at all levels and enables reciprocity as new problems and issues emerge. It enables individuals to sound out new ideas/new concepts prior to putting them into practice in the workplace or other environment. Such sounding out is the key to drawing on the experience and expertise of the members of the community, learning from other people's mistakes, what works and what doesn't. The CoP provides a safe haven.

In order to exist, however, CoPs must be provided with the infrastructure and support to emerge and be maintained. This involves initially bringing the right people together, whose goals and interests are the same, and then to allow the communities to thrive. The key issue is that CoPs should not be over-managed.

There are several advantages of being a member of a CoP. In a business context they can help drive strategy and also help to start new lines of business. They enable problems to be solved more quickly by drawing on the wide range of expertise within the community and help to develop and transfer best practice. This expertise also acts to develop professional skills for those less experienced (Wenger and Snyder, 2000). Moreover the social dynamics are fun: 'they act as resources to each other, exchanging information, making sense of situations, sharing new tricks and ideas, as well as keeping each other company and spicing up each other's working days' (Wenger, 1998: 47). In B823, communities of practice are both objects of study and a means of learning.

Description

Setting up a sustainable but distributed community of practice across the cohorts of B823 presentations involved tutors and students in face-to-face sessions and use of synchronous as well as asynchronous conferencing media. This is the story of how we did it.

The tutor team

For the first presentation of B823 we recruited and trained 78 academically qualified tutors with a wide range of backgrounds and expertise. Some were employed full time by other universities and colleges, but others were practising managers.

Because knowledge management is a new field and because they needed to become familiar with the new technology, all the tutors studied the course as part of their training. This is not common practice at the OU. The training programme included two face-to-face weekend sessions, plus extensive use of online media including groupware (see below). It resulted in a strong community of tutors who continue to support each other daily via electronic media.

Once student numbers and geographical distribution are confirmed for each year, the majority of tutors are offered a contract. Some elect to tutor two student groups, but groups averaged 13 students for the first presentation, rising to 16 for subsequent presentations.

The students

OUBS MBA students are all practising managers studying part time. Up until 2002, 700–850 students had taken B823 in each of the three presentations (October to May). Most were in the British Isles and Western Europe. Almost all were part-way through their MBA, although some alumni and others enrolled to take B823 as a stand-alone course. From 2001, B823 is being presented by the University of South Africa (UNISA), and from 2002 by the Open University of Hong Kong (OUHK), as part of their respective programmes.

Communication

Core learning for B823 is via printed material, multimedia presentations and activities, and audio programmes, all studied in student-directed learning mode. Face-to-face contact in local study centres and residential sessions remains an important aspect of the course, but support for students is also provided by media that enable student–student and student–tutor interactions. Standard OUBS media include CD ROMs, asynchronous computer conferencing and e-mail, as well as the Web. For B823, groupware (see below) enables students to interact synchronously with each other and their tutor.

Face-to-face support

The course has a day school, scheduled early in the programme to bring students and their tutor face-to-face and establish the social group. They can then work effectively from home as a virtual team using communication technology. The group also meets for two structured face-to-face tutorials later in the course.

In addition, a residential school provides an opportunity for students to spend an uninterrupted period focusing on the course and working in groups. The B823 residential schools span a weekend, and each school is attended by around 80 students and seven tutors. Residential schools are an opportunity for students to meet a wider group of fellow students and tutors, and to work intensively in group activities designed to enhance the course and the learning experience. Such activities must be delivered across a range of locations to groups of students who in turn are expected to operate outside their normal tutorial groups. Students are required to apply and explore aspects of knowledge management in the context of various cases and scenarios.

Asynchronous electronic support for learning with FirstClass™

B823 includes complementary forms of electronic support for learning. Lyceum (see below) is synchronous, and FirstClass™ (see http://www.softarc.com) is asynchronous, though both have a synchronous text-chat option for exchange of typed messages in real time.

B823 uses FirstClass™ in its tutor training and for tutors and students during the course, to enable discussion and problem solving, drawing upon the community of practice's knowledge and expertise (see http://www.c2t2.ca/landonline/ for alternative platforms).

For the tutors' initial training in 1999, the online conference was divided into the sub-categories shown in Figure 13.1. At course level these make up a typical set of resources. At the level of the business school and the OU, FirstClass™ provides a virtual campus across which the library, administration and other faculties can be accessed. Figure 13.1, a screen dump originally in colour, shows the Senior Common Room, discussion sub-conferences for tutor-marked assignments (TMAs), resources on knowledge management, etc.

During this initial training the tutors supported each other in working through and understanding the materials, and conducting debates on key issues. They became a distributed knowledge-sharing and learning community, which has been maintained through the first and subsequent presentations of B823. They still contribute new material and references to new sources.

When the course went live on 30 October 1999, the FirstClass™ conference was divided in two: the main conference was for tutors, the course team and students, and the Senior Common Room for tutors and the course team only. Sub-conferences evolved later. In addition, each tutor group had its own private conference.

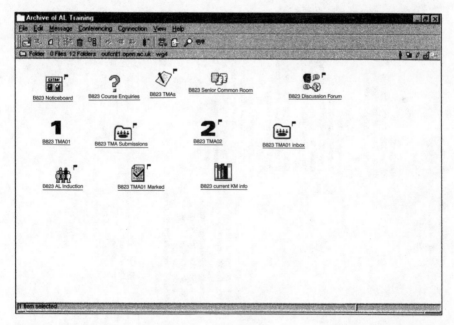

Figure 13.1 *FirstClass™: a screen dump of an online B823 tutor training conference*

The conferences contained prime examples of how the tutor community was able to draw on the expertise of its members. In the first presentation, although most of the course texts were already in print, the tutors jointly developed additional support material and supported and advised each other in getting to grips with the new material. Ideas and/or questions were raised, followed by 'strings' (threads) of contributions from other tutors based on their own understanding, with references to other material.

From a student perspective, FirstClass™ conferencing and developing a CoP is clearly valuable. By discussing course concepts, by grappling with new ideas and what they mean, students also began sharing their own understanding of the course. They produced summaries of materials and new conceptual frameworks, posting these to the conference for all to see, use and comment upon. Figure 13.2 provides an example of a book summary prepared and posted in the conference by Paul Keeton, a B823 student.

Such knowledge sharing supports the definition of a CoP as based on knowledge that is provided voluntarily. In this case (and many others since), students are willing to share their own understanding of the book to support and assist fellow students and indeed tutors, irrespective of the work required to produce such a document.

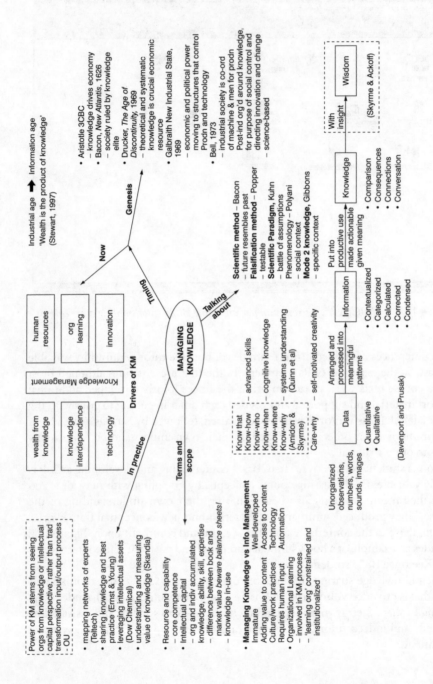

Figure 13.2 *Lyceum: a book summary prepared and posted by a student*

Synchronous electronic support for learning with Lyceum

Lyceum groupware provides a synchronous electronic means of sharing visual representations for discussion and annotation, just as flip charts and OHPs are used in face-to-face tutorials. It was developed by the OU's Knowledge Media Institute (Buckingham Shum, 2000). It delivers audio communication and a shared graphic workspace or whiteboard via a single line. Several tutors have developed 'mind maps' collectively to explore issues around intellectual capital audits. Contributions have been flagged with identifiers by the Lyceum software.

Lyceum provides online meetings and tutorials, with groups able to create separate 'rooms' during a session. This allows a mix of breakout activities and plenary discussion, as with face-to-face meetings. Materials for discussion, such as diagrams or images, are distributed to tutors via FirstClass™ e-mail, and loaded into Lyceum for the session (see Figure 13.3, for example). The screen grabber can capture images from anywhere on the Internet. In Figure 13.3, Bob Roberts, a tutor, is waiting in his 'room' for students to arrive, having set up a screen grab of material for discussion. Sketches and diagrams representing the outcome of a discussion can be captured and archived by the participants.

Lyceum represents the new technologies available for the support of knowledge-based organizations and provides students with experiential learning opportunities. Several commercial applications, such as Microsoft's NetMeeting, offer

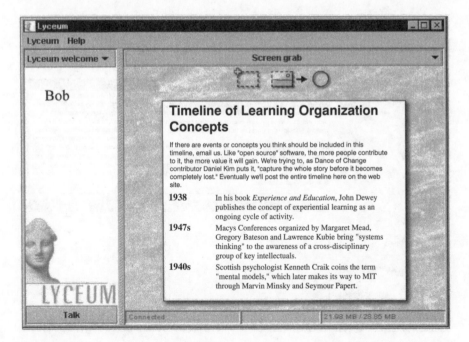

Figure 13.3   *Lyceum: Bob Roberts, a tutor, is waiting in his 'room' for students to arrive*

some of the facilities of Lyceum, but its precise combination of features reflects OU practice and priorities.

B823 students, in small teams, work remotely on assignments and interact in online tutorials, with reflection on this process as a core learning objective. The teams' work is scheduled and directed by students, not tutors, but for the first presentation four formal Lyceum tutorial sessions were prepared and scheduled by the course team and run by the tutors. Later in the course, tutors and students scheduled *ad hoc* Lyceum sessions; for example, one was on revision for the final examination.

Lyceum required preparation of tutorial resources designed for the new medium. Figure 13.4 is an example of tutor notes to support making a concept map, for a tutorial exercise on brand identity and value. Online training sessions were held to give tutors hands-on experience and awareness of the process of using the medium effectively to facilitate learning. To prepare the resources, we set up a tutorial working group with academic, tutoring and human–computer interaction (HCI) design expertise. The group tried out prototypes of sessions in Lyceum to test the effectiveness of the materials and the feasibility of running the tutorials.

Tutor resource packs were provided for each tutorial, setting out the learning objectives, a plan for the sessions (ranging from a single hour to several sessions), visual aids and discussion topics. Tutorials included preparatory asynchronous textual discussion using FirstClass™. In conventional tutorials it is normal for the

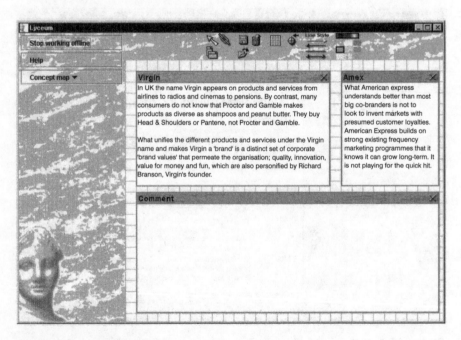

Figure 13.4 *Lyceum: tutor notes to support making a concept map*

more confident tutors to weave their own variations around such resources, whilst others follow the resources more closely. Given the novelty of the medium, a detailed script was supplied, which gave clear instructions to tutors (eg 'Switch to the whiteboard with the Nonaka matrix loaded') and what to tell students (eg 'Now go to your breakout rooms to discuss Q3; record your notes in a single concept node ready to paste into the plenary concept map; in 15 minutes each group should return here'). Learning from these activities was incorporated in support material for subsequent presentations.

The Lyceum Student Tutor Support Team was established to complement the existing support for the Lyceum groupware by providing regular online support and guidance to tutors and students. The support team consisted of two tutors who had completed the training programme but did not have a current student group. The sessions were at first simply reactive to student and tutor problems, but they developed into a 'one-stop market place' of reactive and proactive activities: students and tutors sought answers to problems, obtained information about past sessions or just 'dropped in' as browsers or lurkers.

During the first presentation, this support to the B823 CoP was invaluable in helping students and tutors surmount the problems surrounding adoption of the new groupware. It reminded us that one function of a CoP, which Wenger (1998) illustrates, is enabling workers to get through a working day.

Evaluation

The OU evaluates all its courses, and teams that deploy major innovations in learning and teaching are expected to report success and failure for the benefit of other teams. Evaluation of B823 is carried out routinely by the OU's Institute of Educational Technology but the course team has also conducted its own studies. During the first presentation, the use of Lyceum and FirstClass™ was monitored formally. The discussions and interactions in both media generated material of value to subsequent learners. FirstClass™ conferences are archived during course presentations, but the course team now uses standard Web technology to provide a more widely accessible shared resource.

In this brief account of the development and presentation of B823, a new course in a new area for management education, we have focused on the successful creation of a supported, but distributed, community of practice at a distance. The communication processes used by B823 tutors and students provide evidence that an informal CoP emerged from the formalized processes of recruiting tutors for and introducing students to the course. Face-to-face meetings at the start brought them together and provided a platform on which the community could develop. The tutors' commitment throughout the training programme was a landmark in building and maintaining this community, because they tackled together problems with materials and software and developed good practice for when the course went live.

Salmon's (2000) five-stage model for e-moderating offers a framework for evaluating and comparing the activities and support required by asynchronous and synchronous forms of electronic conferencing (see http://oubs.open.ac.uk/e-moderating):

- *Stage 1: access and motivation.* To participate in online learning, students must each have access and know how to use online learning tools. At Stage 1, they need a welcoming and encouraging environment, in which moderators monitor and comment on their efforts, with some 'hand-holding' where necessary. They learn the difference between one-to-one e-mail and conferencing. In asynchronous mode, tutors help with the introduction of outside resources and support newcomers. In synchronous mode, online meetings and discussions move beyond the group of activists to include others.
- *Stage 2: online socialization.* During Stage 2, participants establish their online identities and find others with whom to interact. They master the protocols and etiquette of online communication. Content starts to become important. Online activities promote learning through meaningful and authentic tasks. Synchronous groups should be attempting the online creation of new learning materials.
- *Stage 3: information exchange.* At this stage participants exchange information relevant to the course. Up to this stage cooperation occurs in that there is support for each person's goals, but the growing engagement of participants dramatically increases the volume of information. E-moderators guide their students through the available material, and help them to learn how to manage the information.
- *Stage 4: knowledge construction.* Course-related group discussions occur and the interaction becomes more collaborative. Communication depends on reaching common understandings. The focus shifts from information content to knowledge process. Students are encouraged to be more technically independent and to engage questions which have no 'right' or 'proper' answers.
- *Stage 5: development.* Participants look for benefits from the system to help them achieve personal goals, explore how to integrate computer conferencing with other forms of learning and reflect on learning processes. They become responsible for their own learning and need little further direct support. The e-moderator's role is usually to stimulate debate, challenge assumptions and promote discussion of course-related issues.

Despite their steep learning curve with Lyceum, tutors and some students reached Stage 5. They certainly learnt about the course content as well as about the new technology they were using.

The mutual support and knowledge sharing between the tutors was a key factor in the success of the first presentation. However much support the central course team provided, the exchange of experiential learning through reflective practice between the tutors was vital. It resulted in a managing knowledge community of practice that has taken on a dynamic of its own, with dialogue continuing across the community well after the end of the course. New debates on knowledge management emerged, and sources and materials were exchanged, essential in such a fast-changing field.

Discussion

Lessons from Lyceum

Tutors and the course team learnt about the new synchronous medium through practice and experiment. Key lessons, rapidly and continually shared via the asynchronous FirstClass™ conferences, included how to:

- manage turn-taking, especially in large group sessions;
- manage silences when images (and sometimes voice) are delayed on the network;
- manage the movement of students between 'rooms';
- pool and present work done in breakout groups;
- deal with technical problems when a student loses his or her connection or is not able to 'attend';
- bring a latecomer up to speed without disrupting ongoing discussion;
- use voice, asynchronous text, and visual media to complement each other when communicating with students;
- use the asynchronous FirstClass™ conferencing and chat tools to prepare for and follow up a Lyceum session;
- take into account the need to be more directive in managing the process in plenary sessions.

These and many other general points were codified in a 'craft skill' handbook that was sent to both tutors and students. However, such documents often remain unread, and process skills in particular can only be genuinely developed through time spent online. Two tutors were employed as 'Lyceum specialists'. Before the course started and during the course's presentation, they ran regular practice sessions. Other tutors knew there would be people synchronously online to talk to, and structured activities or discussion themes relevant to the course such as 'ideas for running tutorial 2' (Buckingham Shum, 2000). Subsequently a report illustrating the best practice from the first presentation was produced.

Lyceum was a major learning experience for tutors and students. Even experienced OUBS tutors very used to asynchronous conferencing found the synchronous sessions a real challenge. Continual learning through reflective practice and exchange among the tutors was a key feature of the programme. Much of this exchange was via Lyceum and FirstClass™ and was captured in a continually evolving 'frequently asked questions' Web site to assist tutors and students. A telephone helpdesk was provided too.

B823 students have identified other software products that offer some of the functionality of Lyceum, and indeed a class of voice groupware is now emerging in the commercial market place. During the 1990s the Open University used both CoSY and FirstClass™ conferencing systems, and students gained value through social learning and pedagogical development. It has taken some time for the OU to appreciate what it means to be literate and socialized in the voice conferencing groupware, and to grasp how student learning can be facilitated. As Sproull and Kiesler (1991) say, technical learning is a prerequisite to the slower and deeper social learning necessary to the effective assimilation of new technologies.

B823 students' enthusiasm for synchronous conferencing was directly related to the amount of travel to face-to-face venues that was eliminated. The Continental and Western Europe region produced the greatest proportions of Lyceum champions. In other regions, students nominally based in the UK but working temporarily as far afield as Australia and the United States were able to participate in online tutorials. Intriguingly, when groups experienced technical difficulties or variable quality of connection, it was usually the most physically remote member of the online group who achieved the loudest and clearest connection.

Some features of Lyceum, such as the online creation of breakout groups, are now reflected in asynchronous conference practice: a corresponding feature is now available to tutors in FirstClass™, enabling sub-groups to be set up at particular points during study.

In the current presentation of B823, use of Lyceum has been made optional, in support of but not substituting for scheduled face-to-face meetings and other informal groups. Elsewhere in the wider OU community, Lyceum is being used in seven language and social science courses, which are developing new practices and supporting technical features (for example, a 'voting' option for groups was requested by Social Sciences).

Lyceum was relaunched in the autumn of 2002 in a new version in which the original licensed voice codec was rewritten. As the software is now entirely the intellectual property of the Open University, it can be used more widely and shared with partners. Across the university a total of 65 groups, involving some 2,500 user accounts, are evaluating the software for both learning and administration.

With the development of a new version of the MBA programme under way, the challenge to OUBS now is to transfer a robust set of skills and technologies for developing distributed communities of practice from a single elective course into the core of the programme as a whole.

References

Buckingham Shum, S (2000) Lyceum: Internet Voice Groupware for Distance Learning, Internal briefing document, Knowledge Media Institute, Open University, Milton Keynes

Castells, M (1996) *The Rise of the Network Society*, Blackwell, Oxford

Cook, S and Brown, S J (1999) Bridging epistemologies: the generative dance between organisational knowledge and organisational knowing, *Organization Science*, **10** (4), pp 381–400

Drucker, P F (1969) *The Age of Discontinuity: Guidelines to our changing society*, Heinemann, London

Gibbons, M *et al* (1994) *The New Production of Knowledge*, Sage, London

Grant, R M (1996) Towards a knowledge-based theory of the firm, *Strategic Management Journal*, **17** (Winter), pp 109–22

Nonaka, I (1994) A dynamic theory of organisational knowledge creation, *Organization Science*, **5** (1), pp 14–37

Penrose, E T (1959) *Theory of the Growth of the Firm*, Blackwell, Oxford

Salmon, G (2000a) *E-moderating: The key to teaching and learning online*, Kogan Page, London

Salmon, G (2000b) Computer mediated conferencing for management learning at the Open University, *Management Learning*, **31** (4), pp 491–502

Schön, D (1983) *The Reflective Practitioner: How professionals think in action*, Basic Books, London

Spender, J C (1996) Making knowledge the basis of a dynamic theory of the firm, *Strategic Management Journal*, **17**, Winter, pp 45–62

Sproull, L and Kiesler, S (1991) *Connections: New ways of working in the networked organization*, MIT Press, Cambridge, MA

Wenger, E (1998) *Communities of Practice*, Cambridge University Press, Cambridge

Wenger, E and Snyder, W (2000) Communities of practice: the organisational frontier, *Harvard Business Review*, **78** (1), pp 139–45

URLs

The background to the development of Lyceum is described at http://kmi.open.ac.uk/people/sbs/talks/Lyceum-CMC-18iv00/.

A technical report on Lyceum and the B823 experience has been produced by Simon Buckingham Shum, Samuel Marshall, John Brier and Tony Evans as Lyceum: Internet Voice Groupware for Distance Learning KMI-TR-100, January, 2001, available at http://kmi.open.ac.uk/publications/papers/kmi-tr-100.pdf.

Contact

Stephen Little
Open University Business School
Walton Hall
Milton Keynes MK7 6AA
e-mail: s.e.little@open.ac.uk

Chapter 14

Assessing student performance

Sue Moon and David Hawkridge

This chapter summarizes and analyses a range of examples of innovative practice in assessing student performance in UK business schools. High student performance is the proof of quality in teaching and learning. Yet the validity and efficiency of methods used for assessing this performance are being questioned. Traditional methods such as essays, short tests and written examinations are giving way to practice better suited to modern courses and the requirements of employers.

In late 2000, when BEST surveyed deans and heads of departments teaching business, management and accounting, they listed their concerns about assessment. A second BEST survey in late 2001 was aimed specifically at finding examples of innovative practice. Innovation does not feature strongly in the literature on assessing student performance in UK higher education. The most fruitful direction for innovation appears to be in electronic assessment, but many questions remain unanswered. The concerns of the deans and heads of departments could possibly be met, however, by one or more of the innovations discussed here, all of which could be adopted elsewhere, given motivation and resources.

The need for new methods of assessing student performance

High student performance is the proof of quality in teaching and learning. For that reason, business schools are delighted when they can announce excellent pass rates and outstanding individual achievements. Equally, they are concerned when their students do not appear to reach expected standards. The blame may be put on the students for not learning or on the teachers for not teaching, but neither may be at fault as much as the methods used for assessing student performance. Are these valid?

All business school teachers have ample experience of being examined, and by and large they have records of success. Most, as students, were examined through traditional means such as essays, tests, three-hour unseen examinations, project reports and dissertations. Most, as teachers, carry on the traditions by using similar methods to assess the performance of their students. Yet there is serious concern about the validity of current methods of assessing student performance.

As Chapter 1 describes, in November 2000, BEST asked deans and heads of departments teaching business, management and accounting in the UK to identify the 'big issues' for them in teaching and learning (Hawkridge, 2001a, 2001b). Among the concerns they expressed on the validity of assessment were:

- Assessment strategies are needed that retain the integrity of the process but reduce the burden on staff.
- The validity of assessment should be maintained despite the increases in volume.
- More programmes should include valid work-based assessment and/or peer assessment.
- Methods should be developed for valid assessment of action learning, including how to tackle the assignment and how to evaluate it.
- Work is needed on the problem of comparing standards achieved by students taking multidisciplinary courses in business and management with those on single-discipline courses.
- The testing of competence in basic skills as well as process thinking should include development of both the type of assessment and its marking.
- The assessment load on students should be reduced, but in a way that is acceptable to tutors.
- Staff competencies and robust electronic platforms must be developed for improved assessment of student performance.

The respondents were also very concerned about the efficiency of current methods of assessing student performance. Among their suggestions were:

- New assessment methods should be adopted to cope with increasing student numbers and reduced contact hours, particularly for largely practical subjects.

- Peer assessment of portfolios should be used for self-development modules.
- Use of case studies in assessment should increase.
- Use of computer-assisted assessment (such as Byzantium software) should support assessment of students in subjects such as management accounting.

These concerns call out for innovation. Indeed, when the deans and heads of department were asked to select (from a list) tasks for the Business Education Support Team, 44 (out of 71) chose 'Improve student assessment strategies and methods'. They ranked this item behind only two others, 'Use electronic resources for learning and teaching' and 'Add, or switch to, e-learning and e-teaching'. These respondents also provided examples of innovations in their business schools. Innovations in assessment were seldom listed, yet they are clearly wanted.

Examples of innovative assessment from the BEST stories

Four of the BEST stories include innovative methods of assessment (Hawkridge, 2002). They cover introductory accounting, public relations, financial accounting and the business environment. Each one safeguards validity and may offer efficiency gains.

Computer-based assessment

As Chapter 6 shows, Byzantium's software for introductory accounting provides students with immediate feedback, so that they can assess their own progress. This form of valid computer-based assessment provides a built-in incentive for students to obtain credit towards the next level of their studies. In Byzantium, students save their assignments to floppy disks for automatic marking. When these disks are returned to them, students can see their assessed work and the marks that have been awarded.

The authors claim that students are motivated by Byzantium to gain numeric accounting skills. As the students use Byzantium on a continuous basis, it helps to spread their workload and they gain confidence as they gradually develop their computing skills and accounting techniques.

High student attendance is reported in the workshops, where tutors can make early diagnoses of vulnerable students and offer them extra support. Students with exam phobia can be identified by the tutors and offered counselling. Hence progression rates can be improved. Although Byzantium is costly in terms of staff resources because of the mode of delivery, the automatic marking offers efficiency gains as well as high validity.

Group and peer assessment

Group and peer assessment comes into the BA in Public Relations at Leeds Metropolitan University (LMU) (see Chapter 8), where a Level 2 module simulates typical scenarios from the public relations industry. The simulation using these scenarios helps students to understand about campaigns and to practise working in small teams, in the public eye and under pressure. The module is assessed through a single group assessment, with peer assessment designed to ensure marks are allocated fairly within groups.

For the simulation students are randomly allocated to teams of four or fewer. Each team selects a scenario by number and receives guidance on information sources and access to past exam papers. The assessment procedure is carefully explained.

During the simulation students are expected to reflect critically on their own and their peers' contributions to the teamwork, but scores for content are awarded by tutors, who then take the peer assessment of participation into account in allocating the final mark. Full and equal participation within the team results in the same mark being awarded to all members of the team for the final proposal submitted. When participation is perceived by the students to be unequal, tutors apply a formula that ensures a fair result. Each team undertakes an important pre- and post-assessment review to check for fairness and agreement within the group.

The key to fair peer assessment is accurate and quantified record keeping. Students dislike team working with individuals who do not pull their weight, but peer assessment ensures that the whole team is not penalized. Student feedback at LMU is positive in this regard. With careful management, the benefits outweigh the drawbacks for both tutor and learner.

The authors say in Chapter 8 that peer assessment encourages cooperative working and ensures fairness in marking. It helps students to take responsibility for their own learning and assessment. Validity is ensured, and efficiency gains may be had too, once the method is established.

Assessment after gaming

In Plymouth University's business school, staff in the Department of Accounting and Law use Monopoly© for teaching during the initial stage of a Level 1 financial accounting module (see Chapter 7). The weekly one-hour Monopoly© sessions, each representing a trading year, are tutor-led. Students play against each other in teams of four, and enthusiastically 'bet' on the outcomes. Each team has to present a 10-minute oral summary of what has happened, financially speaking, after four years' trading. Each student submits a written evaluation of the betting policy he or she used in the game. To ensure validity, tutors award marks for the team presentations and the individual evaluations, which count together for 10 per cent of the module mark.

The authors report that feedback from students has been positive from all but a small minority. Most prefer the Monopoly© approach to traditional lectures. Although this is a highly intensive activity, efficiency gains are available as it is scalable.

Assessment of resource-based learning

Tutors at Sheffield Hallam University's business school introduced resource-based learning (RBL) for a unit on the business environment, to enhance their students' experience and secure efficiency gains (see Chapter 2). The RBL support materials, based on open learning principles, included self-assessment activities designed to encourage deep rather than surface learning. Students can also try to answer a set of multiple choice questions each week for self-assessment.

Assessment of the RBL is based on five explicit principles, say the authors:

- Coursework and the examination are linked, the former being both formative and summative.
- Informal and formal assessment are combined.
- Skills, including application of knowledge, are assessed.
- Direct links are maintained between assessment tasks and learning outcomes for the unit.
- Feedback on each learning outcome is covered by the assignment, on the basis of predetermined criteria stated for students in the unit's learning scheme.

The assessment strategy is thus valid. It blends traditional elements, such as essays that serve to enhance students' critical faculties, with the innovative, such as requiring students to compile an electoral ward profile and analysis.

Based on their own observation, the authors claim that RBL helps students to become self-reliant. Feedback from students suggests that RBL is popular with them. They benefit from tutors' support and encouragement, not least from the feedback they get after assessment. Efficiency gains may be possible using this method, though the authors were not aiming for them.

Further selected examples of innovations in assessment

In an attempt to identify newsworthy innovations specifically in assessment, we carried out for BEST in late 2001 a survey of its contacts in UK business schools. Our 42 respondents indicated first, by ticking items on a list, which types of assessment, most of them innovative, were being used in their business schools (see Table 14.1).

As the sample is small and self-selected, Table 14.1 is merely illustrative, but it appears that a good range of practice is being employed. We were therefore

Table 14.1   *Types of assessment practice reported*

Type of assessment practice	n = 42
Assessment of group or teamwork	23
Assessment of practical skills	23
Multiple choice tests	21
Computer-assisted assessment	18
Continuous assessment plus final assessment	18
Open-book examinations	18
Portfolio assessment	18
Work- or job-based assessment	15
Peer assessment	13
Online assessment	13
Other	2

surprised that most of the leads offered by respondents did not meet BEST's criteria for selecting innovations for further study and dissemination (see Chapter 1). However, we followed the leads and received from various business schools details of what assessment methods were being tried out. We cannot claim that the examples below all explicitly offer high validity or efficiency gains, but we do think they are of interest. They cover business planning, European business law, management accountancy, organizational research and organizational problem solving.

Group assessment, peer assessment and gaming

Payne and Whittaker (2001) report that Leeds Metropolitan University offers in Year 2 an Integrative Business Simulation module that includes peer assessment. The module is based on a game called 'Executive Simulation' (sold by April Training), in which students study European car manufacture and sales. The students are divided into teams, one to manage each company. The team makes decisions, produces a business plan and analyses the company's performance. At 'company meetings', individual students take on roles such as chairman, director of marketing and financial director, and run through five to six years of operating the company. Collectively, students in each team must decide on the product, its promotion and marketing, how many factories to have, how to raise capital and how many employees to take on. Should they close a factory, the team will have to cope with potential strikes or redundancies. Each team must research the company's products and markets, and study likely competition from other companies.

The first assignment is a business plan submitted by the whole team and marked as a group assessment by the tutor. Each member of the team gets that mark, which counts for half the module marks.

The other module marks are awarded at the end of the game. During a series of short annual general meetings attended by the whole class, the company's performance is presented by the 'board of directors' to the 'shareholders' (the other students), who can question the board. Broadly, marks are gained for the team's decision making, the AGM presentation and questions that members pose as shareholders in other companies. Again, tutors award a mark for the presentation, but this time the distribution of marks within the team is determined by peer evaluation of individuals' work during the second semester, when teams discuss their members' progress at their board meetings. This peer assessment is based on 10 criteria (identified by staff), from which students select eight to use (students can also select others). Each team member signs a statement agreeing the criteria finally chosen and accepting the team's final allocation of marks when that occurs.

After the marking, all the teams meet to discuss marks allocated by peers, which must be supported by a written, signed rationale. Should serious disagreement arise, staff can hold a viva: this has not yet become necessary. Validity is thus assured, but there are no efficiency gains so far as we can tell.

Assessing higher-order skills: KCAASE

At the University of North London Business School, in response to concern over the numbers of students struggling with 'higher-order skills', Curran (2001) developed an innovative approach to drafting exam papers. The standard exam rubric of four questions to be answered out of 10 in three hours tends to elicit similar higher-order skills for each question. Curran, using Bloom's taxonomy, graded the questions in sections to identify clearly the intellectual skills called for: knowledge and comprehension (K&C), application and analysis (A&A), synthesis and evaluation (S&E). The requirements for each skill were made explicit to students during seminars as well as in the exam. The early weeks deal with K&C and they progress through A&A, and then S&E. S&E is difficult without A&A skills, and A&A is impossible without K&C.

Under this approach, students can submit practice answers for marking. Their performance is partly assessed on the basis of demonstrated higher-order skills. Feedback from advisers suggests that the 'mark profile' has improved as a result of the change. Informal feedback from students suggests that they like the transparency of the approach, which improves its validity. It is not clear if there are efficiency gains.

Case studies and negotiated assessment

At London Guildhall University Business School, case study reading and annotation is used to develop and test students' higher cognitive abilities. The approach combines the case study method with negotiated assessment and group discussion (Shaw, 2001).

Case study work encourages problem solving. Two weeks prior to a two-hour test on it, the students receive a company case study to read and annotate. They are encouraged to research the case study's background and think about likely questions. On the test day the students choose three questions to answer in two hours. They have 5–10 minutes to read the questions, discuss them among themselves and ask for clarification. All the questions are based on role playing and problem solving in practical managerial situations. The students have with them only the case study and their annotations.

The students are involved in negotiation and discussion about assessment, to give them a sense of ownership in the process. Tutors' comments on students' performance in these tests are very important to them and give an indication of how they will perform in the final exam. Students can get individual comments on their work in tutorials, too. Feedback from students has been positive. The method has high validity, but offers no efficiency gains.

Assessing students' reflective journals

Southampton Institute provides an innovative example of how reflective journals can be used by Higher National Diploma students (Higgins, 2001). The guidelines for students explain that the journal is a tool for reflection, vital for deep learning. The students are told that they must reflect on management theories and applications, and in the journal choose and reflect on the ones that they feel they can defend. The students can develop their knowledge by further reading and adapting given solutions to problems.

The reflective journals count for 25 per cent of the unit mark. The grading criteria are made explicit by offering examples of reflection at different levels, from descriptive to critical. Pure description with no reflection counts as a referral. To achieve a pass, merit or distinction there must be evidence of reflection, for example by having several journal entries at different times, demonstrating that the journal has been revisited. Again, the method has high validity, but offers no efficiency gains.

Assessing organizational skills

Postgraduate students in the University of North London Business School taking European business law must organize a conference to increase their knowledge and experience of the subject matter and develop essential organizational skills (Bamford, 2001). Working in teams, they organize the conference around a relevant theme that they have chosen. The tutors, as facilitators, demonstrate their commitment to research by presenting their own research to students. Each team is required to develop academic arguments to justify its chosen theme, and must also manage the conference – including planning and advertising – for a wider audience.

Tutors observe and assess each team meeting, using criteria such as the team's ability to arrive at a consensus and make future plans, the types of interaction and the challenges from peers. Tutors award a mark out of 50 for the team's performance, with all members of the team getting the same mark. The other mark is awarded, again out of 50, for individuals' performance in presenting and submitting a conference paper. The two marks are added together to yield a final mark. The author claims that, because of the broad nature of the subject matter, student performance on the course is difficult to assess in a more conventional way.

Students like the challenging and original aspects of this approach. It has high validity and may offer modest efficiency gains.

Assessing teamwork on case studies

At the University of Manchester's School of Accounting and Finance, case studies are used to help students understand advanced management accountancy (Scapens, 2001). They aim to locate management accountancy practices in a changing organizational context. The students are introduced to them in workshops. In addition, issues, techniques and the accountant's role are explored through lectures.

Tutorial groups are divided into four teams and, except at the first tutorial, two teams act as analysers and the other two as critics. Tasks are allocated alternately so that each team analyses twice and criticizes twice. Analysers must produce a written analysis and distribute it to the critics' team a week before the tutorial in which it is discussed. The critics must produce written reports challenging the analyses, and present and defend their findings in the tutorial.

The report counts for 25 per cent of the course mark, and the presentation counts for another 5 per cent. A three-hour examination counts for the remaining 70 per cent. The combination provides high validity and possibly some efficiency gains.

Assessing teamwork on projects

At Brighton University's business school, first year accounting and finance students can develop a range of skills by undertaking, in small groups, an organizational research project (Hughes, 2001). This project enables students to apply their knowledge of theories of organizational behaviour in a 'real-world' setting. In addition, the students are encouraged to apply their knowledge, through reflection, to their own experiences of working in a team.

Working in small groups, the students are encouraged to pool their contacts with employers to help decide on a suitable organization. They must produce a project proposal and timetable, which may need to be revised after feedback from their tutor. Assessment of the module is based entirely on the project: 60 per cent for the written report, 20 per cent for an individual reflective document and 20 per cent for a verbal presentation. All students in a group normally receive the same mark for their joint effort but marks may be reduced for non-participation.

The programme has been revised since being first introduced in 1997, when it attracted a prize awarded by PricewaterhouseCoopers for innovation. Then 40 per cent of the marks were given for students' work and 60 per cent for an examination. The project now takes place in the second, not the first, semester. Student feedback highlighted the problem of carrying 'passengers', that is, students in the group who did not do much. The reflective element now enables students to learn from the experience of managing relationships within the group, and to say how they would do things differently next time. Overall, the assessment method has high validity.

Assessing creative responses to problems

The Developing Individuals and Teams unit is part of the Diploma of Management Studies programme at Middlesex University Business School (Jagiello, 2001). Using the Forum Theatre Technique, students taking the unit are encouraged to respond creatively to organizational problems. The technique is based on six steps: choosing a problem; organizing a team of actors; identifying a problem owner or protagonist; performing the scenario; intervening with selected solutions to the problem; and implementing the action in reality.

Based on the notion of all participants learning together – protagonist, actors and audience – this approach aims to provide a safe, creative environment in which students can learn about management styles and rehearse potential solutions to the problem. They must pool their knowledge, tactics and experience in solving organizational problems and perform a scenario to an audience of other students who intervene during the enactment. Predicted interventions are matched against the actual interventions, which are captured on video to enable students to reflect on their actions. For the assessment, all students must produce and enact a script and make a record of interventions during the re-enactment. Feedback from the students suggests that they learn a great deal about themselves and their value systems in difficult situations. The method has high validity, but offers no efficiency gains.

Conclusion

Despite these examples, we notice that innovation does not feature strongly in the literature on assessing student performance in UK higher education, and particularly not in business schools (see, for example, Brown, Race and Bull, 1999). Conservatism rules, it seems, perhaps partly on account of the Quality Assurance Agency (QAA) audits and because universities and colleges feel they must do all they can to 'protect standards'. Indeed, some respondents in the BEST surveys claim that they avoid innovation because of the straitjacket of quality assurance. The QAA does exhort universities and colleges to be innovative in assessment, but not to much effect as far as we can tell.

The most fruitful direction for innovation appears to be in electronic assessment, as already provided quite widely in some disciplines through software such as Question Mark (published by Question Mark Computing), and in accounting through Byzantium (published by Blackwell) and packages such as Understand Management Accounting (distributed by EQL International). In courses where meaningful and rapid feedback to students is desirable, Web-based formative assessment could be provided. Computer software randomly generates different questions, with different numerical values and symbols, using multiple choice and many other question types. Students can practise and assess their progress. The same system could be used for summative assessment, providing efficiency as well as validity.

Significant savings in academic staff time and administration costs would probably be achieved if Web-based online examinations could be held, with automatic marking. Before that becomes universally possible, however, alternative invigilation processes must be evaluated, automatic grading and commenting (feedback) systems made more accurate, and question banks established. The range of types of question, already extended well beyond multiple choice items, may be widened further through using artificial intelligence techniques.

In principle, such online examinations could be held anywhere, given the necessary computing facilities and connections. They could be held synchronously if only one set of questions is available, or asynchronously for subjects such as accounting in which it is feasible to generate multiple sets of questions.

Experience in this field is building up, though there is not much yet in UK business schools. Bridgeman and Cooper (1998) studied whether North American students scored higher when submitting assignments by computer than when using pen and paper. Two equated versions of the Graduate Management Admission Test were both answered by 3,470 students who answered one by computer and the other using pen and paper. Both versions included two 30-minute essays. The pen-and-paper answers gained higher marks than the computer answers, regardless of the students' gender, ethnic group or command of English. Does this result militate against electronic assessment? In the UK, the research has not yet been done.

Many other questions remain unanswered. Can business schools justify using written examinations and tests to assess students' oral communication skills, practical problem solving and multimedia computer-based learning? How good are existing assessment systems for testing for skills required by employers, such as team working? If many students regard as essential only those parts of their course on which they will be assessed, how can staff justify teaching them what is not assessed? Are assessment costs bound to rise in direct ratio to student numbers, or can greater efficiency stem from adopting innovative methods?

The government is aiming for a 50 per cent participation rate in higher education over the next 10 years, and possibly 350,000 more students from increasingly diverse backgrounds will be in the system (Floud, 2002). Innovative ways of assessing their performance must be used, achieving greater efficiency without compromising academic standards and the quality of student learning. Innovative practice takes time to develop and be accepted by stakeholders. Business schools need to find and adapt for themselves what others have tested. The concerns of the deans and heads of departments could possibly be met, however, by one or more of the innovations discussed in this chapter, all of which could be adopted elsewhere, given motivation and resources.

References

Bamford, J (2001) The facilitation of postgraduate learning through the assessment of the organisation of a conference and presentation of a series of individual papers, Paper presented at EDINEB International Conference, June, Nice

Bridgeman, B and Cooper, P (1998) *Comparability of Scores on Word-Processed and Handwritten Essays on the Graduate Management Admissions Test*, Educational Testing Service, Princeton, NJ

Brown, S, Race, P and Bull, J (1999) *Computer-Assisted Assessment in Higher Education*, Kogan Page, London

Curran, J (2001) *An Innovative Exam – Questions Graded*, University of North London Business School, London

Floud, R (2002) Setting the scene: political context for the management of student completion of degrees, Keynote speech, Failing Students Conference, 5 July, Lancaster University

Hawkridge, D (2001a) Learning and teaching business, management and accounting: the UK landscape, Paper for the 1st Annual BEST Conference, 3–5 April, Windermere

Hawkridge, D (2001b) Learning and teaching business, management and accounting: the UK landscape – and changing it, Paper for the 9th Annual Nottingham Business School Learning and Teaching Conference, 27 June, Nottingham

Hawkridge, D (2002) The BEST stories, Paper for the 2nd Annual BEST Conference, 8–10 April, Edinburgh

Higgins, L (2001) *Reflective Journals*, Southampton Business School, Southampton Institute, Southampton

Hughes, M (2001) *Organisational Research Project*, Brighton Business School, University of Brighton, Brighton

Jagiello, J (2001) *Creating an Organisational Theatre of Learning*, Middlesex University Business School, Enfield

Payne, E and Whittaker, L (2001) The use of technology to facilitate collaborative learning and enhance team performance and learning, Paper presented at the EDINEB conference, June, Nice

Scapens, R W (2001) *The Use of Case Studies in Teaching Advanced Management Accountancy*, School of Accounting and Finance, University of Manchester, Manchester

Shaw, J (2001) *Case Study Reading and Annotation*, London Guildhall University, London

Chapter 15

Learning from success

Roland Kaye and David Hawkridge

The BEST stories (Chapters 2–13) are about successful innovations in learning and teaching in business schools. In this final chapter we look for keys to that success. We examine Rogers's (1995) ideas on diffusion of innovations in education and try to apply them to the BEST stories. We then consider alternative means for disseminating these and other examples of good practice. Lastly, we describe BEST's self-profiling tool, based on classic and emergent models of business education: we hope readers will use this holistic and multidimensional tool to judge where innovation is most needed in their own institutions.

Keys to success

Worldwide, 40 years ago, universities and colleges in general were not very innovative in how they taught. Innovations, such as they were, tended to ride on the back of technology. For example, from 1969 onwards there were annual conferences, fostered by the US National Science Foundation, of academics interested in using computers in teaching the undergraduate curriculum. Since then, the US federal government has promoted innovation through the Fund for the Improvement of Post-Secondary Education.

In the early 1970s, the Nuffield Foundation conducted a survey of innovations in learning and teaching, across the disciplines, in UK universities and colleges. The Open University was an innovation on a large scale at that time: its methods and materials have been assimilated to some extent by other institutions.

In the 1990s the UK government funded the Teaching and Learning Technology Programme (TLTP) and the Computers in Teaching Initiative (CTI). The latter's more broadly based successor is the Learning and Teaching Support Network, with BEST as one of its 25 nodes.

All these and other similar initiatives have helped to promote and raise awareness of successful innovations in universities and colleges, but what are the keys to success? On the basis of the BEST stories, we suggest seven.

Key 1: innovative content of high quality

Innovative content must satisfy the demand in our society for current and future managers to achieve higher levels of knowledge and skill than ever before, taking into account the immense impact of information and communications technology. Among the BEST stories, several succeed in this respect. Edelshain and Vielba (Chapter 4) show how, in a collaboration between City University (their own), Fordham University and several multinational financial institutions, innovative content of high quality was brought into a joint course in international business. Clarke-Hill and Kuhanen, in Chapter 11, explain how they developed a public Web site to carry their innovative content on strategic management for the benefit of students in their own and other universities and colleges. In Chapter 13, Little, Fowle and Quintas describe an innovative multidisciplinary distance learning course in knowledge management for the MBA at the Open University.

High quality is not easily achieved: either the champions have persevered in overcoming difficulties or they have won support, backing and institutional investment. Quality reaches beyond the individual innovators' efforts, to allow institutionalization of the innovation or its commodification for transfer to others.

Key 2: innovative delivery and/or assessment

Innovative methods of delivery and/or assessment must be fit for the purpose, as demonstrated in several BEST stories. In Chapter 2, Ottewill and Wall show how they successfully used resource-based learning at Sheffield Hallam University, combined with 'seamless' assessment through coursework and an examination. In Chapter 8, Gregory and Yeomans describe how they introduced peer assessment at Leeds Metropolitan University to encourage cooperative working and fairness in marking. In Chapter 9, Michaelson and her colleagues at Dundee and St Andrew's devised, for a final years honours module, a Web-based portfolio management game that uses real-time stock market data. Little, Fowle and Quintas explain in Chapter 13 how their Open University course includes learning how to build distributed communities of practice through using innovative synchronous and asynchronous conferencing.

Innovations meet organizational and course objectives in these examples. They enable a return on investment in the innovation to be perceived whether or not it is quantified. Those who allocate educational resources can perceive a benefit from the innovations.

Key 3: cost benefits for staff and students

There must be profitability for the business school and pay-off for the students in the innovation. The challenge to business school managers and teachers alike is to attract increased student numbers and operate at lower unit cost each year, while competing against UK and foreign commercial providers. Innovations that meet this challenge are successful. The efficiency gains described by Ottewill and Wall in Chapter 2 clearly count as a major driver in their innovation, resource-based learning at Brighton Business School. Patel, Cook and Spencer emphasize in Chapter 6 that Byzantium offers efficient use of teaching resources: the software provides for economies of scale, although the development costs were high. Stoner points out in Chapter 10 that learning technology was introduced into Glasgow University's teaching of management accounting in order to maintain standards despite worsening staff:student ratios.

Key 4: operability

The innovation must be reasonably simple to understand and operate. If it is very hard to keep up with rapid changes in the innovation and/or the content it delivers, it will fail. If computers are used, there should be no platform compatibility problems that damage or even prevent participation. Bourner and Lawson, in Chapter 5, show that action learning in Brighton Business School has proved to be an operable innovation, and one that has developed slowly while diffusing through the school and beyond. In introducing Monopoly© into Plymouth Business School's teaching of first-level financial accounting, Clayton (Chapter 7) knew that the innovation would be simple for students and staff to understand and operate, and that changes in how it was used would be gradual. There was no danger of platform incompatibility! Clarke-Hill and Kuhanen, in Chapter 11, emphasize that their innovative Web site on strategic management is simple to use and open to all regardless of the browser they use.

These are important lessons given the investment in information and communication technology through TLTP and CTI as well as the continued emphasis on e-issues in our BEST surveys.

Key 5: longevity of impact

The innovation must be sustained in its impact. It should match the changing technology in society and prepare students for the demands of the workplace. It must teach lifelong learning skills. In Chapter 3, Newton, Paine and Flowers outline the development of the intranet for Brighton Business School and emphasize its progressively more sustained impact on learning and teaching, as well as administration. Edelshain and Vielba, in describing the International Consultancy Assignment in Chapter 4, show how this successful innovation has a sustained impact, exploiting the technology. It has prepared students for jobs through them acquiring knowledge and skills required in international business. In Chapter 6, Patel, Cook and Spencer describe Byzantium's long-term impact as computer-aided software for interactive learning of financial and management accounting. The software is now commercially available.

Key 6: observable success

It must be possible to try out and observe the innovation, preferably on a limited basis to begin with. The outcomes should be easily accessible to staff and students, and published for all to see. In Chapter 3, Newton, Paine and Flowers explain how the intranet for Brighton Business School was piloted first. Students were 'overwhelmingly positive'; academics and administrators saw the potential but were more cautious. When the full intranet was implemented, a cultural shift occurred, with all groups wanting to use it more and more. Gregory and Yeomans, in Chapter 8, show how they introduced innovative peer assessment carefully into their public relations planning and management module: its observable success soon led to other courses adopting the innovation. O'Hara, Reeve and Flowers (Chapter 12) describe how they prepared carefully and started cautiously when they introduced their first live consultancy case study into Brighton Business School's MBA programme. After modifications, the method has had success, for all to see.

Key 7: transferability

The innovation must be transferable. Ottewill and Wall (Chapter 2) claim that their approach 'is eminently transferable to other units of study and other institutions' and quote examples. Bourner and Lawson (Chapter 5) show how they were able to transfer 'self-managed action learning' to another institution, in another field (health), in another country (Ireland). In Chapter 6, Patel, Cook and Spencer demonstrate the transferability of the Byzantium software between universities in England, and Stoner, in Chapter 10, describes its adoption in a Scottish university. Michaelson and her colleagues at Dundee state in Chapter 9 that their FINESSE software for learning portfolio management is now in use at two other sites. Clarke-Hill and Kuhanen, in Chapter 11, provide data to illustrate how widely used is their public Web site on strategic management. O'Hara, Reeve and Flowers (Chapter 12) argue that their innovative live consultancy case study method is easily transferable to other courses and disciplines.

For transferability, the innovation must have passed beyond the individual enthusiasm of the champion: the innovation will have become established and the knowledge about it will have been commodified.

Research on diffusion of innovations in education

The BEST stories, and other stories like them, deserve wide dissemination. How else can managers and teachers in business schools learn from and adopt or adapt the successes described in them? But what does the research suggest about the diffusion of innovations?

There is no need to refer to Schumpeter (1934), Deutsch (1949), Argyris (1965), Freeman (1974) or Freeman, Clark and Soete (1982), all of whom studied and wrote about the diffusion of commercial and business innovations. Research on diffusion of innovations in education began in the late 1960s, when US communications scholars began applying to education their ideas about diffusion of innovations, gained from studies of agriculture practice in developing countries such as India (Rogers and Shoemaker, 1971).

According to Rogers (1995), adopters of change fall into five categories, which he believed were normally distributed:

- innovators (about 2.5 per cent of any population);
- early adopters (about 13.5 per cent of the population);
- early majority (about 34 per cent);
- late majority (about 34 per cent);
- laggards (about 16 per cent).

Kaye (1985) applied a similar classification to examine the adoption of IT in accounting education. However, he went on to examine the alternative strategies that could be pursued: reject, minimize or adapt. Rejection of disciplinary developments was seen as not feasible, while minimization was viable in the short term, though long-term it would lead to uncompetitiveness. Adaptation was seen as essential for the long-term health of the discipline.

Rogers's categories are easily recognizable. Clearly the BEST stories have been written by some of the innovators. However, if Rogers's estimate is right, there must be many more in business schools: 2.5 per cent of their 8,500 teaching staff equals over 200! We shall continue our searching. As for the early adopters, several of the BEST stories include evidence of these, where the innovations have spread to other departments and institutions.

Another way to view diffusion, Rogers suggests, is on five perceived attributes of innovations. These attributes are related to but not identical to the seven keys to success listed earlier in this chapter:

- *Attribute 1: relative advantage.* Does the innovation offer a better way to do something? As we said in Chapter 1, 'better' can be judged against a range of criteria (see Table 1.3 for our list), none of which may be based on improved examination results. Perceptions do vary about what is better or successful. Readers of this book may feel that a particular BEST story does offer a better way to learn, or that it does not. All the innovators, on the other hand, were convinced that there was relative advantage in what they were doing.

- *Attribute 2: compatibility*. Is the innovation compatible with the adopters' values, beliefs and needs? Adoption or rejection of an innovation in a BEST story will depend on readers' values and beliefs (regarding content or method). We are pleased to see that the innovators' values and beliefs come through clearly in the stories in this book.
- *Attribute 3: complexity*. Is the innovation not too complex? Does Byzantium (Chapters 6 and 10) sound too complex to adopt? Despite the name, learners do not find it so, though the developers may have found the programming byzantine in its complexity.
- *Attribute 4: trialability*. Can the innovation be tried out before adoption? All the innovations in the BEST stories can be tried out before adoption, but it would be more difficult and expensive to do so with some than with others. Moreover, testing education innovations has implications for the learner and teacher. The trials have to be undertaken in a manner that is ethical and equitable for all learners.
- *Attribute 5: observability*. Does the innovation have observable benefits? We looked for observable benefits in selecting the stories but we also depended on opinions to some extent (see Table 1.3). Opinions of the innovators, being biased in favour, were not enough.

Rogers (1995) also theorized that successful diffusion of innovations has five human aspects:

- *Human aspect 1: change agency*. A change agency is an institution whose functions are to initiate, support and institutionalize beneficial change for its client system. The Learning and Teaching Support Network has this general function, and BEST is charged with supporting that function in the fields of business, management and accounting, within UK higher and further education.
- *Human aspect 2: client system*. The clients of educational innovation are the learners and the teachers, as well as the policy makers, within the client system of education. BEST's main clients are the teachers, though we seek to influence policy makers too, all for the benefit of learners.
- *Human aspect 3: change agent*. A change agent is an individual who influences clients' innovation decisions in a direction deemed desirable by a change agency. BEST staff aim to serve this function, the change agency being the Learning and Teaching Support Network, funded and operated within guidelines set by the government.
- *Human aspect 4: innovator*. An innovator is one who launches the new idea in the system. Again, the innovators are the authors of the BEST stories, plus others in the business schools whom we have yet to locate and work with.
- *Human aspect 5: developer*. This is the innovation developer or there may be a team. Many of the BEST stories are about development of innovations by a team made up of teaching, technical and other staff. Even if there is only one author for a particular story, a team probably supported the innovation.

Rogers writes about innovators who are venturesome and ahead of their time: our authors are like that. Some have managed to persuade their own colleagues to become early adopters, willing to try the innovation before it had proved successful. Some went even further and persuaded colleagues in other universities and colleges to be what Rogers would call 'early majority' members, deliberate in their decision making. Late majority members are sceptical even after others embrace the innovation. Laggards are traditional and do not see a need to change.

Disseminating examples of innovative good practice

This book is one means of disseminating examples of innovative good practice in teaching and learning in business schools, but certainly not the only one. BEST's Web site disseminates the BEST stories too. BEST has published the individual stories as booklets and publicizes them at workshops and conferences. Besides these stories there are many more examples that ought to reach a wide audience. We suggest below two other means by which diffusion of such examples can happen.

Benchmarking clubs

Performance benchmarking of the kind used by the Quality Assurance Agency is unpopular in the academic sphere. It is usually based on output and resource use comparisons of whole entities, with the findings presented in league tables. The winners benefit, perhaps, but there are too many perceived losers with little or no recourse to natural justice! Such benchmarking is resource-intensive and does not yield much useful information on how to improve.

The kind of benchmarking provided by a formal standard of good practice may even have a negative influence on innovation. Standards such as Investors in People (IIP), ISO 9000, the Business Excellence Model and so on may not serve well the cause of successful innovation.

In the business world, another kind of benchmarking is becoming a valuable form of information exchange between companies. Benchmarking clubs are usually made up of small to medium-sized clusters of organizations in which there are concerns about a particular issue or key process. They are represented by staff responsible for and involved in that process. The meetings are private, to share experience and solutions under 'Chatham House'-type rules. A club may only meet once or twice, and then lapse. Or it may be longer lasting with confidential data collated and presented (perhaps by third parties) and visits arranged to observe processes.

Competition, it is often argued, is a block to sharing knowledge. The reality is that leading organizations are keen to learn and will share knowledge as a means to access new ideas. However, this learning happens in a climate of trust amongst peers. If commercial organizations can adopt these approaches there is surely little disadvantage to business schools in following their example.

Business schools are used to arranging meetings between staff of different schools, for sharing and comparing, in confidence, the challenges before them and practices that address these. There is no reason why such benchmarking clubs should not tackle issues that this book raises. Knowledge sharing through visits can be very valuable: for instance, those responsible for assessment in one organization can visit another, to see how it is being done and how the issues have been approached.

Good practice exchanges

Already familiar to many business schools is the good practice exchange: staff from different schools come together to share and compare, in confidence, the challenges facing them and the specific practices they are using. BEST recently ran a good practice exchange on the practicalities of internationalizing management education and of running overseas partnerships.

A more public mode of knowledge sharing is practised by large consulting groups and some professional bodies such as the Institute of Housing. Original documents relevant to a hot issue are registered or lodged centrally (often on the Web these days) and can be accessed by network members seeking ideas on how others have tackled that issue. The Case Clearing House is a well-known example, and libraries of course outlines and reading lists are now springing up on the Web. A good practice library for assessment of student performance, say, could include assessment policy documents, details of procedures and guides on matters such as plagiarism. It would probably become a library-cum-database as contacts, listings, directories and so on were added, to provide a signposting service for questions like 'What is known about…?', 'Who can advise me on…? and 'Where can I find out about…?'

Classic and emergent models of business education

BEST has also developed a self-profiling tool to assist staff in evaluating their progress in meeting the challenges of change and innovation (BEST, 2002). This tool is holistic and multidimensional, comparing the 'classic' mode of business education with the 'emergent'. It emphasizes the strong links between characteristics of the market, programme governance and curriculum renewal, learning and teaching, staff, and learning support and customer care. In the classic form, for example, assessment, as part of learning and teaching, is overwhelmingly based on individual coursework and traditional exams. In the emergent form, assessment depends on methods such as group projects, individual project exhibits, placement reports and portfolios.

Characteristics of the market

As Table 15.1 shows, there are clear differences between the markets for classic and emergent business education. The former serves mainly local markets, though a few players draw on a wider national hinterland. Partnerships between business schools and corporate bodies are unusual. Emergent business education serves a broad range of markets locally, nationally and even globally. It engages with industry and corporate partners.

The classic model is based almost exclusively on campus teaching, whereas the emergent one is campus-based or company-based, or is even a dispersed online community scattered across countries or continents. The emergent combines campus and distance teaching.

In the classic model, the business school stakes its reputation on selecting the best students, the research standing of its staff and the employability of its alumni. In the emergent model, the school still adheres to these standards but also aims for industry specialization, is responsive to corporate requirements, practises successful inclusivity or widening participation, and works to provide 'added value' of courses for careers. The emergent model recognizes market segments and seeks ways to serve the markets in a heterogeneous manner rather than treating all students as some homogeneous body.

Table 15.1 *Differences between the markets*

Characteristics	Classic business education	Emergent business education
Market(s) Served	Mainly local; a few national players. Partnerships unusual.	Variously local, national, global and sector/industry, including online and corporate customers.
Spatial Organization	Campus-based.	Campus-based, company-based or dispersed online community. Partnerships widespread.
Basis for Reputation	Selectivity; research standing of staff; alumni employability.	As before, but also: industry specialization; responsive to corporate requirements; successful inclusivity; 'added value' of courses for careers.

Programme governance and curriculum renewal

Table 15.2 shows the differences in programme governance and curriculum renewal between the two models. In the classic one, programme oversight and regulation is largely in the hands of external examiners and assessors. In the emergent model, these methods are complemented by subject benchmarking and industry kitemarks.

The classic model involves employers and professional bodies in an *ad hoc*, variable and generally limited manner. The emergent calls for substantive linkages: dialogue occurs through review panels, partnerships with corporate universities, in-house programmes, placements, teaching companies and the like.

There are notable differences, too, between the two models in how their programmes of study are progressed and integrated. The classic model often has no more than an assembly of discipline-based courses, with few integrative elements. Students do the integrating, so far as they can. The emergent model includes disciplinary and interdisciplinary elements, integrated through learning outcomes. The differences are even more marked in the theory taught: the classic model is based on what can be called the 'Anglo-Saxon generic' management theory, undifferentiated, whereas the emergent model has a small core of common theory backed up by extensive contextualization for industries, sectors and national cultures.

Learning and teaching

Differences between the two models are particularly marked when it comes to learning and teaching (see Table 15.3). The aims and pedagogy for the classic

Table 15.2 *Differences in programme governance and curriculum renewal*

Programme governance and curriculum renewal	Classic business education	Emergent business education
Programme oversight and regulation	External examiners; external contributions to course review.	As before plus QAA subject benchmarking, industry kitemarks (AMBA, Equis).
Involvement of employers and professional bodies	*Ad hoc*; variable but generally limited.	Substantive linkages and dialogue through review panels, corporate university partnerships, in-house programmes, placements, teaching companies, etc.
Progression and integration of programmes	An assembly of discipline-based courses, with few integrative elements.	Disciplinary and interdisciplinary elements, integrated through learning outcomes.
Management theory taught	'Anglo-Saxon generic' body of theory.	Limited 'core' with extensive contextualization for industries, sectors, national cultures, etc.

model are largely limited to knowledge acquisition through curriculum-centred methods, with standard progression of students by cohort. The emergent model calls for student-centred and resource-based learning and teaching.

The classic model is based on the written word: in fact, students must learn from it and demonstrate their knowledge and competence almost entirely through it. The emergent one calls for a much wider range of primary media, for learning and for testing.

The experiential elements in the classic model are limited, particularly outside the course: even within it, use of simulations is infrequent. In the emergent model, students frequently draw on their past and current experience and learn via a wide range of experiential elements.

In the classic model, the scope for learner dialogue is restricted to tutorials and seminars, supplemented by informal discussion. In the emergent one, group activities are common, including those in online conferences, as well as what happens under the classic model.

As we noted earlier, there are clear differences, too, between the models with regard to assessment.

Business teachers

The teachers differ, under the two models, with respect to their characteristics, professional development and roles (see Table 15.4). Teachers under the classic model have much autonomy and are proud of their subject expertise; they know little about educational technology, however. If they get any professional development at all, it is through occasional informal and voluntaristic schemes. Other grades of staff are regarded as limited, second-class contributors.

Under the emergent model, business teachers sacrifice autonomy by becoming team members and are proud of their capacity to support learners, not least by means of their knowledge of educational technology. Their professional development is formal, passing through various grades, and they are expected to become members of the Institute for Learning and Teaching (ILT). Under this model, other staff are widely used and appreciated as important for a balanced team.

Learner support and customer care

Learner support and customer care are also different under the two models (see Table 15.5). The classic model expects the student body to be largely homogeneous within particular programmes in which quality is designated as high standards and low drop-out. The emergent model sees students as very diverse customers of educational services of formally assured quality as seen by academics, students and employers or sponsors. In the classic model, student workload is not an issue, but in the emergent one there are policies and metrics that are monitored, linked to learning outcomes and skills. Scant student services under the classic model are properly organized and resourced under the emergent.

Table 15.3 *Differences in learning and teaching*

Learning and teaching	Classic business education	Emergent business education
Aims and pedagogy	Knowledge acquisition through curriculum-centred standard cohort progression.	Practice development or preparation through learner-centred and resource-based models.
Primary medium	Written word for both learning resources and to demonstrate competence.	Varied, but e-intensive for both learning resources (CBT, multimedia, CD ROMs, Web, etc) and demonstrations of competence.
Experiential elements	Limited experience external to the course, barring occasional use of simulations, activities, case studies, projects, etc.	Participants' prior and current experience integral, plus substantial use made of wide range of experiential elements.
Scope for learner dialogue	Tutorials/seminars; otherwise informal.	As before, plus group activities and online conferences.
Assessment	Overwhelmingly, individual coursework and exams.	Also group projects, individual project exhibits, placement reports, portfolios.

Table 15.4 *Differences between business teachers*

Learning teachers	Classic business education	Emergent business education
Characteristics of role and skill set	High autonomy; low on educational technology know-how, but subject expertise critical.	Reduced autonomy; often team-based; high on educational technology know-how; learner support critical.
Professional development	Informal and voluntaristic occasional staff development schemes.	Training grades and formal development widespread; ILT membership expected.
Roles of other staff	Limited, second-class contributors.	Widespread, important for a balanced team.

Table 15.5 *Differences between learner support and customer care*

Learner support and customer care	Classic business education	Emergent business education
Learner role and characteristics	Students largely homogeneous within particular programmes.	Customers of educational services, often very variable by age, gender, and educational, employment and cultural background.
Approach to quality issues	Understood largely in terms of academic standards and limiting dropout; student feedback informal.	Quality negotiated in terms of academic, learner and employer/sponsor desiderata; formal quality assurance processes in operation.
Student workload	Basic guidelines, but left to individual staff and not seen as an issue.	Clear policies and metrics, with monitoring, and links to other issues such as learning outcomes and study skill development.
Student services	Basic counselling and careers advice; *ad hoc* remedial and resit support; rudimentary back-office systems; technology infrastructure variable.	Explicit policies and systems for learner support, retention, diversity, etc, and customer-focused administration with appropriate technology infrastructure.

Implications of classic and emergent models

Readers may note that many of the innovations originate in the new universities and colleges (post-1992) that have a strong tradition in vocational education. The classic model might be seen, inappropriately, as a reflection of the old (pre-1992) model with an emphasis on the scholarly strength of its staff engaged in research and sharing their knowledge through traditional teaching methods. This would not be a fair division as many of the leading business schools embody elements of both models. However, there is often a significant difference in approach between undergraduate pre-vocational and post-experience teaching. In many cases this difference extends to a division of staff resources, which might explain why BEST surveys have had difficulty in gaining a more comprehensive set of responses about innovations.

Conclusion

The Learning Teaching Support Network was established to encourage and disseminate improvements in the learning and teaching of disciplines. It was designed to complement and act as an 'honest broker' to the Higher Education Funding Councils' quality improvement agenda. BEST, as one of the 25 discipline centres, has a role to capture, monitor and disseminate good practice, and to build resources that will enhance the learning and teaching of the disciplines, and improve support networks within the disciplines.

The BEST stories are highlights of some of the innovations that have emerged in the fields of business, management and accounting. The range of stories and institutions provides a cross-section of developments in the disciplines. The significant presence of ICT-related developments reflects the concerns about these developments expressed in the surveys. The presence of innovations that enhance realism and vocational context reflects the government agenda on 'employability' as well as the vocational nature of the disciplines.

The other two issues of national concern identified in various recent proclamations are widening participation and retention. The lack of innovations expressly addressing these issues reflects their complexity. Further, they may be seen as generic rather than discipline-focused.

With regard to widening participation, we would express our concern over the Anglocentric nature of much management and business education, which is at variance with the multicultural nature of the UK. It surely is incompatible with the significant number of overseas students who either study in the UK or study this material in different national contexts. Innovation of content must come if there is to be greater participation.

Retention is becoming a more significant factor than before, associated with problems of funding higher and further education as well as increases in the catchment communities. Study methods will have to change, with more flexible student-centred and resource-based approaches, plus the development of independent study skills. Innovations in these areas emerged in our study and we expect to see more of these developments in the future.

Finally we should note that the reports of the Council for Excellence in Management and Leadership (2002a, 2002b) and the subsequent government response (DTI/DfES, 2002) all stress the need for improvements in the supply of management and leadership development. The emphases of these reports are on the competitiveness of UK plc and on the suggestion that our management and leadership cadre is underdeveloped and poorly equipped to compete internationally. While this view can be disputed, it is likely to influence educational developments in these areas for some time to come. Universities and colleges are likely to face increasing pressure for improvements in business, management and accounting education, to meet international competition. The positive side of these recent reports is the gap they identify between supply and need for management development, which should stimulate expansion of the market.

BEST remains fully committed to the diffusion of innovative good practice in learning and teaching business, management and accounting in UK higher and further education.

References

Argyris, C (1965) *Organization and Innovation*, Irwin-Dorsey, Homewood, IL

BEST (2002) *Managing Better: UK business schools today and tomorrow*, Business Education Support Team, Learning and Teaching Support Network, Open University Business School, Milton Keynes

Council for Excellence in Management and Leadership (2002a) *Excellent Managers and Leaders: Meeting the need*, CEML, London

Council for Excellence in Management and Leadership (2002b) *The Contribution of the UK Business Schools to Developing Managers and Leaders: Report of the Business School Advisory Group*, CEML, London

DTI/ DfES (2002) *Government Response to the Report of the Council for Excellence in Management and Leadership*, DfES–CEML, Nottingham

Deutsch, K W (1949) Innovation, entrepreneurship and the learning process, in *Change and the Entrepreneur*, ed A H Cole, Harvard University Press, Cambridge, MA

Freeman, C (1974) *The Economics of Industrial Innovation*, MIT Press, Cambridge, MA

Freeman, C, Clark, J and Soete, L (1982) *Unemployment and Technical Innovation: A study of long waves and economic development*, Pinter, London

Kaye, G R (1985) Teaching strategies in computers and accounting, *British Accounting Review*, **17** (1), pp 22–36

Rogers, E (1995) *Diffusion of Innovations*, 4th edn, Free Press, New York

Rogers, E M and Shoemaker, F F (1971) *Communication of Innovations: A cross-cultural approach*, Free Press, New York

Schumpeter, J A (1934) *Theory of Economic Development*, Harvard University Press, Cambridge, MA

Index